MW01599606

Wight

is the chronicle of a love affair with the Isle of Wight by a travel writer who first visited Seaview in 1951 and over nearly forty years has returned to find many changes and many features unchanged: the magic is in the enduring character of the Island, and the people it has attracted to live there and take their holidays there.

So much still surprises: the intimacy of Bonchurch, the wilderness of St. Catherine's Down in winter, the 15-mile Tennyson Trail from Alum Bay to Carisbrooke in spring, the loyalty of generations to Sandown sun in summer, and the woods in autumn, round Rookley or Borthwood, Gatcombe or Parkhurst. The unsung splendours of Shorwell and Niton are described, as well as the characters of Cowes and East Cowes, Mottistone and Ryde. The Isle of Wight has something for everyone, from Brading to Yarmouth, and Wootton to Blackgang. Roman villas and modern vineyards, village churches and historic manor houses: Wight is a haven for those who seek identification with the spirit of England, in pubs and guesthouses, quiet chapels and rowdy amusement arcades. Philip Ward has visited farms and bingo halls, museums and great hotels, watermills and beaches, talking and listening, recording banter and wisdom in an attempt to define and present the magic of Wight to those who wish to preserve it for all time, like a fly in amber.

PHILIP WARD is a poet, novelist and traveller whose many previous journeys have taken him from Peru to China. His latest volume of poems is *Lost Songs: Political and Other Poems*; his latest work of fiction *Forgotten Games*: "the games played between Hernán Cortés and his captive, the Emperor Moctezuma, in the Aztec capital city before its conquest by the Spaniards. The Renaissance and Christian mind jousts and feints with the imagination of the divine nature-worshipper. Brilliant in concept, written in prose as spare, lush and pointed as a cactus-garden, *Forgotten Games* is as powerful and evocative as a rational nightmare, a logical daydream" (*The Times*). Philip Ward's recent travel books include *Polish Cities* (1988), *Rajasthan, Agra, Delhi* (1989), and *Bulgaria* (1990).

Wight Magic

Tales of the Isle of Wight, its
islanders and overners

Philip Ward

The Oleander Press Ltd

The Oleander Press
17 Stansgate Avenue
Cambridge CB2 2QZ
England

The Oleander Press
210 Fifth Avenue
New York, N.Y. 10010
USA

British Library Cataloguing in Publication Data

Ward, Philip, *1938-*
   Wight Magic: tales of the Isle of
   Wight, its islanders and overners.
   (Oleander travel books; V. 17).
   1. Isle of Wight
   I. Title
   942.2′8085′8

ISBN 0–900891–98–X

Typeset, printed and bound in Great Britain

CONTENTS

Acknowledgements

Authors seem to be grateful all over the place, and I am no exception. Without the wit and wisdom, good conversation and bizarre behaviour of islanders and overners, good fun even when misunderstood, *Wight Magic* would be less magical than it is.

For unlike every other book about the Island, and heaven only knows there are plenty of them, *Wight Magic* actually allows real people to say what they think, without too much editorial intervention. I have had to make some cuts, of course, to keep the book to a manageable length, but I have found that visitors and residents alike have a great many things to say, and here they are allowed to say some of them. The Isle of Wight is not just a collection of wondrous manor houses, beautiful churches and strange events: it is more than anything a society of good folk democratically disinclined to agree with each other but inclined to be tolerant. Overners make an impact, and this too must be allowed for in a book attempting to anatomise the Island's fascination.

My father and late mother introduced me to the Island when I was thirteen. My wife and daughters enjoy it just as much as I do (Carolyn lives in Ryde and Angela appreciates the Island equally). Sir John and Lady Nicholson gave me the run of Mottistone. Shaunagh Aylmer spent a full morning at Nunwell, and Mrs Denys Oglander a full afternoon in John Nash's Coach House and gardens. Janusz Trzebski introduced us to the pleasures of Morton Manor and Alix Goddard to the delights of Barton Manor. Ron and Pat Winter of Whippingham have helped, so has June Thirlby at Cowes. Elaine Shaw at the Isle of Wight Tourist Office in Newport kindly allowed me the use of some illustrations. Jan Peters at Islandwatch (Gurnard) kept me up to date with successes and failures in the march of redevelopment. It would be invidious to attempt to name everyone who helped, from Joan Wolfenden at Bonchurch to Diana Webber at Brook and back, so let this word of general gratitude go out to all who spoke to me, or spoke while I eavesdropped. I have of course changed names where embarrassment might result from unconsidered trifles dropped in the course of gossip.

PHILIP WARD

PROLOGUE

The English Tourist Board currently promotes the Isle of Wight as one of its nine leading resorts, with (in alphabetical order) Blackpool, Bournemouth, Brighton, Eastbourne, Great Yarmouth, Newquay, Scarborough and Torbay. Of these the Island and Great Yarmouth are poor relations in bed-night terms, a league table with Blackpool way ahead (12 million), followed by the Torbay area (7.5 m), Bournemouth (6 m), and both Newquay and Skegness (5 m), followed by Scarborough and Weymouth (4 m each) and a cluster of resorts on 2 m bed-nights: Bognor, Brighton, Eastbourne and Lowestoft.

We must be careful to distinguish travel from holidays. Travel involves a degree of preparation, often linguistic, artistic or cultural; holidays are intended as relaxation, and are mainly passive in character, sitting on a beach or lying by a pool.

Why the sea? The Lake District has greater natural beauties, the Yorkshire Dales and Moors solitude and wilderness, the Cotswold tradition and charm. But in the early 19th century the Prince Regent made a celebrity of St Tropez, and Brighton began to acquire the reputation that made it forever London-by-the-Sea. The Victorian period saw the spread of railways and the enrichment of the middle class, followed by the increasing prosperity of the working class, which together allowed the rise of seaside resorts from Blackpool to Llandudno, and Margate to Ventnor; paid holidays became the rule, and people could take two weeks away from urban grime to fresh seaside breezes.

By the late 1950s, however, the resorts which failed to modernise lost out and the fashion of Continental holidays began. Margate and Weston-super-Mare lost ground, while Blackpool and Torbay fought back, proliferating in discos and Illuminations. So as soon as holidaymakers could afford to travel to sunny Mediterranean resorts, with cheap charter flights, in the 1960s, Benidorm and its like sprang up to satisfy the need for beer and pubs, fish and chips, and English resorts had to fight a rearguard action.

It is, perhaps, relatively easy to describe the fantastic and grotesque, the bizarre, curious and outlandish, from Kufra in Southern Cyrenaica, to Yazd in the Iranian Desert, from Albania's mountains to Oman's Musandam Peninsula, from the Zen monasteries of Kyoto to the Orthodox monasteries of central Bulgaria, from Lappish fells to Polish market-places.

Now I face the challenge of the familiar: Tesco's stuffed shelves and village post offices, branch libraries and seaside guesthouses. People not travelling, that is to say, but going away for a holiday, that activity so ordinary that very few ever write about it. Yet a woman is no less worth listening to, a man no less interesting to watch, because they are in Shanklin instead of Shanghai, Seaview rather than Sioux country.

The view of the Isle of Wight here offered is not tidy, like ranks of showcases in a museum, but quirky, like the strange diversions and cul-de-sacs of our own limitless lives, with all their breathtaking possibilities and bifurcations, choices made, not made, or not even considered. This is, to be sure, the only book that this particular Englishman will ever write about a patch of England, because I believe in snatching the strange from the jaws of time, even at the prospect of being bitten. Kant says that we perceive and transform the outside world according to the structure of our intellect. Fair enough: but what was the outside world like before we perceived and transformed it?

Is the Isle of Wight the outside world, more or less, to Caulkhead or overner, or is it different? Does it really change according to the manner in which each of us perceives it? If so, my perceptions will hardly assist readers in their own perceptions, since each will become unique. I do think we are changed by what we experience, and the more we choose to experience, the more intensely we experience it, the more radically we change. I do not know that I can be trusted to remain the same man ten minutes together, which is one of the reasons why I find teaching creative writing to the mentally disturbed not only fascinating in itself but significant in its consequences. For it is wrong to think that the world is naturally well organised, easily intelligible; we know that chaos and catastrophe are natural when two apparently orderly processes meet, in train crashes or mathematical theory, in religious disputes or the gradual warming of the earth. It is just that most travel books (many of mine included) do not convey that sense of disruption or rapid change so apparent in real life. I have tried in *Wight Magic* to provide such disruptions, so that your experiences there might be recognisable from the shifting patterns of description and dialogue in the book, alarming as their confluence might seem to those accustomed to a quiet life.

List of Illustrations

OFF WIGHT

I am forever classified by Wighters as a overner from the mainland. By this they mean that I come from a slightly bigger island called Great Britain. The same thing happened on Hoy. I had taken the boat from Stromness and at about five that burnished purple-grey summer evening my boat lolled on the beach like an opened white shellfish on a plate. "Time", waved the boatman as I sat dreaming by a rockpool, "to go back to the mainland". He meant Orkney, seven miles from the northernmost coast of Scotland.

Islands are separated as much by emotion as by water and an expanse of unalloyed air; Man had its own language, Celtic in distinction to English, as different as the Norn of Shetland. Scolt Head off Norfolk was the life study of the geographer Alfred Steers; Northumberland's Farne Islands stimulated a bibliography of more than 600 items in the 1970s; the Seigneur of Sark ranks with the Bishop of Urgel, co-Prince of Andorra, as one of Europe's tiny handful of feudal rulers. Skye, Jersey, Lundy and Lindisfarne apparently have nothing in common except the fact that they are bits of rock adrift from larger bits of rock. But they do: people think of them as isolated, separate, eccentric, and in quirky Britain these are virtues prized and exaggerated for effect. Why, indeed, should one want Benbecula to become like Guernsey? Is it not better that we differ? Yes, it is.

The Isle of Wight is not only the quintessence of Englishness: it is explicitly recognised as such by many who persist in returning there, despite no lack of alternatives. If you think of the Dordogne as the Frenchest Frence, and Heidelberg as the Germanest Germany, then Wight is the Englishest England.

So, as I trudge round Portsmouth, to Wight as the Ile de Ré is to La Rochelle, my glance keeps straying to the shape on the horizon, clear or misty, bright with sparkling lights at midnight, or businesslike, bedrizzled, penny plain. Shall we go?

About twenty thousand years ago the sheets of ice receded from the land we know as Wight and it gradually acquired forests, with settlements around what are now the West Yar, Medina and East Yar rivers. About seven thousand years ago the chalk heights from Studland in Dorset to Freshwater crumbled, letting in the thunderous sea, and Wight was no longer part of mainland England, but an island where Neolithic man fished, caught shellfish, and hunted boar and deer. For centuries, men could ford the Solent at low tide. Paddling became a normal Hampshire activity. The round-headed Beaker folk colonised long enough, around 1850 B.C., to cohabit with long-headed natives. The Iron Age silently advanced Wight in hand and brain, techniques and social skills from about 550 B.C. The dead were no longer buried, but cremated; millstones crushed cereals. The Belgae from Northern France, arriving around 100 B.C., introduced coin-age and the chariot, trading with the Romans who soon conceived the desire to own lands beyond Gaul. Caesar raided Kent in 55 B.C. and 54 B.C., but it was in 43 A.D. that old Crab-and-Claws was seized by Vespasian, and renamed Vectis, without a fight. What use would it have been to fight against the might of Rome? No camps – no military roads – nothing was needed to subdue the peaceful men of Wight. Several fine villas (like that on Brading Down) indicate a peaceful purpose for Roman settlement on Wight: retirement. The Romans would have been tongue-tied as the natives of Freshwater stroked the wheels of the chariots, and asked about real horse-power to the milia. And can I try on your helmet, mister? We have a fortification at Carisbrooke, but this is very late Roman, probably achieved against the Saxons shortly before 530, when West Saxons conquered the island under Cedric and his son Cynric and colonised Vectis for Wessex. In 534 Cedric died and ownership passed to his nephews Stuf and Wihtgar, renaming Carisbrooke and its castle 'the fort of Wihtgar': Wihtgarasburh. But for the grace of Wihtgar, we might now be visiting the Isle of Stuf. In 661 Wulfhere of Wessex granted the island to his vassal king of Sussex.

The Norman Conquest changed sovereignty of Wight for a while: to William FitzOsbern, but by treason his son Roger forfeited the prize in 1078, when it reverted to the King. The castle earthworks must have been raised during these years because in Domesday (1086), the Castle of Avington (the manor in which Wihtgarasburh lay) is recorded as standing on twenty acres of land.

Portsmouth to Fishbourne

Cyril, a retired bus-driver from Nottingham, was taking his thirteenth trip to the Isle of Wight in eleven years. Eighty-three years of age, he had seen Australia, Spain, Holland, three or four times Germany, but all in all, the Isle of Wight's your best holiday anywhere. The first couple of times he and his wife from Matlock stayed at the Sanmay Guest House, 51 Station Avenue, Sandown (Reductions for children, No hidden extras, Regret no pets), but ever since they've stayed at Daish's in Old Shanklin. The people all over the island are very friendly, and Daish's has a good chef, very polite waitresses, and Jeanne makes you feel at home for the whole week. There's a full-day tour on Monday to Alum Bay and Freshwater, three half-day tours, and there's a grand weekly market in Newport. You sail round Portsmouth Harbour on a boat from Ryde. Cyril remembers when Arthur Lowe played Mr Swindlehurst in the Coronation Street grocer's before Alf Roberts. The best time at Daish's is the Christmas and New Year week, with fancy dress. Cyril and the missus had their best fancy dress party over Christmas and New Year 1987, with a mile-long buffy, when she got herself up as an Austrian peasant and Cyril dressed up as an Arab sheikh. "Nothing to it", he said, enthusiastically. "Give me two corks, half a cup of Guinness and the cork dipped in the Guinness will go brown. Then you rub it on your face, stains lovely, and your own mother won't recognise you. To get rid of it when the party's over, hot soap and water's all you need. That night I went to a pub in Godshill and met a couple from Daish's. I went up to them and said 'memsahib' to her and all that twaddle. Didn't recognise me! Next morning at breakfast I said 'You enjoyed yourself at Godshill!' They said 'How do you know we were at Godshill?' I said you didn't know but that were me in the Arab dress. Well I never! They did laff!" The pace of life hasn't increased a jot since Cyril started to come to the Island in 1978, he said. "Eh, I got a shock of my life when I went into the church at Whittingham. The verger's son is a teacher at Chesterfield! It's all gone downhill in Nottingham. You can go into a shop and call out 'Is there anyone about?' Here on the Island they can't do enough for you."

A trinity of seagulls overhead debated whether to screech out to me news of impending disaster: their unanimous warning of shipwreck I ignored again, as I ignore fretting turbulence below aircraft. There is a sublime quality of the carefree among those of us who have seen so many countries that the law of averages about catastrophes no longer seens to apply. Like centenarians, we gobble up each fresh day gluttonously. It's all strawberry sundaes and fresh linen-white Mondays.

Forty minutes is all it takes to cross from the dockside between Portsea and Old Portsmouth to the jetty at the head of Wootton Creek for Fishbourne. Within twenty minutes the car ferry has unloaded its vehicles and passengers and has loaded again ready for the return journey, every hour on the hour between 6 a.m. and 8 p.m., with additional weekday trips at 3 and 5 (from Portsmouth) and 4 (from Fishbourne)

Fishbourne. The Sealink car ferry arrives from Portsmouth

and extra evening trips at 9 and 11 (from Portsmouth) and 10 and midnight (from Fishbourne).

On Fishbourne jetty a yellow graffito announced THE LORD JESUS CHRIST IS WITH YOU, to which a frustrated football supporter had appended in red I'D RATHER HE WAS WITH WEST BROMWICH ALBION.

Once on the island roads, you realise that they are different (a sign tells you so) and one has to resist the instinct to drive on the right, as if one had crossed to France. Everywhere is so close (23 miles in all east to west, and 13 miles in all north to south) that speed is something only overners think about. There's always time, on the Island. Seen from above (and NASA's Challenger saw it from 240 miles up on 11 October 1984), the Island looks like a flat fish, with Newport north of centre and the Medina running almost due north to Cowes from its source near St. Catherine's Down. The Ordnance Survey map shows two Rivers Yar, but locally they are known as the Western Yar (Freshwater to Yarmouth) and the much longer Eastern Yar (north of Niton to Bembridge). We have seen the short, heady progress of the Wootton emptying into Wootton Creek by the Fishbourne Ferry. Apart from these the only river of any size is the Newtown River within the National Trust reserve which incorporates the entire estuary, the 78 acres of Hamstead, the 12 acres of Quay Fields, the 12 acres of Town Copse leading to Clamerkin Lake, the occupied late seventeenth-century inn, De Francheville Arms known locally as Noah's Ark from the inn-sign; and the Town Hall.

1 Seaview and the East

Ryde

Portsmouth is linked to Ryde Pierhead by Sealink ferry, departing roughly hourly, and Lymington to Yarmouth. From Southampton a Red Funnel service currently operates to West Cowes (Pontoon) and East Cowes (Trinity Wharf) and a Red Funnel hydrofoil takes only twenty minutes (a third of the boat service's time) from Southampton's Royal Pier to West Cowes (Pontoon). The fastest connection with the mainland is the seven minutes taken by Hovertravel's hovercraft between Southsea (Clarence Pier) and Ryde (Quay Road).

Ferry services that we now take for granted were started as recently as the 1850s, and it was only then that seaside holidays in the Island could develop as an attraction for large numbers of overners. Popularity among island resorts quickly diverged, leaving northern, western and southern areas relatively untouched. The current annual Holiday Guide published by the Southern Tourist Board to advertise hotels and guesthouses in the Island devotes one page each to Bembridge, Cowes and Newport, 3 to Ryde, 8 to the whole of West Wight, 15 to Ventnor and 66 to Sandown and Shanklin, so there is no doubt where to go for your seaside holiday if you are sociable and enjoy plenty of human contact, often with people who choose the same guesthouse year after year.

Ryde, we have just seen, is mysteriously not one of the favoured seaside holiday resorts, despite its accessibility from the mainland, its attractive sands west and east of the pier, and Puckpool's bathing huts halfway to Seaview. Prehistoric man staked out St John's, Haylands (axe-finds) and Swanmore (urn-trove), but by the Middle Ages, La Rye (Ryde is a variant spelling) had diminished in importance to a dependency of the manor of Ashey, now a hamlet on the downs west of Brading. Even in the mid-17th century, the population barcly exceeded two hundred souls, rising to a thousand in 1800, ten thousand

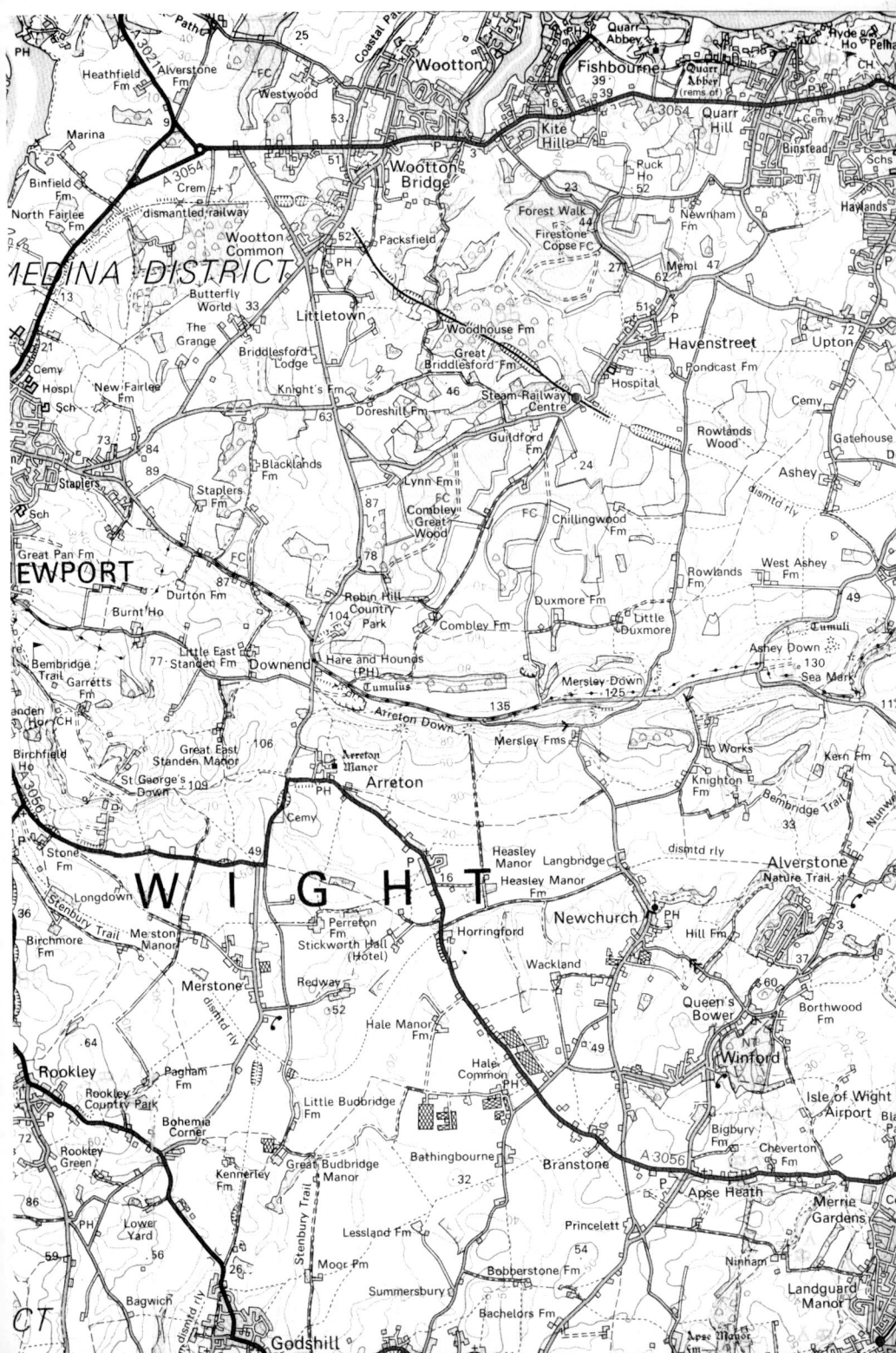

Map of the Isle of Wight, East

in 1850, twenty thousand in 1950, and thirty thousand today, when it outpopulates the Island capital. The difference in that crucial half-century to 1850 can be found in a number of apparently unrelated factors, such as the founding of Yelf's Hotel (1810) in the Union Street that had connected Upper and Lower Ryde since 1781, and the construction of a little wooden jetty (1813), many times improved and extended until it became, with a shank-length of 2,305 feet, the second longest pier in the country, with a promenade, tramway, and its own railway track and station. The tramway started in 1864, horse-drawn trams being the only mode of transport until the railway started operation in 1885, with a station at each end of the pier. The railway pier was built in 1879-80, and the fortune of Ryde was made, even if many purblind overners merely passed through the town on their way to other resorts.

Captain Marryat recorded in the 18th century at Ryde how "wherries came in as far as they could, and were met by a horse and cart, which took out the passengers, and carried them through the mud and water to the hard ground". On Ryde Esplanade one rainy autumn day in the Sixties, an evangelist's milling, raving, waving arms had cut a great open swathe so that he had to shout to make himself heard among the unsaved and the barely saveable. "Open your legs", he yelled, "and let the sin out". I'd never before heard constipation equated with damnation.

I spoke to Steve, dredging the mud from the boating lake in March 1989. "Three years since it's been done", he confided, "should by rights be done every year. It's on clay, not on concrete". Below the lake lie the mortal remains of many of the eight hundred victims of the sinking of the Royal George. England's greatest warship suddenly kneeled over and sank in Spithead in 1782 while families and friends of the sailors were bidding them fond farewells and many corpses fetched up in Ryde harbour. Nowadays kiddies use the lake for harmless fun above the grisly makeshift cemetery. A sign 'ROYAL MEDINA Boat Club. Sandy Slip.' bore a blank 'date' and a blank 'High tide will be at', with the permanent 'Warning. Beware of wash from passing ships. Get off Appley Sandbank 2½ hours before high water'. Below me the sands shrieked with

4

Ryde. Esplanade. Three icecreams, with ladies attached

running boys and girls, and dogs scampering ecstatically off the leash. I found four old boundary stones near the boating lake, one marking the St Helen's-Newchurch boundary and three the later Ryde Borough boundary.

Union Street has, understandably, changed a great deal since its creation in the 1830s, but the Royal Victoria Arcade – with its original shops – makes an enchanting exception. Gladrags, Moonfleet Antiques, Yvette Clairvoyant (does she mean 'clairvoyante'?) 10.30-3 p.m. Mon-Sat, Antiques Uriah's no. 9 Heap. 'Hole in Your Garment: cover it with a badge'. 'You don't have to be suicidal to talk to the Samaritans'. In the basement, records and bric-à-brac can be found on Fridays and Saturdays. At the back of the Arcade, with a narrow kitchen just out of sight, is the friendly Cockney-style Jay's Place, with a placard outside offering 'Toms on toast 70p' and 'Steak-kid Pie-Pots plus Veg £1.95', excellent value for these times. 'Just like a family', Jay assured me, as I settled down to a cupochar. "Jill comes in at all hours, look at that! She's done a day's work here, goes 'ome and cooks for the family, comes back and blimey, she's done us another dozen cakes. She is

5

bloody fabulous". Jay's wife, described by him as 'a toff', was born in Gibraltar, and sort of migrated. Jay from Fulham and Judy have been in Ryde for two years, working seven days a week. Why? "Cos I'm a greedy bastard, en I? No, seriously we 'ad a long weekend, fabulous three days, you know where I wen?" "Spain?", I hazarded. "Try again." "A Romany caravan around Ireland?" "Naa. Albion Hotel, Freshwater Bay, all the way over there!"

"Do the locals like you muscling in on their catering territory?" "Solid if they like you, otherwise..." He chopped air guillotinishly. "Oo's that?" – he waved at a late-night customer finishing egg and chips with industrious gusto. "I don't think I've had the..." "Smick", asserted Jay in conclusive triumph. "Tell em, Mick." Mick swallowed, and cleared his throat. "I'm a milkman", proffered Mick in a Solihull accent. "Sry", assented Jay. "Mother and father, Brummies. Mick, Brummie. Girl-friend, Brummie." I nodded a smile. "Get married, Isle of Wight, comes in for all his meals, 'blige me if 'e doesn't end up doing 'is washing up!" "Not today", contradicted Judy, "Today I'm doing his washing up." The quiet milkman walked over to the kitchen with his plate and cutlery. "See wot I mean?" snorted Jay. "One word from us and 'e treats the place like 'is 'ome." "I enjoyed the tea, thanks", I said. "Bloody fabulous".

Anyone interested in life 'upstairs, downstairs' will readily imagine earlier generations in the five-storey terraced houses in George Street, dating from the late 19th century, and intended as homes for the gentry or retired naval or army officers with an establishment to keep up, with one front door for 'the family' and guests; the other 'below-stairs' for tradesmen and servants.

Four free-standing statues representing the four seasons top Bernard Mitchell's, built in 1865 for a royal photographer called Jabez Hughes. One of his assistants, William Robert Hogg, though of Southampton origin, worked in Ryde from 1870 to 1928 and a selection of his work has been edited by Roy Brinton, Curator of Carisbrooke Castle, and published by the County Council.

The King Lud (Well Matured Wines and Spirits) faces the entrance to the pier, and is reckoned to be the closest pint to a new arrival. The man Lud was in fact a sixth-century invader from the Norse countries, and no more a king than the Staffordshire potter resting his elbows on Bob Jones's bar.

"That's the last time I come on 'oliday with a girl", moped the potter. "We'd barely got 'ere and she found a Rastafarian with an E-reg Porsche."

"Don't tell me about women", retorted another Midlander with a draught Guinness. "She wanted this flat in Sutton Coldfield to be near 'er work, and what 'appened?"

"She ran off with the first Rasta to toot 'is 'orn", nodded the potter.

"We'd no sooner moved in than the council tore down the block. They said it'd cost one and a half million to mend the places for ten years. It'd be cheaper to start again."

The conversation away from the bar encircled the subject of television so dear to the English even before the boom in satellites.

"I'll never forget the day", announced a woman in a beige cardigan, stroking her ginger moustache with an index finger, "when my Cousin Alice was on TV. The sixth of March 1989, it was, they had her on the possessive mothers show in that Kilroy. Bang in the middle of the front row, turning her 'ead this way and that, putting up 'er hand like she needed the loo, would that Kilroy look at 'er, would 'he ECK! I was watchin' loopy, like the end of a murder programme, waitin' for 'er, when bang, she's on. 'What is your experience then, Alice,' he said, scooping up a line of flex and poppin' the mike into 'er jaws. I was all ears. She'd just opened 'er mouth and bang, she's off again. 'Sorry to interrupt the lovely Alice', he goes, only we've run out of time and see you all again tomorrer'. I felt that deflated, you could have scooped me up with a trowel."

The semi-circle of lager-and-limes sat in sympathetic dismay. "An' that was it?" ventured a bright red hat with a bow from the bingo hall down the road.

"I thought I'll never get to the bottom of that one now".

"They say everyone's to be famous for fifteen minutes", offered a grey woolly beret.

"Thew," retorted the beige cardigan, "our Alice never got fifteen seconds. Sometimes you feel like weepin'."

Ryde. Pavilion, threatened with demolition

"Does you good, does a good weep," asserted a green-and-white striped blouse with cream buttons.

"I've had plenty", assented the bright red hat.

"Doris Day", nodded a grey jacket flecked with blue.

"Aye", said the bright red hat, "I know just how you mean."

Ryde is still an important shopping town for villagers. At Burton's, hopsack trousers cost £16.99. Hobbs Jewellers purvey a ghastly flamingo for £224.00, and real goose and hen eggs hand-decorated for £24.00 or £15.95. A wooden fretwork map of Great Britain for use as a thimble rack is priced £7.95. Outside Gateway a poster proclaims 'National News. It's War. Free can of top crop baked beans 440 g. when you buy any pack of Meatmaster Beefburgers'.

Wight Rabbit 'one-hop shopping' is claimed on Union Street. At number 34, the Gibbs and Gurnell 'Dispensatory' displays a collection of little green frog soaps. 'Come and have a complimentary makeup with Lin Bucknall'. Scottish Weavers at number 7 reduce 100% wool full-length coats, from £55. Jack's Beauty Shop offers earrings, necklaces and bangles with ladies' and men's hairdressing. First Stop at number 23 suggests gifts, souvenirs and lighters, with watches from £1.25. The view to the Esplanade, the Pier and the Solent seems to change minute by minute with variations in sunlight, cloud and mist. Hogg Robinson Travel list a one-year return to Dubai for £352, Bombay £397, Tampa £259 and Sydney £774. The County Press hoarding announces 'Ryde Heart Swap Mum Tells of Will to Live'.

I met Mrs Dickens, a regular at Ryde Coral, whose grandson plays soccer for West Ham United, and the amiable manageress Lynn Waldron. "It's a social service more than anything else", she explained. "It's warm in here when it's freezing in some of these old folks' homes, and it gets them out for a good laff." There would have been seventy women and a handful of men, all between about fifty and eighty. As well as the local prizes (£10, £15), there are regional prizes of around £5,000 and a national prize of £50,000, won not so long ago by a Ryde widow, Mrs Margaret White, who has since emigrated to Belgium. The caller, Neville Clark, reads out the randomly selected numbers on the television screens, so that devotees do not have to raise their heads. "Thirty eight, three eight, thirty eight", he chants, like a Tibetan monk reciting mantras, "fifty seven, five seven, fifty seven, eight, on its own, number eight, thirty three, all the threes, thirty three." In the neon-illuminated hall, with desks, pens and paper, we might be in a numerological examination hall for ancient druids. Fruit machines in the entrance foyer stood plopping, bleeping, and whistling, unheard and unwatched.

The interval gave us merciful release from the tension of all those numbers shooting up all over the place. The ladies relaxed, and carried on their conversations where they had left off forty minutes before.

"No, but *are* you *surprised* that our Denise got the shock of her life when she went to clear out at our Percy's after the funeral?"

"I'm not."

"Would you credit it what she found stacked up against the spare room door?"

"Filthy magazines?"

"Try again."

"Bird droppings. A sparrow 'ad been locked in and couldn't get out."

"It was bursting out with those giant catalogues, wasn't it?"

"No."

"It was. They write and say you can have this toaster and this carriage clock free if you take in our catalogue. The big ones like telephone books, with pictures of women in their nighties."

"He forgot them."

"Forgot 'em, eck. 'e didn't crack on that you were allowed to chuck 'em away after the carriage clocks had come. He'd upwards of a thousand all crashed down from piles like wossname."

"Haemorrhoids."

"Lockerbie. I was that fed up wi' traipsin' down the stairs to the rubbish with four at a time that I gev up, didn't I, and started throwing 'em out the window. I killed that Mrs Jarndyke's poodle with a Grattan's but I warn't to know it was leavin' its message in our Percy's carrots."

"It's a crying sin where they *do* go sometimes."

"Not that poodle it won't any more. Contribution from on

high that were."

I tucked in to lasagne in the fondue cellar at the Biskra House restaurant in St Thomas' Street, then emerged to the drunken songs of pool-playing lager louts.

This Johnny-come-lately of Island towns, Ryde had no place of worship at all, apparently, until the 18th century: its population in 1795 was barely 600. Ryde did not become a borough until 1868, when a clock tower was added to the Town Hall of 1829-31. In 1974, Ryde became a part of the Borough of Medina.

James Sanderson, who built Brigstocke Terrace, rebuilt St Thomas' Church (1827), with a strange churchyard using broken tombstones to walk on. This may not be sacrilege, but hardly suggests the best possible taste. Two stone lions guard the grave of Elizabeth Maynard (1799). The Medina Borough Council exhort us: 'Please do not allow your dog to foul this rest garden', a plea ignored by at least one dog-owner.

I chatted to Reg Barnes, an affable islander born in Brook in 1913, who has lived on the island all his life. His grandfather and father worked on a farm in Brook, in a tied farm cottage. When Reg was eleven, the family moved to Newport. He started life as an errand-boy, but took all sorts: cowman, general farmland, stable boy. On Sundays he'd be able to go home at eight or nine o' the morning if the animals were all fed and watered, but he went back two to four to see they was all comfy. All his adult life Reg has made concrete blocks: a good job with security, a living wage, and no rat race, not like today, no violence all year long. He'd walk 1½ miles each way to Yarmouth. He could have had a tricycle for ten shillin but he couldn't afford that, leastways not in them days. Food cost next to nothing.

"We used to forage for swedes and turnip tops: they're lovely. We used to have our own potato patch in the farmer's field, and there'd be a good crop every year, that'd see us through. Then there was mushrooms in the fields, fresh picked there's nothing to beat 'em. Blackberries along all the hedgerows: that's a good meal, with them apples. We raised chickens in the yard". Since retirement in 1978, Reg lives in Binstead, just before Quarr Hill. "The youngsters reckon they have to get their car out now to get to Binstead", Reg shouted

11

with laughter, shaking his head and wheezing at the folly and weakness of the younger generation.

I wandered into Star Street, to the Coral Bingo and Social Club, in the huge Commodore Cinema which backs on to Ryde Public Library and Art Gallery. The Star Inn (1683) was built as a private house in 1613. 'Afternoons, doors open 1.30, main session 2.10-2.50: 2nd session 3.05-3.45. Closed Sunday afternoons. Evenings, doors open 6. 55p afternoons, 65p evenings'. But senior citizens get in for nothing on Tuesday afternoons, and enjoy a free hot drink and biscuits. It felt a long way from the draughty village halls of South Yorkshire where I had first come into contact with bouncing balls and Kelly's Eye.

Posters announced Stainer's "Crucifixion" at Ryde Methodist Church and Tippett's "A Child of our Time" by the Isle of Wight Cantata Choir and Orchestra at the Medina Theatre, Newport. Shops announced "Over 60 pipe tobaccos in stock", including Borkum Riff, Escudo, Amphora Fall Aroma and Skandinavik"; and joke mugs marked 'Property of H.M. Prison, Parkhurst. Not to be Removed.'

Vernon Square Preservation Society, founded in 1986, used workers from the employment training scheme to clear the great jungular brambled wasteland in the centre, unkempt for more than forty years, and create the idyllic public amenity the whole neighbourhood enjoys today. Vernon Square is not just bricks and mortar on four sides with the air between. It is a microcosm of England: the dinky laid-out lawns and flower-beds, flitting up a pre-existent slope. It is the wrangling society and its committee, concerned as to who should get the credit, the memory of David Bellamy's opening in May 1989, to cast his cheery, bearded avuncularity over gaping children. Vernon Square is a busy housewife's shopping bag beside a bench; an elderly man bending to smell a rose, anger against passive vandals who see cigarette butts but do not pick them up, and the single yellow lines saying that you can't park here except at night.

The houses and flats, some of them coming down slightly in the world in a rakish, haphazard fashion, are called Vernon Lodge and Gray Lodge, West Point and Summerville. Gentility raises its hat a little more self-confidently with the renova-

Ryde. Vernon Square, after landscaping, 1989

tion of the square's green party piece.

By the Royal York Hotel, I found a graffito on a very tall lamp-post, "Does Neil's Head Swell When he Had Plants?", and at the next one, "Why Doyle Need a Haircut. Because He Look Like a Hippy." The Taj Mahal's sign read "Take Away Meals at the Front Door Please". A shop called 'Imagination' stood next to Ryde Washeteria, lacking the whingeing hypochondria of *Eastenders'* Dot.

Ryde Esplanade rejoices in a 16th-century creeper-hugged hotel, the Ryde Castle, built by order of King Henry VIII in the 16th century and nowadays providing weekly accommodation at £155 to £225. Nothing could be more convenient for the buses, hovercraft or ferry.

If you have to regret the passing of any one building in Ryde more than another, it must be the Theatre Royal in St Thomas' Square, where Ellen Terry as a child played Puck in Shakespeare's *A Midsummer Night's Dream*. Erected in 1871 on the site of an earlier Theatre Royal, it was converted to a cinema but gutted by fire in 1961. In latter years the *Red Guide* complained that "entertainments are generally of the 'variety' order", but regrettably even those came to an abrupt end when National Westminster Bank tills began to ring where a box office had once sold tickets.

All Saints' Church (1869) allowed Ryde its grand spire, a Sir George Gilbert Scott monument to Victorian self-confidence in an island where Queen Victoria felt more at home than she did anywhere else. All Saints' could seat a congregation of 1,300 in lordly competition with St John's at Oakfield and St Michael and All Angels' at Swanmore. From the top of All Saints' Tower it is said that the spire of Chichester Cathedral is visible on a fine day; on even the mistiest day you can make out within the opulence of its Decorated style, with elegant arcades between aisles and nave, and an alabaster pulpit with a white marble base proclaiming the distance of the Victorian God from the paupers whose case was passionately advocated by Dickens.

Whenever two taxi-drivers have a chat they seem to take endless pains to avoid looking each other in the eyes. They face the same way with their hands clasped behind them or lean over each other's shoulder, polish their hubcaps, adjust wing mirrors, wipe their windscreens and generally admire the view. I've never found out why they don't look at one another, but Ryde taxi-drivers behave in just this universal fashion. Is it due to lonerism, gazing straight ahead while driving and talking to passengers, or to cab radio, which never allows them to see their interlocutor?

"Got a Whippingham at four o'clock," said one driver, in a blue short-sleeved shirt, crumpled and sweat-stained. "Hunny Hill Technical School at four twenny", responded the other, "is old Mike back yet?" "Nah'" offered the first, "zonny zollidez".

In 1846 Prince Albert laid the foundation of the Royal Victoria Yacht Club just west of the pier. Now it has become the Prince Consort Theatre. A year later the Royal Isle of Wight Infirmary and County Hospital opened its doors, and in 1899 Queen Victoria opened the extension. The Esplanade, which caused the levelling of shore-side houses between Union Street and the Solent waters, was opened by Princess Beatrice in 1902, by which time the rail network had spread from the Pier to St John's station (1871), nine years after the first line had opened: the four and a half miles from Cowes to Newport, amalgamating in 1887 as the grandiloquently-named Isle of Wight Central Railway with lines completed in 1875 from Newport to Ryde and Newport to Sandown. The company opened a fourth line in 1897 which connected Newport with Godshill and St Lawrence, but this closed in 1952, the Newport-Sandown stretch in 1956, and the rest in 1966. A number of private railways once existed, the earliest being John Nash's at Hamstead, which opened as early as 1832, but nothing remains to view.

The most successful railway system was the Isle of Wight Railway which began operating from Ryde Station (now St John's Road) to Shanklin in 1864, with a defunct branch to St Helen's and Bembridge closed in 1953, and a Shanklin-Ventnor extension which ceased operation in 1966. Stations still served by former London Transport Underground rolling-stock (and a signal box from Waterloo Junction at St John's) are Brading, Sandown, Lake, and Shanklin. A typical timetable between eight in the morning and five in the afternoon would be Ryde Pier Head 2.18, Ryde Esplanade 2.20, Ryde St John's Road 2.24, Brading 2.30, Sandown 2.35, Lake 2.38 and Shanklin 2.41.

Rail enthusiasts might like to explore St Helen's to find part of the platform and a wooden extension to the main building; the station building (1877) has been transformed into a private house. If you want to hunt down more stations converted into homes, ask in Ashey, Blackwater, Godshill, Horringford, St Lawrence, Whippingham and Whitwell.

Almost as interesting are the tunnels: Ryde Tunnel is actually a covered way, being a cutting subsequently roofed over and opened in 1880, despite the date 1881 above the Esplanade entrance. Newport Tunnel (75 yards) is visible from waste ground near Fairlee Road. Ventnor Tunnel is the longest on the island, at 1312 yards: it opened into Ventnor station, which is regrettably demolished. The most interesting tunnel is that between Whitwell and St Lawrence, threading 620 yards below the downs south of Whitwell, now a mushroom farm.

One year I stayed at the Strand, using Philip and Diana Brown's Teneriffe Hotel as a base. Every morning I reversed into the parking space at number 14, where a balefully glaring old woman screeched down at me, "It's a good thing I'm queer, otherwise my car would be where yours is now!" I am still trying to think of a reply combining dignity with sense, but "I'm glad you're queer too, so I can spend thirty seconds in the space your car would otherwise have occupied" sounds as lame in retrospect as it would have done then, if I had thought of it. But I didn't.

The little Dotto train was carrying adults and excited children along the beach front from the pavilion in Eastern Gardens to Appley Park. "If you're going straight back again, there's no extra charge", an anxious Dad with a brood of six was told, to his visible relief. By the public bowling green, a maintenance man told his colleague, "I jis saw Barry, 'e come down garden way."

In Ryde Public Library I spoke to an assistant about local reading habits.

"They're quite reticent about language", she murmured, nibbling at her lower lip. "There was one of our Elim Pentecostals in a dirndl on her way to the chorus in *The Sound of Music* who brought back a Jean Plaidy and complained that it had the word 'breast'."

"I didn't think they were allowed to enjoy themselves", I said, "or is that the Exclusive Brethren?"

"I think she got a special dispensation because of the Trappists. Then we had that quiet little lady from East Hill Road, had been an emergency dentist in the War, in the brown fur collar and walking frame. We thought she was interested in ornithology, borrowing all the bird books, four at a time every week for seven years, she'd been changing 'tit' to 'nightingale' throughout."

A balding man peered unobtrusively over his pebble glasses as if trying to count absent friends. "Was she the one who sewed blankets for Bob Geldof?"

"No, that was Mrs P. from the Havenstreet Railway. She had a quavery bass soprano, if you catch my drift, and she never quite caught on to decimal fines. She heard about all the censorship rumpus and said she didn't know what all the fuss was about. 'Tropic of Ruislip indeed,' she said to me by the pelargoniums one afternoon when it was quietish: 'We never *had* any of these natural functions when I was a girl'."

I stopped at a shop called 'Not Just Beds' on the corner of St John's Road and High Street. "How much is a not just bed?" I asked them warily, gazing at the beds. "About £196.99", answered a Michelle in a pink suit. "What about the beds?" "About £246.98". "It sounds as though you've got a bargain in not just beds", I mused, leafing through wallpaper pattern-books. "I'm really more interested in not just mattresses". "Those would be very reasonable indeed", smiled Michelle, encouragingly. "You can get quite a good not just mattress for £94.97". "Is that a pillow," I guessed wildly, "or not just a blanket?" "That," she said, wondering at my slow uptake, "is not just a mirror." I edged uneasily towards the not just window. "Did you want to see the curtain materials?" "No thanks," I replied hastily, "not just now".

West Hill Road winds its way like a flat coil invisibly tensed. Behind those curtains gentility lulls itself with hot water bottles and Horlicks into a comforted certainty that there is nowhere better to be. Paul Daniels and Annabel Croft can flicker into your home with technicolour fidelity, their voices more familiar than your neighbour's. You have to put a mental rectangle round next door's husband's face to recognise him at all.

Tesco's outside Ryde stands on a redundant airport, with the cheapest petrol on the island, and daily bus services: from Shanklin, Lake and Brading; from Bembridge, St Helen's, and Seaview, from East Cowes, Wootton and Binstead; from Newport, Wootton, Binstead and Ryde town; and from Ventnor, Shanklin, Sandown and Yaverland. There is something anti-Wightish about this neon-lit brazen cathedral of Mammon in a gently-rolling isle of village churches and manor houses, as though Gateway were to open stalls between the monoliths at Stonehenge. "Strawberries are now reduced to 79 pence from 98 pence", seduced a languid soprano over the loudspeaker, another temptation to St Anthony. "Mrs Charlton", mysteriously, "to the F.S.C. Room", like a priestess being called to the Pythian oracle. The assistants wear red coats, as at Butlin's, giving a faintly sinister, mock-festive air to the sacrifice of your housekeeping money. "Mr G. Armitage" I read on the badge of one comedian-confessor, who would point you in the direction of leeks or radishes, Jeyes or Radox. Another heavy bore a badge with the legend 'Roy Trow, Tesco Security Guard", against raiders, looters, shoplifters, hijackers, kidnappers. A girl of nine or ten was dragged screaming past an aisle with cakes. I went over to the cause of her distress: a display marked 'Large Birthday'. Her mother stamped off with her friend. "She'll only scrape the top off," she shouted.

East of Ryde, by contrast, there is nothing of Tesco's clicking cash-registers and airport-type announcements. You can stroll to Appley, with its little folly a droll landmark, and then to the wide sands of Puckpool, where seventy beach huts painted bottle green stared enviously at the sea; nobody has thought to give them wheels, unlike the bathing machines of once upon a time.

One summer in the 1970s a matron in a dress badly afflicted by measles confided in a fresh acquaintance at Puckpool Holiday Village, a mile and half from Ryde, "I would have gone to Turkey, but I discovered at the airport that they wouldn't agree to take me on one of those visitor's cards. So I ended up in Puckpool. It's great here, isn't it?" "I don't know, I'm afraid", responded the peroxided widow in all turquoise blue, with a white leather belt where her waist should have been, "I'm only here for three nights."

Quarr

I first came across Quarr Abbey (the origin is obviously 'quarry', for several ancient stone quarries are well attested in the neighbourhood) when reading about the rabbit-mad clerk Hardekyn in C.J. Cornish's *The New Forest and the Isle of Wight* (1903). Three times his bow and arrow hit the mark, and our poaching friend seized the illegal prizes. "Tres cuniculos sagittas transfixit", notes the record of his transgression. Since Cistercian rules required monks to abstain from flesh, it was only by relaxing somewhat that they were able to vary their diet. Hardekyn claimed he possessed a dispensation to keep domestic rabbits in his cell, and they made abundant increases. Naught availed him: he was put in chains and finally absolved only after throwing himself on the *misericordiam dominae*, on the mercy of the Lady of the Manor.

Until myxomatosis decimated the British rabbit population, rabbits formed a vital part of the Island diet, so it is interesting (but fruitless) to guess how the word 'rabbit' became a mild oath there.

There is an odd reference to Quarr in the sixteenth-century topography of England by William Lambard, compiled by John Nichols in his *Bibliotheca Topographica Britannica* (1780-90), to the effect that "the inhabitants of this island be wont to boast merrily that they neither had amongst them monks, lawyers, wolves nor foxes, yet I find them all save one in a monastery called Quarr."

Baldwin de Redvers, son of that Richard who became Lord of the Island, built the original monastery for grey-clad monks from Savigny-le-Vieux in Normandy whose order was founded in 1114 by the hermit-saint Vitalis. Eighteen years in the building, it was completed in the first half of the 12th century and became Cistercian by default in 1147, when the Order of St Vitalis merged with the white-garbed Cistercians. By appointment, you can be taken to see the ruins of the ancient abbey, already inhabited by Savignac monks in 1132, when the foundation charter of Quarr was issued. Quarr owned many lands on the Island, such as Haseley and Arreton and the Lord Abbot attained such wealth and status that he sat, as a spiritual peer, in the Upper House. Younger sons of the gentry were appointed rent-gatherer, chief butler, treasurer and steward. The Abbey owned its own fleet of ships, being permitted to import wine duty-free, and the abbey became a fortress against invasion. The shallow stone pits (they are called *pitts* not only here but in Bonchurch for example, *quarr* being the name used even now in Dorset) gave up greenish-creamy, hard limestone from the upper Osborne beds, not as previously believed a kind of Bembridge limestone.

Outside the ruins of Quarr Abbey, a County Council sign urges 'No galloping please'. The Old Abbey Farm has a barn and back wall dated 1103 with tall stepped lancets later reset. The farm manager, Mark Carter, with one cowman, administers 160 acres. Prior Leo showed me over the western range of the cloister, on which the barn rises above the vanished storerooms and cells for lay-brothers. Nothing much survives of the church south of the cloisters, the kitchen in the north range and refectory, joined by a chamfered hatch. So what happened to Quarr?

After the French invasion of Newport and Newtown in 1377, the abbey fortified, with gunports in the northern enclosure wall, first itself, then Fishhouse (now Fishbourne) and its mill on Wootton Creek. So when the Dissolution of the Monasteries was decreed in 1536, Islanders argued that Quarr remained as useful a fortification against the French as any; that the abbey was not a wealthy foundation; and that only ten monks were then in residence. But nothing helped Quarr: after some time its stone (and lead) with stone from other abbeys, such as Netley and Beaulieu, went to create new castles, such as Yarmouth (still standing) and East and West Cowes (both vanished). Imagine the great elms that once surrounded Quarr, now gone forever. But one of the abbey's three bells still rings out from the Holy Cross Church in Binstead.

Monasteries in France were not suppressed until assailed by 'liberté, egalité et fraternité' in 1792, and then in 1833 a young lay priest called Prosper Guéranger founded a new contemplative community in the priory of Solesmes. Compelled to quit France in 1901 by the Law on Associations, they sought refuge first at Appuldurcombe House, under Dom Paul Delatte, whose community numbered about a hundred monks. But when Appuldurcombe's lease expired in 1908, the monks could not afford to buy the house, and they moved to Quarr with their wooden chapel. The Abbey House here had been occupied by Admiral Sir Thomas John Cochrane (1779-1872) but after Queen Victoria's death the Cochranes no longer visited Quarr, and the Admiral's son Lt. Thomas Cochrane, Deputy Governor of the Island, sold the oak-girt house, built of stones from the ancient abbey. By the most fortunate coincidence (G.K. Chesterton might have called it, with characteristic extravagance, 'the hand of God'), the community of Solesmes included an architect, Dom Paul Bellot. By 1914 he had completed his design, using local bricklayers to lay hard, durable Flemish bricks outside and inside, an uncompromising brick in golden and reddish layers, arching like the struts of a great barn illuminated evenly like heaven at dawn or dusk, without those columns and capitals which typify the English parish church.

Transverse pointed brick arches flow like the Marsh Arab dwellings of Iraq up to the high roof above the long choir which dominates the church and overwhelms a casual visitor in the short nave, who rightly feels an intruder in the daily round of monastic offices which will have begun long before his visit: at five thirty a.m., with Matins, followed at seven by Lauds in Latin, and at 8.45 by the Conventual Concelebrated Mass. Sext at one; None at 4.30; Vespers at 5.00; Compline at 8.30: the obligations and opportunities recur like a dove's beating wings, without which it would fall and die. The public is permitted to enter the church and attend services every day.

The Solesmes community under Dom Germain Cozien returned home with dignity in 1922, leaving behind 25 monks to maintain an English foundation under Dom Émile Bouvet, who presided over his first ordination of an Englishman in 1936, before his death the next year, when the priory was raised to the rank of Abbey it holds today. The first English abbot, Dom Aelred Sillem, was elected in 1964.

Charles Fitzsimons kindly showed me round the computerised library (the great Solesmes library is back in Solesmes as one might expect), but I received the impression that – unlike the mediaeval scriptorium – the library is not the heart of modern Quarr but its brain. Days are divided between the life of direct prayer and the working periods from about 10 to 1 and 2.30 to 4.30. The two hours after Vespers are spent reading, meditating or praying in the church, the cells, or the garden. Work may include craftsmanship, manual labour or administration in the buildings or on the farm.

As modern life seems to become ever more hectic, stressful, and changing, and people seem to become ever less dependable, more neurotic, it is essential to recognise that the seeds of growth and maturity are in ourselves. We may have the resources to develop our own personality in secular or religious life; or we might require the intervention of external discipline, like the Benedictine Rule. For Benedict said "Let him not be granted an easy entrance but, as the Apostle says, 'Test the spirits, to see whether they come from God'."

One test of a great (as opposed to a large) religious building is whether it would enhance a performance of Eliot's *Murder in the Cathedral*, a test that St Mildred's at Whippingham fails with clutter, but *sobrio* Quarr passes with decorous ease, its chanted atmosphere contagious with awe and spiritual plentitude. I connect it with that resonant German adjective *hervorragend*: prominent, distinguished. One does not gossip here, as one may do with comfort in Niton's John the Baptist, or St Mary & St Rhadegunde at Whitwell. One listens, and the spirit is allowed to speak, we know not whence or whither, or why or how, but it speaks.

Quarr makes it difficult for a novice. He is invited to stay in the guesthouse several times, then to stay in the monastery, and if he is compatible with the monks he may enter the community for two years before taking temporary vows. A further three years must elapse before he may take his final vows, and even then, of course, it may be that he is unsuited to the task. He may lack tenacity or celibacy or he may lose his convictions. But, a few hundred yards from the main Ryde to Newport road, near the shadow of millennial oaks, he may find the peace that passes all understanding while uttering Gregorian chant below the narrow verticals of stained glass augmenting the six pale lamps above the choir. At Lent and Advent he may wear a purple chasuble over a white alb during Mass; he may, as if in a dream of early Solesmes, see distant black monastic habits, red for the martyrs' feasts and for Whitsun and Pentecost, or the asymbolic green. He may join one of the fifteen priests or twenty-five monks who inhabit time without time, transitional between birth and eternity.

Long before the Christian religion overtook parts of humankind, Plato had written (in the *Phaedrus*), "Those who have once begun the heavenward pilgrimage may not go down again to darkness and the journey beneath the earth, but they live in light always."

On Ashey Down, in Newtown's Town Copse, and in Quarr Abbey church, the heavenward pilgrimage appears in starry steps it is almost easy to attain.

Perhaps, amid the racing of little children on Sandown beach or Blackgang's Wild West Town, the deepest Magic of Wight need be sought no farther from Wootton Creek than Quarr. Who knows?

I suppose St Edmund's at Wootton and the Holy Cross at Binstead may lay claim to be the quietest churches on the Quiet Island, for they both lie distant from the highway, each at the northern end of a Church Road.

Binstead's church, originally of Norman date, antedated the Island's other foundation dedicated to the Holy Cross, in Newport. First look for the sheela-na-gig, locally called 'the Idol', a pagan grotesque set up on the Norman gateway along the perimeter to the right of today's entrance gate. This sculptured cult symbol is here, as usual, connected with female fertility, and similar examples can be found in Ireland at Cashel's cathedral and the 16th-century church of Killinaboy. Good Binstead stone built this church, as it contributed to Winchester and Chichester (11th century), Quarr itself, and the abbeys of Beaulieu and Netley (13th century) among others.

The 13th-century chancel is the most distinguished part of Binstead Holy Cross, with 16th-century Dutch carved panels on the altar far superior to English work of the time; particularly beautiful is the Last Supper. The 19th-century nave was severely damaged in a fire of 1969, but much of the chancel was spared, and the new hammer-beam roof of Sussex oak faithfully reproduces the original, in virtuoso craftsmanship by Morey and Sons of Newport.

During the season, roses flourish and scent the churchyard with their fragrance. A pathetic gravestone depicts the innocent vessel of one Thos. Sivell "who was cruely shot on board his sloop by some *officers* of the *customs* of the Port of Portsmouth on the 15th of June 1785 at the Age of 64 years, leaving a disconsolate Widow & family." Ironically, many a guilty man eluded the customs men.

Grace Yealland of Binstead remembers how the village institute provided somewhere for the boys to play cards or billiards, and the older men to read or chat. They regularly plagued the lady 'in charge', on one occasion placing underneath a painting of a man and horse a pile of what on closer inspection proved to be horse manure.

A nightingale's ravishing song glittered in the air like a chain of diamonds, a star-burst, and I stood bewitched at Binstead until its tones eventually fell silent, and the echo dropped into bracken, and died. A century had passed.

Not all the endless ferry to-and-fros in the world can spoil Wootton and its creek, though a new Brewers Fayre was springing up at Wootton Bridge, north of the Ryde-Newport highway, which threatened to upset the rural calm. I followed Wootton Church Road almost as far as the cul-de-sac. Farm Lane would take you to Woodside and Warner's Holiday Camp but, like Judith in *Duke Bluebeard's Castle*, I wanted every door to be opened, and St Edmund's Church was to be no exception. The old Saxon church, defying the Danish compulsion to worship Odin and the gods of the north who still penetrate our daily calendar with clever subversion, has vanished, as well it might. It is a wonder, after the Norman invasion, that the Norman church kept its Saxon dedication, but Edmund was a saintly king and martyr never likely to be forgotten among the English, killed like Sebastian by archers after he had been bound to a tree. You can see the origin of the little church as private chapel to Wootton Manor House in its intimate dimensions, with room for barely forty-five seated in the nave. The nave dates from the first generation after the

Wootton. St. Edmund's

Conquest, since when the church was long connected with the de Insula or Lisle family, who provided the Rector, again an Edmund, 1283-93. The south doorway is proclaimed by Ron Winter the finest Norman doorway on the Island, and he has seen them all. Sun slanted down, peering as if to read the hymnbooks. Nobody came. Nothing stirred. Hell, Sartre decided, is other people. Heaven is possibly somewhere like Wootton. A hollow tree invites the curious hand beside the tomb of Louisa Groundsell (d. 1 May 1910 aged 80) and her husband James Young Groundsell whom I think pined for lost love, for he died aged 80 on 28 October in the same year.

For some reason I found the most painful, awkward, frustrating, moment in Wootton churchyard was that standing before a new tombstone, not yet afflicted with the lichen gnawing at the great Norman doorway:

'Here our pretty daughter lies,
sung asleep with lullabies.
Holly Elizabeth Sines,
in heaven 24 June 1988,
1 day old.'

At Warner's Holiday Camp, a plump lady lolled in a deckchair, overlapping both sides so that painful ridges sawed into her thighs and she had to keep moving, like a do-it-yourself cow on a spit.

Her mother was turning the pages of a magazine called *Best* with the restlessness of a ticket-vendor asked to look up a timetable for Goole in the middle of a morning rush-hour. "I don't understand this twenty-four hour clock. I needed this 17.10 the other day. I don't know whether that's seventeen minutes past ten or ten past seven. So I cracked it by setting two alarm clocks, one for each."

"Does it work?"

"I s'pose so. Only, I was so nervous, wasn't I, I woke up before either of them went off."

Wootton has the distinction of being one end of Havenstreet Steam Railway, but it also possesses an indoor garden with a 'Butterfly World', next to Medina Garden Centre. A White Admiral gorged on a banana slice set on a bird-table, and an infant called Christopher was trying to hit the butterfly under the indulgent eye of his mother. Fifteen butterflies a day emerge from the chrysalis here, taking ten minutes to pump their wings and two days to dry them out. The whole entrancing tent is a dithering, dancing melée that would have made Ronald Firbank squeal among the duchesses, especially on catching sight of inquisitive, lightfoot Chinese quails employed as cleaners to demolish the spiders and ants that would devour the butterfly eggs. Fountain World, a new attraction next to the Medina Garden Centre, has computer-controlled fountains with ten different spray patterns, but the 'Italian' and 'Japanese' gardens fail to capture the idiosyncrasy of their originals, and are saved from tweeness only by the rapacity of Japanese koi carp which Penny feeds three times a day. Some of these eccentrically-marked fish live for sixty years and more, with an uncritical diet including brown bread, plants and prawns. In Japan they live in mud pools, but here at Wootton they swim around a clear pond where visitors can see their hungry, snapping, swirls.

Seaview

The Flamingo Park four hundred yards up Oakhill Road is open from Good Friday to May, 2-5.30 and from May to September, 10-5.30. You don't have to love birds to find these enchanting gardens full of interest, with waterfowl so tame they will eat out of your hand. By a willow, I joined a convention of ants. I tried to listen to their main speaker, but he had just finished, the meeting had already broken up and the delegates were excitedly greeting each other. "Maurice, fancy seeing you here! How's the missus?" "Larry old son! Fancy a bite round the oak-roots down the field?"

A little girl was wearing a plastic ring in the shape of a brown bat which she had rescued from a Christmas cracker before her tidy mother had silently scooped it away with the torn wrapping-paper. I too, little Effie, had done the same with a tin frog that craaaked at me very satisfactorily every time I pressed its tail.

I rejoined the coast road where Springvale Road met Duver Road, with its tollgate. The first inland bend brings you round into Salterns Road. Saltern cottages date from the early 19th century, when saltworkers in the pay of one James Fitzpatrick brought summer sea water into shallow pans (called salterns) at high tide until a strong brine was produced, being boiled in autumn until salt crystals were formed and could be packed for sale. In 1819 the Seaview saltworks collapsed, but in 1824 it is known that 29 such workings survived in Hampshire and the Island of 35 throughout the whole of England and Wales, though by the end of the century the industry had died.

I was thirteen, a miserable, spotty, homesick adolescent when I was dragged screaming for my first seaside holiday to Seaview. In April 1951 the proprietress of the guest house wrote to my father,

'I am in receipt of your letter of the 18th, for which I thank you. I can offer you a large bedroom on the 2nd floor, with the single bed for your son for the week July 28th to Aug 4th, inclusive terms for your wife and self 6½ gns each per week, and as you do not give the age of your son, I quote for the following ages. Up to 8 years 4 gns per week. 8 to 12 years 4½ gns per week. Teenage 5 gns per week. Children not taking the evening meal, a tea is provided for them at 5.30. Thanking you in anticipation of an early reply'. Her brochure explained that the Yacht Club and Starboard Club were each within one minute's walking distance, the view over the Solent was unrivalled, spring interior mattresses, hot and cold water and gasfires were provided in all rooms, dogs could not be accommodated, and ferries would be met by arrangement. 'Extras: Early morning tea, 3d per cup; meals in bedroom, 1/- each'.

It was a fearfully hot summer, at least in my memory, and I cowered against the merciless sun in the lee of a wall until exhorted to come out. My bucket and spade were no consolation. I wanted to go back home, and I began to feel the first stirrings of lust, which I thought to be unique, as I had been reading the Greyfriars stories in which the only female mentioned was a porcine joke. My public school was single-sex, and although masters (and even a chaplain) disappeared unaccountably for reasons unconnected with academic promotion, I had remained as baffled about homosexuality in those early years after the War as about heterosexuality. Without a sister or girl-friend, I didn't know what *anyone* was doing or talking about. There was a girl at the guest-house, possibly eleven or fifteen (I had no yardstick for guessing their age) who smiled at me twice across the lunch-tables and once in the passage. I was of course too shy to smile back, much less speak to her of my overwhelming, inchoate, passions. No-one else of my age was staying at the guest house, and I was too tongue-tied to approach anyone else. The rest of my life has been an ocean of bliss compared with those frustrated, powerless, incoherent years when school and homework imprisoned me in hours, days, weeks and months seemingly endless, with the agony of exams like a Golgotha after carrying the cross all that way.

I promised myself that if ever life stopped ganging up on me, and I became master of my own destiny, I should never have another miserable, dank day and so it has turned out. Seaview should have been different, but I had been too happy reading and daydreaming back at home to benefit from a week spent reeling with sunstroke from a bookless room to a mute passion for a distant girl in the dining-room, and then back to the shrivelling, burning beach. Sun-tan lotion of rather poor quality just made me cook more deeply and furiously. I suffered at Seaview.

Seaview. The author in 1951, aged 13, shortly before destruction of the pier

It seemed awful retribution when, a few months later, Francis Caws' 1880 suspension pier was totally demolished in a storm. Yet at the time, around me, youngsters were skipping and shouting, building meticulous sandcastles guarded by Dads in shorts who behaved like Doberman Pinschers at any threat to their colonised territory. I had finished *The Mowgli Stories* and *Swallows and Amazons*, and riffled through the official guide for clues to seaside behaviour. 'The Laurels' anxiously told me about the 'small ideal family guest house, right on sea front with garden adjoining beach, absolutely central, separate tables, really excellent meals, every comfort, children and elderly people especially welcome, hot and cold running water and Slumberland beds in each bedroom, personal attention in every department, open all the year, most reasonable terms', but forgot to mention their address. Separate tables, that key to English isolationism so deftly magnified by David Niven (who lived on the Island from 1919 to 1933) in the film of Rattigan's play, are also featured in half-page advertisements by 'South Winds' (old garden with fruit trees, putting green, 'buses stop at the gate'); Quay Rocks Hotel, a 'superior hotel charmingly situated on the Sea Front, hot and cold running water in all bedrooms and interior spring mattresses'; Green Gates, with 'every modern convenience, central heating, two bathrooms, H. & C. Water in all Bedrooms, also Electric Fires, Bedside Lamps'; and the Madeira Hotel, Madeira Road, with 'comfortable lounge, spacious games room, and modern dining room.'

Such guest houses and little hotels offered a base for impossible hopes. Girls of eighteen would encounter an admiral, tanned and travelled, desirous of whisking them away to romance under eastern skies. Pimply youths would find Rita Hayworth incognito at the pictures, sitting alone nearby and smouldering for a kiss. Bank clerks with worried, willing helpmates concerned about the housekeeping money feigned jollity and camaraderie with the same people they would pass without a nod once home in Surbiton. Elderly ladies with a pekingese, two poodles, a woebegone dalmatian, would regret having to consort with their social inferiors. "It was never like this in my day". A rowdy family of six from Hackney would set one's delicate nerves on edge with family jokes and earnest plans about Sandown. It was all intolerable.

But Seaview is doomed, crumbling into the briny, a process accelerated by recent winter storms. One old lady steadfastly refused to leave her subsiding home even though it could be observed slipping daily farther into the sea. It was reported (though I cannot vouch for this at first hand, luckily) that she arranged for her bed to be strapped up to the bedroom wall, as it sloped at such an angle that it would have otherwise carried her outside and into the waves, an occurrence all too familiar to fans of the Marx Brothers from the disappearing orchestra finale in *At the Circus*.

Seaview stubbornly clings to the divine right of two pints of gold-top milk, left on the doorstep at the break of day, not only to be left untouched by thieving human hand, but even untapped by passing sparrow's beak.

In Seaview, the sloping High Street leads to a plaque: "During the last invasion of the county, hundreds of French troops landed on the foreshore nearby. This armed incursion was bloodily defeated and repulsed by local militia, 21.7.1545". The French were actually defeated by archers at Fairy Hill. Just above the pebbly beach, where waves wash over sea-weedy boulders, I stood beside two retired men, their cheeks betraying the combined effects of liquor and fresh air in doubtful proportions.

"Oh yes," confided the walking stick to the rolled umbrella, "she was a very *strong* woman, was Emily, my first. She wouldn't let a book in the 'ouse. Everything 'ad to be *that* tidy, you couldn't put a newspaper down the way she wanted it."

"Nerm?", enquired the rolled umbrella.

"Folded once, with the front showing, not the back, so she could tell what day it was. A *terrible* strong woman."

On a boat-ramp, little row boats (one ominously named *Titanic*) lay daydreaming upside down like stranded turtles. I strolled again (how many times, over how many years?) along the path above the beach to a blue door marked Northbank Hotel, and wanted, yearned to *go in*. But I never did. Again and again I patrolled that path with the mania of an obsessive to own that door, and that hotel, to prevent other people from going through that private door – then I shut the possessive anxiety from my mind and concentrated on the sensational embonpoint of a twenty-year-old girl, whose lime-green sweater, stitched MARVELOUS in a rainbow curve, drew Monroeish attention to her best, possibly her only feature. I found inscribed benches, e.g. 'The Kennedy Sisters. This seat is given by Jean, Tisha and Elizabeth to their mothers Cynthia and Joan and to Rachel (Lawrence) their aunt'. The four sea forts were built by Lord Palmerston in 1850, against the threat of Napoleon III. Built of granite, they have walls twenty-one inches thick, laminated with teak and iron, each with its own artesian well.

Outside a High Street ladies' outfitters called Shore Things, a wizened witch with twigs for fingers was using a hooty voice to explain to a heartily lipsticked roly-poly in a red hat: "No, I *used* to be a Catholic, but when I heard they grab a new Pope on the throne and shout 'He has testicles!' I thought, 'Well, really!' "

I took a cup of tea and scone in Winter's Tearoom but was disappointed to find the only company was a morose man with wandering black eyes, who turned them away whenever I glanced in his direction. I am not gregarious, and gladly jail myself when the muse instructs if nobody else does it for me (as the Libyan authorities did, on suspicion of espionage, in the oasis of Sardalas many years ago). But if I am alone with another person in a café or hotel, I find the need for dialogue overpowering, and when the antagonist fails to respond, I feel deflated, unwanted: a brick in the wall that might be removed without effect on the strength of the structure.

Nicholas and Nicola Hayward, at the picturesque, unobtrusively luxurious Seaview Hotel on High Street amply made up for my Winter's tale, however. The date on the façade is 1909: but that is only the date of the façade, the interior central square dating from 1820. On a sepia postcard dated 1918, the virtually empty High Street is the scene of a decorous stroll by two groups: one in white and the other in darker clothes, with a child the cynosure of attention.

The Good Hotel Guide (1989) pronounced the Seaview Hotel the best seaside hotel in Britain, and I can well imagine that this might be true, judging from the range of original paintings and drawings on the walls, and a dinner that might be expected to include chicken livers wrapped in bacon with prune purée or lamb with Burgundy and fresh rosemary. Nicola Hayward was born in a hotel (her mother, Pamela Bailey runs the Royal Esplanade in Ryde), and Nicholas has been deputy general manager at the 120-bedroom Athenaeum in London's West End.

Nicholas told me he was virtually full all year round, with Home Counties clients predominating in short-break holidays and long holiday clients coming more or less evenly from the whole of Britain.

Upstairs, a bay-windowed lounge with a small library provided a cosy ambience for afternoon tea, but even the ghosts of 1909 had departed to the beach. This is the room where one might expect to find a flawless, pallid English beauty as painted by Meredith Frampton.

Next to Winter's I checked in the Bookworm to see what was selling: the answer, from the window-display, seemed to be Collins' *Field Notebook of British Birds*, Flora Thompson's *Lark Rise to Candleford*, and Susan Higginson's *Needlepoint Miniatures*. Outside Watson Brothers on Madeira Road corner a poster announced a Barn Dance. The Seaview Garden Society was hosting a talk by K.J. Hosking on 'Your Gardening Weather' at the Beulah Chapel Schoolroom. Seaview Girl Guides and Brownies in the Masonic Hall, a ploughman's supper and tombola. Seaview F.C. were due to play Shanklin. You would think that the Isle of Wight Conservative & Unionist Association would have swept all before them in this apparently contented community of the retired, the prosperous, the aged, embroiderers and birdwatchers, but at the time of my last visit the County Council had fallen to the Liberal Democrat alliance, though the M.P. was a Conservative, Barry Field, who was announcing the oddly-named 'surgery', as though he was volunteering to mend political bones and do ideological transplants.

Clubby Seaviewers were invited by the Royal British Legion to the anniversary dinner and dance at Hotel Ryde Castle, tickets £11, dress optional, and the Women's World Day of Prayer at St Peter's Church, speaker Mrs J. Quarrington. The preoccupation in the neat, spick and span Church of St Peter seems to be less with the untidiness of holiness, or the smelliness of hermitages and the ravings of ascetic and mystical enlightenment, but more with the regular cleaning of the window ledges (assigned to Mrs L. Edwards on the notice while I was last there) and provision of flowers on the altar frontal (by Mrs. Daish). A 'Soup famine' lunch was being arranged for Friday: 'A little help', exhorted the notice,' is worth a lot of pity'. The church of 1859 might stand for that whole burst of ecclesiastical building in the Island during that period, like St Saviour's in Shanklin (1869-87) also by Thomas Hellyer of Ryde. The stone is from Swanage in Dorset. The church remained unconsecrated for many years, until 1906 in fact, and the first Vicar, F. Rowland Dawson (1907-11), provided at his own expense altar linen and electric light.

On the corner of Old Seaview Lane and Madeira Road the estate agents Watson Bull & Porter were advertising local properties. In 1989 a two-bedroom ground floor flat on Bluett Avenue, Seaview could have been snapped up for just under £70,000; a detached three-bedroom bungalow on Horestone Drive (near the sandy beach on Seagrove Bay) for £87,500.

Cullifords were offering spencers for £3.90 reduced from £7.75 and a Chilprufe quilted dressing-gown in pale green for £30, down from £59.95, leading the odd cynic to suspect excessive profit margins in the first place. Everybody entering the newsagent's greeted a miserable dalmatian wagging its tail like a whisk outside the door. The morning papers aiming to interest the good folk of Seaview headlined 'MPs demand air traffic control reform' (*The Times*); 'Cabinet to back Pamella enquiry' (*Daily Express*); 'Guardians of the Streets' (*Daily Mail*, on civilian vigilantes); 'Come Clean Channon!' (*Daily Mirror*, on bombers); 'Yarwood sees shrink' *The Sun*, on a popular impressionist's nervous disorder; 'Army in Jap Jeeps Shock' (*Star*) and 'Thousands join Moscow parade in support for Yeltsin' (*Daily Telegraph*).

St Helen's
St Helen's is unlike anywhere else I have ever been, like strings straggling away from a kite of the National Trust Common, one strand flying north to the neatly quarantined Nodes Point Holiday Centre, another flung eastward to the slight mediaeval tower (with 13th-century details) on the

shore. Southerly lie the causeway and Bembridge Embankment Road; westward Upper Green Road ends up at Field Lane Holiday Park, a quiet caravan setting some way from the sea. 'Regret no dogs or parties of youths' was the message from Field Lane. Old Mill Holiday Park stands nearer the sea, overlooking Bembridge Harbour.

St Helen's village green is a good place to eavesdrop for verbal *graffiti*, those burning brands I rescue before the fire of conversation dies down to black embers. Near the playground, two grandmothers were jockeying for the conversational lead.

"Did you see the Coronation of King George VI?", enquired the one in a brown dress the colour of malt loaf. "No," sniffed the other, in crumpled cream, "but I've got the cigarette cards."

A mother in scratched jeans chewed gum in the approved Californian fashion, pushing a pram back and forth as if doing arm exercises for a Jane Fonda audition. On the hut, St Helen's Parish Council proclaimed a Social Car Scheme to provide transport 'for people who are unable to use public transport or private services'. Bingo is played on Thursdays at 8: all welcome. Changing rooms were marked 'Home' and 'Visitors'.

Booksellers are the most welcoming people on earth, with the exception of geologists, and Val Edmondson at The Mother Goose Bookshop proved no exception, introducing me to her husband Michael (Island Book Sales) in their nearby home, West Green House. Together they welcomed me as Founder of the Private Libraries Association and gave me a welcome coffee while I rummaged eagerly through their bookpiles and shelves. Michael acts as a courier for Shearing's Coach Tours of Shanklin from early May to early December, concentrating on his book business in the winter, when the tourists have disappeared. They moved to the Island from Waltham Abbey in 1971 and have felt thoroughly at home ever since. In the quiet, behind-the-scenes struggles between conservationists and modernizers, the former seem to be still dominant in St Helen's, though the latter wish to surround the village green with kerbs. Overners seem to relax in the few minutes it takes to cross a six-mile stretch of water to the mainland and, once on the Island, many hanker to remain, or to come back and retire, the watchwords 'nice', 'pretty' and 'beautiful' proliferating like freckles. No muggings, no rapes, but the holiday camps have given the Ryde-Seaview area the hushed-up distinction of the highest illegitimacy rate in Europe: incoming boys and local girls. Fifty seven per cent of the population is retired, so this relatively wealthy age-band dominates the housing market and youngsters cannot afford to live on the island, with its relatively low rates of pay. A four-bedroomed house started in August 1988 and expected to fetch £135,000 was sold in 1989 for £195,000 and even a little cottage made £66,000.

I tried to envisage those days in 1798 when Nelson's fleet lay off St Helen's awaiting the down-channel wind that would carry them round Spain and Portugal, through the Straits of Gibraltar, finding the enemy near Toulon and finally defeating them in the heat of August, at the Battle of the Nile. St Helen's then was a tiny village of two hundred souls, but it would flourish in the course of the next fifty years to supply the fleet with water, beer, eggs and meat, till two thousand inhabitants could rake off a good living, some smuggling, some farming, some providing free and easy girls: who knows? *We* know, since Marjorie Bowen's *The Scandal of Sophie Dawes* (1935), which cunningly narrates the rise of the daughter of Dicky Dawes the smuggler. The one-time-whore became wife to a French officer and mistress to the Duke of Bourbon, last Comte de Chantilly, and her name was bruited around the Island as Queen Chantilly. She it was who probably murdered the Duke, but came back to retire in St Helen's, her meddling and malpractice done.

The Duver of St Helen's, a sandy shingle spit, was given by the Royal Isle of Wight Golf Club to the National Trust, and its clubhouse has become a holiday cottage for the disabled. A ferry will carry you from the end of Duver promenade to Bembridge Embankment Road, where the Pilot Boat Inn makes a rare shelter from raw winter winds. John Hurst found me a prawn salad and draught cider, and I listened to two ladies from London on their annual holidays.

"I've had no trouble with dirty underwear lying about the 'ouse since I bought that Laundry Shoot for twelve ninety-five."

"What's that then?"

"Didn't you get one? They send you a fibre-board back, a basketball net, two brackets, nuts and bolts, and you put it on your bathroom door so they can chuck their smalls in it."

"Does your Eric play with the laundry too?"

"I couldn't get him and Jerry away from it. They kep on scoring, taking the laundry out again, missing, picking it up, backwards and forwards, passing, it goes out the window and on the soil."

"The laundry gets a lot dirtier now then?"

"Mm, there's always that side, but at least they never leave the dirty underwear lying about the 'ouse".

Bembridge

After Sir William Russell bridged the Yar, at Yarbridge, the zone to the east was called 'Within Bridge', dialectally contorted to 'Binbridge', then broadened more euphoniously to Bembridge.

Bembridge astonished me, with a magic all its own, yet its two most attractive buildings were derelict at my last visit, and the latter has been pulled down. The first is the handsome neo-classical house Hill Grove on Ducie Avenue; the second the three-storey Royal Spithead Hotel of 1882, beautifully situated on the Point, where I mooched in disappointment around rooms recently fouled by squatters and party-goers. Islanders feel passionately about dog-mess and parking-space: too much of the one and not enough of the other. Dog wardens patrol Ryde beach from 8 a.m. to 6 p.m. from May to September, and will be on call throughout the year from 6 a.m. to 9 p.m., and Medina Borough Council gardeners and beach inspectors add their beady eyes to an informal neighbourhood watch against dog-owners who should know better.

Bembridge has taken the lead when it comes to parking, abolishing the irritating yellow lines in 1988 and coming up with... no problems at all. Oh yes, every so often a thoughtless deviant will park outside Lloyds Bank, rendering it dangerous to turn the corner, but by and large drivers park where they want to, shop nearby, and are quickly away. This satisfies local shops like the chemist's run by John Steane and restaur-

Bembridge. Royal Spithead Hotel, shortly before demolition in 1989

ants like Ann Monk's Fox. The idea is that people should know their Highway Code and act accordingly. As the Bembridge experiment sign announces: "There are now no yellow lines in this village, but please take great care how you PARK, and remember it is ILLEGAL to cause an OBSTRUCTION."

Lord Brabazon is convinced that the idea should operate throughout English villages, allowing drivers to shop locally instead of heading for a big supermarket miles away where they would spend on petrol all they save on lower-priced goods. "I believe", he told me in Bembridge, "that places suffering particular pressure might have thick yellow lines, and others should have no yellow lines at all. You might save villages and their shops by the simple experiment of removing the yellow lines."

After chatting with John Steane about the success of the parking system, which he had vigorously opposed to begin with, I talked to him of island cures.

He shook his head in dismay at the pharmaceutical remedies noted by Sir John Oglander against the scourge of English port-imbibing gentlemen: the gout. One required the binding of fresh oysters to the place infected with a cloth. Another involved beating a quarter of a pound of the best washing soap with four eggs, and spreading the ensuing compound on the 'grieved place' with a cloth. Yet a third (the man was desperate) consisted of shredding a handful of rue, and beating it with twenty snails, mixing the concoction with a pound of badger's grease and applying it to the place. Sir John – nobody will be amazed to learn – suffered from agonising gout throughout the last two years of his life, and presumably these 'remedies' made no difference whatsoever even as a placebo.

Bembridge High Street is totally different from similar shopping streets in Ryde or Shanklin: it retains that quiet English miniature feel familiar to visitors from Dorset or Suffolk. Tricia Hair Salon, Bradley's the Butcher, the Sweet Shop, Jade Garden Chinese Takeaway. Roast duck with beansprouts, £3 (closed all day Tuesdays in winter– what is it that the Chinese of Bembridge do all day on winter Tuesdays?). Next door stands Ye Olde Village Inn (Licensee David Hamilton-Warwick), offering Strongbow draught cider and Whitbread White Label. Robert F. Andrews, Bespoke Joinery, exhibited dolls and patchwork as well as 'house names and numbers made to order by Bill Cox.' At the Square Rigger licensed restaurant local dover sole could be found at £7.95, crab salad at £5.75 or lobster at £12.50. The Maritime Museum (Easter to October) offered six galleries of nautical history to those nostalgic for old smuggling days, old fishing days, when (as around 1820), smugglers managed to thrive so well that they replaced old shacks in Bembridge with a row of new houses.

The Ordnance Survey map shows Bembridge as a swinging bough nearly severed from the Island's trunk by the searing lightning of the river Yar as it scythes southwest from St Helen's through Brading towards Sandown. Norman Bembridge was indeed cut off by the sea, whose waters lapped the high walls of Brading itself. A tiny hamlet, cut off except from the treacherous sea, Bembridge found transient hope in a causeway at Yarbridge south of Brading, in 1336, but nothing more happened until the time of James I, when another short-lived attempt was made, this time to fill in the sea to the north of the causeway, and the steadfast locals, suffering a setback when the sea breached that embankment, tried again later on until by the late 18th century the sea had been constructed into a channel, which nevertheless still remained tidal, making permanent agriculture impossible. It was in 1878 when Brading's wall and embankment took their modern shape, and the railway line (long abandoned) extended to St Helen's and Bembridge. Six hundred and fifty acres of land were thus rendered manageable for farming and gardening.

The public library in Church Road might never win a competition for buildings, or size of bookstock, but surely someone must stand up from time to time and praise to the skies Britain's unobtrusive public library system that has worthily spread across the globe, no matter how diluted in degree, to become a cornerstone of freedom, two cheers for democracy where otherwise none might be raised. Mike Cunliffe and Mary Cullimore in Bembridge exemplify that neat, thoughtful, imaginative approach to modern librarianship that transcends all niggling budget cuts. Even jigsaw puzzles and talking books are being lent here; the growing collection of large-print editions reflects an ageing community with fading sight; a notice-board links it with community life and leisure such as the Bembridge Friendship Circle. The Circle is open to all village residents over 60, the disabled and the lonely, keeping them mobile by the aid of a minibus and arranging a social evening once a month.

"That dreadful Warner's Holiday Centre!" tutted one salmon-pink lady to a lady in turquoise, who replied, "I know a girl who used to go there, that Estelle from where was it, Arreton?" "No," rejoined the salmon-pink, "I know everyone in Arreton. There's no Estelle. There's a Marcia." "What a mix-up it all is. My Cliff's bought a house in St Helen's: I don't know what he'll do with it. Live in it most likely, I shouldn't wonder."

All that Pevsner can find to write about Bembridge's Holy Trinity Church (1845-6) is rather depressingly "quite large". This is not quite fair. From the harbour its spire acts as an elegant landmark on the wooded hill and the internal proportions feel just right. The *Parish News* is ecumenical, with room for the Methodist Church, St Michael's Roman Catholic Church on Walls Road, and the Hillway Mission Hall near the entrance to Bembridge School. Bembridge's first public place of worship was the Bible Christians' Chapel opened in 1826. These were democratic Methodists, who believed in arranging their own meetings and as 'enthusiasts' found little support elsewhere. At Brighstone, the rector Samuel Wilberforce tried to prevent farmers from employing labourers who attended Bible Christian meetings but the curate of Brading, Legh Richmond, gave the Bembridge Bible Christians encouragement. He wrote three passionate stories defending the poor: *The Dairyman's Daughter*, on Elizabeth Wallbridge (buried at Arreton); *The Young Cottagers*, on Little Jane of Brading; and *The Negro Servant*, set in Sandown, written in 1809, after he had left the Island. In 1814 they were together reprinted by the Religious Tract Society as *Annals of the Poor* and sold over two million copies. Richmond's life has been written by T.S. Grimshawe (1828).

Bembridge School was founded in 1919 as a boarding-school by a visionary influenced by Geddes and Ruskin: J. Howard Whitehouse. Whitehouse believed that arts and crafts should take their rightful place among academic subjects and sport, fulfilling William Morris' ideas and anticipating the work of Sir Herbert Read's *Art and Education* and such enlightened schools as Dartington. Culver Cottage (1914-15) is in fact a miner's cottage designed by Baillie Scott and transposed from Scotland, but New House was purpose-built in 1925 by Scott, with some advice from Whitehouse. The chapel of 1931 is due to W.A. Harvey and H.G. Wicks, the architects at Bournville, where Whitehouse had previously worked.

Near the crumbling Royal Spithead Hotel (since demolished) the little Tollgate Café served desultory ice-creams to young teenagers on the razzle, turning its back on the beach strewn with cola cans, butane gas canisters, and cans of John Smith Bitter 'brewed in Yorkshire'. Some vandal had tossed away an empty BQ Multigrade motor oil container, and a Cuprinol Bilgex awaited high tide before it could sway and dip off, temporarily at least, into flickering waves.

Bembridge's activities are mostly centred on the L-shape made by Foreland Road abutting the High Street, and the shorter squiggle of Church Road before it debouches into Kings Road (downhill) and Sherbourne St. I sat in Bo Peep's coffee shop on Foreland Road as expectantly as a caged parrot in the window of Pampered Pets.

A nice aunt of about thirty-five was giving her freshly-washed schoolgirl niece a cream tea, with quite generous helpings of jam, and éclairs. "Who's your nicest teacher to take you this year, Charlotte?", asked the Nice Aunt brightly, her pudding-basin ginger hair craning forward around her chubby head, with its carefully-elided anxieties of harassing job and unstable boyfriend. "I haven't got one," answered Charlotte, eyes escaping in search of a jeans-clad youth with long greasy hair and dirty fingernails, patently derived from long hours at the temple of Kawasaki. Nice Aunt tried again: her name was probably Henrietta. "Who do you sit next to?" "Cheryl Binns," stated Charlotte, rolling her eyes in horror. "She's disgusting. Her nose keeps bleeding."

I like the Nice Aunt and all of Henrietta's contemporaries, sympathising with her hang-ups. The recipient of many alleged advantages from the Germaine Greer-Betty Friedan feminist generation, she had in fact lost out on almost every count. Not allowed to be feminine, and constitutionally incapable of becoming masculine, her birthright had been mortgaged for her. Nothing had really changed in the eighties, except that the world expected more of her, but was unwilling to give as much in return. She would suffer from stress in her underpaid job, she would be disillusioned with the selection of men-friends still available after the first choice had been snapped up by the dolly-birds and the sexually available gels from naice schools who met high-fliers at Oxbridge May balls and breakfasted with them late, oh so late, the morning after. She would write confidentially to Dateline and receive inappropriate replies. Her c.v. would limp embarrassingly behind those with access to the Old Girl Network. She would have no husband in the Masons or the Rotary Club or the Oddfellows. She would not be taken where it mattered: to Glyndebourne, Ascot, garden parties, Henley. She would see Wimbledon on television, and wince inwardly at Sabatini's grace and Mandlikova's strength. Her inhibitions would keep her from experimenting with lesbianism, her best friends would all be married, with threatening children, often precocious, called Charlotte and William, playing the fiddle like

41

Menuhin and solving maths like Ruth Lawrence, the Oxford prodigy. She would fall into debt, paying more than lip service to the rule of holidays abroad. She would try to get a better job, and fail through a combination of shyness and over-compensating arrogance. She was, after all, a pet. A man would try to comfort her, and be resented for showing pity. A man would try to understand her, and be scolded for invading her privacy. He would, in the end, turn to his secretary Sophie, a little feather-brained perhaps, but not so much trouble. Wait, impatient man, she is more worth the trouble than Sophie, who spends more time at the hairdresser's than at the theatre. Don't lose her!

'Nice' is what she is, was and always will be, middle-class, worthy, sensible, trying to be a housekeeper, professional woman, gardener and cook. She would make a clever, resourceful, good-humoured, diligent wife superior in many respects if not all to the men who will not marry her. She is not beautiful to look at; she is hardly pretty in any conventional sense. But she is like the Isle of Wight: she has her own magic, her enduring good nature, her ability to prefer the right to the wrong at almost any cost. Stable, conventional, preferring Mozart to Stravinsky and Constable to Graham Sutherland, she is moved more easily to pity than to condemnation. She agrees easily with friends, neighbours, and even people who do not matter. For she has a sense of worth, of dignity to maintain, a certain manner to keep up, a façade that may be breached only in fugitive thoughts but never in letters or telephone conversations. She comes to the Isle of Wight because it is manageable; more to her scale than London, Paris, or Texas. Let us prize her dearly, for the world she fears will not.

There's no end to the surprises of Bembridge. Arriving at the foot of Lane End Road, with Warner's Chalet Hotel behind you, the lifeboat station is on perpetual alert. Down Egerton Road, cross Howgate Road and a winding descent brings you to the inviting Crab and Lobster Inn, beside the coastguard station. Or you could look for the old station building and the Row Barge Inn on Station Road.

At the Crab and Lobster, two ladies looked suspiciously at their light ales and changed the subject.

"My Alf knew a geezer 'oo suddenly turned into an anti-vegetarian one day."

"You mean, 'e didn't like vegetables?"

"Didn't like vegetarians. Brought 'im out in a rash in allergy. Couldn't stop sneezin' when they waved bits of lettuce about. 'ad to go on a excloosive diet of steak, and 'amburgers, an' all that stuff. Not a blade of cress."

"Did 'e get over it?"

"Well, evenshully he got over it. 'E was knocked down and killed by a pleece car in a chase round Canvey."

But whatever you do, don't miss the windmill, because it is the last on the island. Windmills throve from the Middle Ages wherever no local stream could drive a mill-wheel. Bembridge Windmill (c. 1700) is opened by the National Trust from April to September, and can be found by driving along to the end of High Street. Functioning until 1913, it still preserves most of its wooden machinery, and its stone tower. From Steyne Wood it looks like a mushroom.

A lady in a navy blue suit and white court shoes looked out of place in the kind of mill that Don Quixote would have treated as a giant enemy, to be overcome. She kept puckering up her nose, as if the cattle food it once produced had continued to leave a bad odour. "I will say this for Cedric," she informed a knobbly woman with iron-grey hair and Cratchit specs, "he does like his toast lightly done. Only with my last husband the noise at breakfast over that burnt toast was that deafening I could never concentrate on my crossword."

I knew that a number of airfields had existed, with grass runways, prior to World War II, but only two remain. One of these is at Sandown (though it started operations inland from Shanklin near Apse Manor Farm) and the other, between Brading and Bembridge, began as a club airfield but opened scheduled passenger services to London in the 1930s, though the present hangars, for making Britten-Norman Islander aircraft, were built as recently as the 1960s. Worldwide, over a thousand of these aircraft are in service, many as nine-seater commuter planes or one-tonne freight carriers.

I don't normally call in at airports where I have no business, but the Propeller Inn at Bembridge Airport, situated below the airy expanse of Culver Down, tempts you to call in, not least to inspect the historic flying photos and other memorabilia on show during licensing hours.

Several youngsters were playing noisy, beepy, crashing games in the room next to the bar. Eleanor Hewitt provided an excellent ploughman's lunch, and regulars on bar-stools gazed up at the propeller that gives the inn its name with an air of not seeing it, as is usual with whatever you put up on walls. A young lady in a magenta scarf reminded me of one of George Formby's girlfriends, pert and giggly. "No, but Mandy won the Trivia Quiz down our pub the week before I came away, because she was the only one who could remember Simply Red."

"I thought you said it was Deep Purple."

"It was, it was. They got everybody else in the famous people of the Seventies, like Paul McCartney. It was just a few they missed out. Mandy was ever so good.

"D'you go to a lot of those Trivia Quizzes, then?"

"Wouldn't miss them: Colin says it's the most important thing in my life."

Brading

Six minutes after leaving St. John's station in Ryde you are in another world, just before the River Yar meets the line below Brading. Brading Station is a neat introduction to the topography of Brading, whose heights dominate the shoreline from Bembridge Foreland on the north to Culver Cliff and Sandown in the south.

Historically, it makes a great deal of sense to head first for the Roman Villa (April to September), near bus routes 16, 16A, and 36, with free car parking. The best general source for the period is David Tomalin's *Roman Wight* (Newport, 1987). A courtyard is surrounded by buildings on three sides, and presumably by an undiscovered fourth, if the usual Roman villa pattern is followed. The main west wing, with thirteen rooms, and parts of the north wing are currently open to visitors.

Like Schliemann's Mycenae, Brading's Roman villa is a victim of early archaeological naïveté, ignorance, and arrogance. Found in 1879, it was excavated in 1880-4 in so much haste that little was recorded, excavators concentrating on the finding of treasure and discovering the plan of the site. But then, the dilemma is when to dig at all. The Saudi authorities even now feel that it is too early in the history of archaeology to excavate Mada'in Salih, the Nabataean city on the trade route from Yemen to Petra, and who is to say they are wrong?

We think Brading was a wealthy farm complex, for its many stylish mosaic floors and painted walls denote a degree of luxury in the main house, or western range. The northern range comprises an aisled farmhouse, and the southern range was a farm building. The main bathhouse was probably adjacent to the southern range, but there was a secondary bathhouse near a well 96 feet deep adjacent to the northern range. The date of the main complex we see today is the 3rd century and, though the area is covered, it is regrettably open only from 1 April to late September. The entrance-hall has an Orpheus mosaic, showing the god of music attracting with his lyre a fox, birds and a monkey. Orphean iconography is common but the extraordinary half-human, chicken-headed figure in room 2 has been identified by some scholars (though not all!) with the Gnostic god Abrasax or Abraxas; numerologically, the spelling does not matter, because whichever way you spell it, the sum of the numerical values of the Greek letters still comes to 365, the total days in some years and hence the number of heavens in gnostic terms. The heresiologist Irenaeus thought that Abraxas was the gnostics' almighty god, but Schwartze's translation of the *Pistis Sophia* from the Coptic in 1853 showed up this Abraxas as merely the lowest powers, taken by the ignorant populace to embrace 'powers' such as good luck, magic over one's enemies, and ability to change the future. Followers of Abraxas abound today, even among those who have never heard his name, and recognise only those of the fortune-tellers in popular magazines and newspapers. A roundel of Bacchus shows another aspect of the Brading Roman's belief, quern stones reveal the existence of grain harvests, and imported Continental pottery sherds prove links with the mainland, to which excess farm produce could be sold from Brading harbour. Fishing-weights are indicative of the obvious: sea harvest to supplement the diet and possibly also for trade: barter and sale. Bones of oxen, cattle, hare and deer have been found, and rather more surprisingly cherry stones. Windows were glassed high in the walls. 'Samian'-type bowls of fairly crude quality have been found.

Room 12: last seen, best loved. The triclinium was a reception and dining-room area, with opulent mosaics. The central Medusa was prefabricated in a workshop, and moved here later. Clockwise, the surrounding mosaics portray Ceres, goddess of fertility and agriculture, with Triptolemus, inventor of the plough; a satyr pursuing a maenad in the Bacchic cult; Lycurgus with Ambrosia, the mythical origin of viticulture; and a shepherd with naiad, exemplifying the life of the fields and flocks. A sea panel, showing Brading's marine associations, depicts three tritons protecting sailors, and two nereids. It is a shame that the curators do not keep the mosaics damp, bringing out the colours as they were intended to be seen.

The mosaics are distant provincial work which we cannot compare in quality with the Villa Borghese in Rome, the Piazza Armerina masterpieces in Sicily, or the brilliant effects from Aquileia, all roughly contemporary with Brading. Nevertheless they are not to be missed, especially in the company of a youth from Poplar with his girlfriend who waved his hand across scenes of classical mythology and told her: "I like the wosname." So, friend, did I.

Back in Brading, at the bar of the *Bugle*, totally redecorated by the Strettons in May 1989, two strangers seemed to be trying to bruise the wood with the weight of their elbows.

"Relaxing 'ere, enni'?"

"Sunning *reely* great. You know", said the portly character with stained trousers and moustache, "where I come from round London it's all Asians now. Look oucher front winder, yer bay winder, wotcher go'?"

"Asians."

"Prams, push-chairs, carrycots, more prams, more push-chairs. They're all brown as yer bitter."

"Yer bitter?"

"Too right I will, thanks. Make it a large one, I've 'ad a dehydranging day round the pitch and putt you wooden bleeve."

I visited the exterior of the period thatched cottage (1790) pointed out to me as 'Little Jane's', then headed for the notable church of St. Mary, for the heroine of Rev. Legh Rich-

Brading. Little Jane Squibb's Cottage

mond's moral tale is buried in that churchyard. An exemplary child, she died at fourteen and might have become a Wightish Thérèse de Lisieux if the Islanders had just been a little more prone to mysticism or the aura of sanctity and the worship of pure little girls. However, with a surname like Squibb, little Jane was unlikely to capture the imagination of the sceptical British, who bought the book all right but failed to see her as a rôle model for themselves.

On my way down to the High Street, the postman greeted me as he might any grinning overner. "Daatanoon." "Good afternoon." "Binup sill undidza tyimes nit doan simta genny flaater." To which I worked out an answer about a undid yaards down the road but by then he had turned the corner. Tlate agin.

The metal bull ring in the traffic island recalls those rough and vicious days before the R.S.P.C.A. was formed when a terrified bull would be fastened to this ring and a ceremonially-beribboned dog called the 'Mayor's Dog' would be set at the bull until one or both animals expired. Sir John Oglander of Nunwell recorded that "it was the custom from

47

time immemorial for the Governor of the Isle of Wight to give five guineas to buy a bull to be baited and given to the poor. The mayor and corporation attended at the bull ring in their regalia, with mace-bearers and constables."

One of the first churches on the Island may have stood on the site of the present St Mary the Virgin's, which dates from the late 12th century. Saxon bones dated to 680 or so prove the existence of a graveyard here at a time when Ceadwalla, King of the South Saxons was imposing his rule and gave the Christian missionary Wilfrid (Bishop of Ripon, later Bishop of York) a quarter of the island and its spoils. At that time some three quarters of the Island's population were said to have been massacred, though we cannot surmise whether it was due to Ceadwalla's wars or Wilfrid's attempts to impose the new religion on pagan islanders. Since the time of Edward I – to be exact from 1285 – it has been known as the King's Town because of the 'grant of market and fairs' he accorded it eight years before the Island was purchased from the Countess Isabella de Fortibus, for 6,000 marks, on her deathbed.

St. Mary the Virgin has a 12th-century nave, a 13th-century tower, 14th-century chapels and chancel and additions and monuments of every succeeding age. You might view it as a living history of the English parish church, even to signs of fanatical desecration by Cromwell's louts and hooligans, who were responsible for smashing a doubtless valuable figure of the Virgin once ensconced in a niche above the west-facing tower entrance. The transitional Norman nave can be dated to the late 12th century by the round piers and scalloped capitals. The west tower, resting on piers, is open on three sides and was evidently constructed onto the existing nave.

Though in no sense minimising the interest of the de Aula or northern chapel, I stress that the Oglander Chapel must be the highlight of any visit to St Mary's, with the beautiful oaken effigies, locally believed to have been brought back from France by Sir John Oglander, and therefore not representational of him and his father. The 'Sir William' figure is supine with hands at prayer; the 'Sir John' almost comically refuses to lie down, his staring eyes still clearly thinking about this life, and his head propped up above his right elbow, resting on a partly rolled mat as a pillow. William died in 1609 and John in 1655. Oglanders have lived at Nunwell Manor, Brading, for eight centuries, possibly coming into possession between 1100 and 1135; in the latter year Henry I gave land at Nunwell to a Roger Dogelander, the 'd' abbreviating the Norman 'de'. The Oglanders play a central part in our understanding of the Island. Sir John served as Deputy Governor of the Island in the period before supporting the Royalist cause and for loyal friendship to Charles I himself. He wrote a fascinatingly detailed *Notebook* edited by Francis Bamford in *A Royalist's Notebook*. The tomb of Sir Henry (who died in 1874) is a charming example of Arts and Crafts Jacobean by J.C. Powell, 1897.

Opposite the church stands a garish, Disneyish Wax Museum which disturbs the finest timber-framed building still extant on the Island, and the only surviving case of close studding, a method of constructing timber-frame walls with many vertical timbers a whole storey high set close together. Because of the expense of such lavish use of timber, close studding was confined to homes of the wealthy, and some parts of this carefully-restored mansion are said to date from before the Conquest. 'If you insist on smoking inside', warned a notice, 'kindly let us know to whom to send the ashes'.

Much more interesting is the Old Town Hall, with its lock-up and open 18th-century brick arches through which you can see the stocks. The upper floor is dated 1875. The New Town Hall (by James Newman) is of 1902-3.

I nearly missed the Lilliput Antique Doll and Toy Museum, which would have been a mistake, for Margaret Munday-Whitaker is a knowledgeable and enthusiastic advocate of doll-collecting. The best dolls are French, such as the Jumeau fashion doll of 1870 which led to her obsession. Detailed captions add to the interest in, for instance, the wooden Queen Anne doll of *c.* 1725 and the wax Princess Caroline doll of *c.* 1790. I liked best the Käthe Kruse dolls from Berlin (1910-30), but you will have your own favourite. The shop is an outlet for locally-made Isle of Wight character dolls, such as the Primrose Picker (£5.95), Morris Dancer (£8.95) and the St Helen's notoriety, Sophie Dawes (£11.95). A middle-aged lady with enormous beads was gazing half-abstractedly at a Fanny Wheeler doll.

"It doesn't make a noise, does it?" she asked of a girl in floral pink and green behind the counter. "No, you're thinking of squeezy toys," the girls replied. "Only my husband can't sleep if there are owls, dripping taps, babies, barking things, parrots, or trains." "It's not a train," said the girl. "Sometimes he wakes up and shouts 'That's a brass band', and it's the hall clock ticking downstairs. One barrel organ, and he's awake for four days and five nights." She sighed, straightening at the wrist lilac gloves of the mode entitling her to sing 'I dreamt I dwelt in marble halls' before a select gathering.

I made my way to The Barn Tea-rooms on High Street, dating to 1699. I was there so early for cottage pie, two veg and a pot of tea that I had the whole place to myself, except for the chatty cook, who had come here in 1979 from Manor Park in the London Borough of Newham. She and her husband both worked in banks. Now he drives a heavy-goods vehicle for Sandown Borough Council and she works in the tea-room. Their children go to schools with classes of twenty instead of forty. While pregnant, she spent a few months in Hackney, where her car was broken into and her house burgled. In their spare time they go for walks on the downs now, and in summer the children enjoy the beach every day: on the Yaverland side of the pier. The boy was a slow reader in London without attention in a large class; here on the Island he has caught up with the rest. "Do you not miss the shows in London?" "Not a bit of it," she answered, "we've got nice pier shows in the summer."

Another time I dined off prime roast topside of beef at the Bugle in Brading next to a gloomy couple who avoided looking at each other, giving marriage a bad name. The woman craned wanly over an ash-tray and said to her tall husband, equally listless in matching tweedy brown, "It's more of an ash-tray than anything else", to which he responded in the sombre manner of Alvar Lidell announcing another bombing raid over the Kent coastline: "I haven't had my third pint of water today yet. Dr Morris will be livid" and advanced heavily towards the toilet. The reason for the Bugle as an inn-name is that the bugle, or young bull, was supporter in the arms of Henry Beauchamp, Duke of Warwick, crowned King of the Wight by Henry VI in 1443.

Nunwell, reached from the north of Brading and Morton from the south, we have already considered, as the ancestral home of the Oglanders, and the house is now occupied by Colonel and Mrs Aylmer; the Colonel traces his lineage back to the Saxon King Ethelred, and shows wondrous diligence in maintaining the fine mansion with such gems as the Italian ceiling in the Georgian Library, and the round-arched Venetian window. Homogeneous Nunwell is not, nor should we wish it any the less eclectic, for it is a three-dimensional palimpsest of English building and could be set as a walking examination to test your knowledge of Jacobean, Queen Anne, Georgian, Victorian and Edwardian styles. It is open every afternoon (except Fridays and Saturdays) from late May to late September.

You visit Nunwell in guided tours at roughly hourly intervals: sometimes they are given by Tony Aylmer, sometimes by Shaunagh Aylmer, and Mr Coulson comes in several days a week to help out. The visit begins in the Edwardian music room of 1906, a spacious and light addition to the east and the last important extension, so as generally one goes back in time through Nunwell, rather than forward, one might choose to begin with the World War II Home Guard museum, especially if a tour is not ready to depart.

The paintings, lent by the Oglander family, include portraits of Sir William (6th baronet, 1769-1852) and his wife Lady Maria-Anne, forever honoured as the instrument by which Nunwell was rescued from the hands of the Regency architect John Nash, whose idea in 1810 was to demolish Nunwell and start again. Lady Maria-Anne, seeing how Nash had modernised the stables block and replaced the fine oak panelling with fashionable wall paper, managed to dislodge him shortly afterwards. Look for Joan Oglander's portrait by Olive Snell; it was her second husband, General Cecil Aspinall-Oglander, who wrote the memorable Island book *Nunwell Symphony* (1945) after commanding the East Wight Home Guard during World War II.

The Victorian dining-room (*c.* 1896) benefits from a fine Venetian window, but the cynosure of all eyes is a double portrait of two sisters by the important Dutch artist Adriaen Hanneman (*c.* 1601-1671), who worked in England from 1625 to 1640, and has a painting of Charles II in the National Portrait Gallery. As a successor to Van Dyck, he created a marvellous portrait of his mentor now in Vienna. The present morning-room was a library in the time of the writer Sir John Oglander, and features double doors based on the idea of Thomas Jefferson, a system of weights pushing open one door if the other is pushed.

The drawing-room has a painting attributed to Van Dyck known as the *Sunflower* because of the royalist symbol the artist is holding to indicate his fealty, but the most attractive work is one of those *fantasie* which Hubert Robert calls *caprices*, taking elements of Roman architecture and allowing them by artistic licence to pose together, like human models placed for the artist's convenience. The artist is Gianpaolo Pannini, and if his studio played an active part in the work, and the figures are as usual by another hand, the *caprice* lures the eye, fascinates by detail and compositional values, and dignifies the marvellous room by its majesty and classical restraint.

The Library of 1762 has wallpaper of 1833 and a brilliant plaster ceiling by Florentine craftsmen brought from Italy by the Lady Oglander of the day – Sukey Serle – to carry out her intricate design. The books stress the military aspects of life, from Sir Winston Churchill to Maclean's *Guns of Navarone* and the maritime novels of C.S. Forester, as well as Compton Mackenzie and Kipling, Dickens and Thackeray, Arnold and Byron.

The Jacobean rooms begin with the notable Hall, with French prints portraying the tragic life and death of Charles I. Two 18th-century Irish chairs bear the Aylmer crest. The early 17th-century staircase, oak-panelled and evocative of those days when the Oglanders were a force in the land, leads to the King's Room, where in 1647 Charles spent his last night of freedom, before being escorted to Carisbrooke. John Nash removed the oak panelling and replaced it with wallpaper in 1810, the Victorian fireplace was added fifty years later, and the south windows in 1930. The four-poster bed, alas!, is a copy, but the velvet-covered Spanish chest dates from the 17th century. The fans are selected from the family's collection, one of the most interesting being of chicken-skin, a fact leading one confused visitor to remark on her way to the military rooms, "I wonder who they got to fan the chickens?". This room and the little adjacent Equerry's Room are the only two not still in regular use.

The military memorabilia belong to the Aylmer family, and most refer to one or other of the World Wars. Major-General Sir Edward Spears, cousin to Colonel Aylmer, and his wife, the novelist Mary Borden, once owned much of the library, some of the furniture, and more of the military objects. Winston Churchill called on Spears to bring Charles de Gaulle from Bordeaux in 1940 to found the Free French Movement.

Nunwell gardens and woodlands are as sturdy and long-lasting as the house itself, some oaks over three centuries old surviving the dreadful hurricane of October 1987. The old bowling green of Sir John Oglander's time has become a rose garden, and the lower gardens was planted in the 1930s around a former swimming-pool, now a graceful lily pond.

I spoke to Shaunagh Aylmer about the trials and pleasures of running a great house. Good-humoured, indomitable, and courteous with the unmistakable stamp of good breeding, she

Nunwell House. Shaunagh Aylmer

was born a Guinness in County Kildare, and has two daughters and one son from her marriage to Colonel J.A. Aylmer in 1961. He was made Governor of the Isle of Wight in 1965. The Oglander baronetcy became extinct in 1874 and the property passed through the female line, keeping the name Oglander by deed poll, but in 1982 the Trustees sold the house to the Aylmers, who spent the next two years repairing and renovating the mansion and have never really relaxed. "It is true that it takes up all your waking life," she smiled, in her pink work top and comfortable trousers. Nothing is too much trouble, from the kitchen to the weeding, and yes, she does her own vacuuming, makes her own marmalade, and rushes to auctions which may turn up a piece of old Nunwell furnishings, or something that she knows intuitively will 'fit', like an original Nunwell Georgian four-poster bed she bought at auction in Ryde, or the fabulous recent Pannini, acquired from the sale of a nondescript portrait. Mrs Reichard, who once kept house for Major-General Sir Edward Spears, stays on at Nunwell as a housekeeper *en famille*, and Mr Coulson helps with the tours. Apart from these stalwarts, Mrs Aylmer has only a cleaner, a part-time Australian gardener, and an odd-job helper who also polishes the floors and cleans the brass. This is not the dreamy, wispy existence of a cosseted Victorian grande dame, but an active, energetic, even exhausting life fulfilling because it is enjoyed by so many beyond the immediate family. Myrtle cuttings from Queen Victoria's wedding headdress are found all over the island, linking one great house with another: Nunwell too joins in this convivial fraternity, this freemasonry of climbing plants which gives the Island yet another secret magic, like Van Dyck's sunflower or the sempiternal oaks, bowing before the storm but not breaking.

Mrs Denys Oglander welcomed me into her studio in John Nash's Coach House, close to Nunwell but not too intrusive. Her husband suffered a stroke, and the difficulty of maintaining a stately home and a disabled husband forced the decision to sell; the happy compromise is that she is so near her former home, and is welcome there at any time, "though," she said, "I don't go very often because I don't want to intrude." Her Spanish help comes up every day from Sandown, and she finds

Nunwell's Coach House

that she can manage the much smaller three-bedroom property quite well. Much of her time is taken up with ceramics and oil-painting, and she possesses some fine Oglander portraits, including one of Sir John (though 'William' is written on it in error), and another of his son. She showed me a very fine petitpoint working on the Brading Medusa mosaic that it had taken Sir Denys eight years to complete. Though born in London, Mrs Oglander has been at Nunwell for more than thirty years and never wants to leave these idyllic surroundings, protected as she is by a fierce dog who sounded and looked inclined to have me for afternoon tea. Her father Sir William Erskine was Minister in Bulgaria in the 1920s and Ambassador to Poland in the 1930s, but she was such a little girl at the time that she can hardly remember anything of those times. Her hydrangeas spread and flourished about us like harbingers of Paradise. Neat, congenial, sympathetic and committed to self-expression – at the moment in the still life – she dreams of Tuscany in the green swathe of Nunwell, but seems as happy here as anywhere. "I knew an old boy who had never been out of Brading," she mused. "One day, the farmer asked him to take a cart over to Yarmouth and he grumblingly agreed to go, saying he'd best be back afore nightfall, otherwise there'd be no place to stay." Mrs Oglander's young acquaintances do not seem to want to leave the Island any more than the old folk, "but if there's a living to be earned, I'm afraid the mainland seems to be the only answer nowadays."

Morton Manor opens at 10 a.m. (closed Saturdays) from early April to late October.

It has been a historic home since 1249, when the Norman de Aula family built the first Morton. The Tudor period brought a hall extension, and 1680 saw major rebuilding. The Elizabethan sunken garden and a charming turf maze beside the car park are only two of the reasons for visiting Morton: the vineyard and wine museum, the rose garden, herbaceous displays and specimen trees such as the huge *Magnolia grandiflora* and London plane 130 feet tall, transform this historic private home, still very much owner-occupied, into a quiet Elysium where you feel genuinely welcome. The owner, Janusz Trzebski, guides his own tours of the manor, which finish by a four-hundred-year old box hedge growing so slowly that it needs trimming only once a year. They start in the gun-room, with a fine 18th-century oak table originally in the Long Hall. The Victorian library is established in the part of the house built in 1540, with 18th-century Delft tiles in the fireplace; this continues (imagine the dividing wall away) into the stately dining-hall, with panelling of around 1840 and a Victorian fireplace in front of its Tudor predecessor. The green maritime tiles are by William de Morgan, contemporary of William Morris. With a marble bust of Ellen Terry and late

Georgian chairs of about 1810, the dining-hall is the only room at Morton used not daily, but only on special occasions. Imagine away if you can everything you see, and replace the flooring with flagstones, the ceiling with a vaulted roof. The new wing of 1680 stands on mediaeval foundations, the very large cellar comprising the kitchen of the earlier house. The Georgian drawing-room sagged in the early 20th century – as the mediaeval foundations failed to support modern weights – and it has been underpinned with stabilising pillars. The influence of Robert Adam is felt in the two round arches flanking the fireplace and the two symmetrical doors, one being false, not so much a *trompe l'oeil*, perhaps, as a *trompe le pas*, for it does not open. The late 18th-century Italian parquet floor is only one eighth of an inch thick.

Janusz, born near Kiev, stayed in Britain when demobilised from the Polish Air Force, and lived in London. He was a friend of the Fardells, Morton's previous owners now in Zimbabwe, and when he heard that the manor was to be converted into a light industrial complex, destroying the age-old traditions of the place, he rescued it to magnificent effect, nurtur-

Morton Manor. Raised granary

ing rhododendrons and allowing water-lilies to flourish, lazy with dragonflies.

A vineyard was established in 1981. During the next four years 2,500 vines were planted on 1¾ acres; as they take up to seven years to become established, the vineyard had not yet begun full production at my last visit, in Autumn 1989: 1985 production consisted of 672 bottles of white wine, 1986 2,300 bottles of white and 2,000 bottles of apple juice, and 1987 – despite the terrible hurricane – 4,000 bottles. Morton seems set fair for its second millennium, thanks to the loving care of its owners. Yes, there is a younger Janusz.

In the Thatched Cottage Tea Room, a woman and husband tinkled teacups on saucers and spoons in cups ritually, like chimps grooming. "No," he was saying, "only I'd just like to know what you and Stephen Pocock were doing behind the bicycle sheds."

"I've told you, nothing at all."

"You've forgotten."

"Well it *was* forty-six years ago."

Another vineyard, the Adgestone, can be found along Upper Adgestone Road, taking a left fork from Brading Mall when a right fork would lead to Newport. Adgestone is open every day but Sunday throughout the year: you can see a working winery as well as buy local table wine. I visited Adgestone with a bewildered Welshman whose view of a Celtic twilight was that it should be permanent, assisted with the haze of wine. His confusion about the end of the Welsh twentieth century emerged in the course of his explanation of a concert he had recently attended by Peter Singh the Rocking Sikh from Swansea, and the rich pickings of joyous beggars, who demand such fantastic sums in the churchyard of St Mary's, Swansea, that they earn more than the people who pay to be let alone. "Our vicar, the Reverend Lewis, says he has been in the British Army, he has been in the Butlin's Redcoats, but he's never seen the violence of our winos. It gets to the point where the happy beggars can afford the best sherry and cider. After all, you don't want to break a leg in the middle of Swansea, do you?"

Of course, the main road from Ryde to Sandown via Brading misses Yaverland, but that is, in England, all the more reason

Leisure is Sandown's birthright, with the sandy beaches and seas cool even in the scorching days of June 1989, when I noted at breakfast that Sandown was warmer than Istanbul, Ventnor hotter than Venice. It's on days like that when the canoe-lake comes into its peerless own, and Elise asks Deirdre, on the front: "Have you tasted that new grape and chestnut ice-cream?", to which Deirdre answers with the immortal line: "No, I prefer those vermilion coons".

TV's snake man Jack Corney runs the Zoo at Sandown, inescapable in the granite fort of 1866. Jack loves pumas best of all, and the big cats – panthers, leopards, tigers – always seem to be the biggest attraction. I joined a couple gazing abstractedly at a Royal Bengal tiger, as if none of the three had any business to be there.

"What wor the name of that bungalow in Canada?" enquired the plump man in a check jacket of his birdy wife.

"They called it Vietnam, after that country in Asia, with the war."

"That wor a funny name."

"It wor a funny bungalow."

A sad rentable homosexual in its stubbly forties shuffled off to a promising lad of twenty or so. He was the kind of mackintosh who looks down at other men in public urinals.

Culver Parade's Jolly Sailor pub and amusements and restaurant above Culver Beach seemed a promising source of pithy sayings, but word must have gone out that my notebook sat ready by my lasagne and everyone spoke in whispers. Outside the restaurant, two hairy-chested paunchy men in shorts, still pasty-faced as computer printouts, sucked ice lollies sheepishly, wondering if anyone within eyeshot could guess that back in London they're civil servants at the Department of Social Security. The amusement arcade barked 'Definitely No Loitering' but as that is definitely what I do, with no ulterior motive beyond curiosity, I loitered anyway. 'No Alcohol Allowed Thank You' snapped another notice, to which I answered a polite "Don't mention it." I rolled three tenpence pieces on the 'Silver Strike' game: they fell like three stones, instead of performing the obvious service of pushing heaps of other silver coins off one of the ledges and down a chute into my waiting hands. "There!" nagged my puritanical ego, reasserting its nasty self-control over my greedy id, "you thought you'd break into the big time, and you've been taken to the cleaners, mac, whaddI tellya?" More complex machines, beyond my technological infancy, whirred, beeped, bopped and pinged in a darkened fairground cacophony, as though everyone was wearing sunglasses. King Fruit, Street Fighter, Operation Wolf, Silver Ghost, Snapping Viper lulled the players into a kind of standing lethargy. What could they all have been thinking? An attendant in a T-shirt suspected my intentions.

"Wockaneye dooferya ma'e?"

"I'm taking notes for a book about the Island. Where do these people come from?"

"All over, all year round. July and September it's mos'ly London crowds. Welshmen in August."

"They come from Aberystwyth to stand in the dark by a Snapping Viper?"

"Some do. The best is Hillbilly Moonshine."

This was a diorama-type rifle game put in five years ago, with unwanted prizes for machos keen to show off their noisy prowess to bubble-gum chewing *bimbe* in short sundresses.

Behind the amusement arcade, I watched with increasing apprehension as a foul-mouthed, ugly-tempered East End git in navy overalls, waving his arms at a bald Glaswegian in pebble glasses, tried to pile up boxes. First one box would fall, then another, as though he were losing a fight with intelligent cartons from outer space. But then men are the clumsiest creatures I have ever come across, making even the most lumbering camel look dainty. Cats leap deftly and wash with elegance. Birds assemble nests with speed and efficiency. Horses canter with grace, and even millipedes co-ordinate all their feet at once, while rugger players can't seem to keep their balance on two. Only a man can drop plates during washing-up, spill soup on his clean tie, and hit his head on the door when entering a cottage.

Yet just a few yards away the sun danced like crystal stars in the soft waves. Nymphs with huge bouncy beachballs cavorted as in a Hollywood version of Greek gods and goddesses. Infants paddled and shrieked with a joy that would mark them for life as seaside junkies, ready for a fix each summer at

Rhyl or Cleethorpes, whichever is nearer. 'Deckchairs 30 pence per session, 9-1 and 1-5; or 50 pence per day' read the sign, jumbling up its Latin and English. Who cares, at the seaside? 'Please sit. The attendant will call.' Not if I see 'im first, squire, I'm off dan the chippy till the coast is clear. St Moritz Hotel, Trentham Hotel, Jesmond Dene Hotel, Vancouver Bar. Culver Parade is a long line of holiday dreamfactories, providing leisure the way a bakery provides bread.

"Excuse me, madam," I accosted a splendid marchioness all white hair and straight back, with expensive glasses in place of her preferred lorgnette, "but I'm grading ladies' toilets from O (Addis Ababa's University Library brown squat-hole) to 10 (the opulent chandelier and perfumed marble of Beverly Hills Hotel) and I wonder if you'd be so kind as to suggest a vote for the ladies' latrine on Sandown seafront."

"Five point one", responded Her Magnificence, and raised her back at the road's turning heads, their surprise tempered with deference.

At the Belgrave Hotel on Beachfield Road, I took a cool cider in the bar, while watching a noisy little boy of six rant and yowl around the lounge, deafening the scattering of old folk, when at last a sharp Ena Sharples voice emerged from above industrious knitting needles to the left of a white-haired bridge game by the window.

"Pardon me," she addressed the parents of the little boy, "is he mentally retarded, or do all your family behave like that?"

The fat-cheeked father with sprouts of ginger hair fluffed up to conceal incipient bald patches responded, "All youngsters can let their hair down a bit on holiday."

"I'm glad you approve," darted back the pink needles. "Only if the I.R.A. ever need a terrorist, I should put his name down right away. The regular army wouldn't stand a chance."

Along the High Street, a poster advertised a day tour round the island, 10.15–5.30, £5.50 adults and £3.50 children. Creekwood Gifts were taking delivery of boxes from Taiwan and Korea. The shelves, watched by zealous assistants, were filled with oriental wares such as a framed Donald Duck at £3.50 and soft green frogs at 60p, a pebble 'Rock Concert' made in the Philippines (70p), and mugs lettered 'I used to be conceited, now I'm absolutely perfect'. The choice of badges varied from 'Get even: die in debt' to 'Life's a bitch, then you marry one'.

A family of four trooped, with melting plastic bags, into Penelope's Restaurant where gammon steak with pineapple, mushrooms, tomatoes, peas, beans and French fries came to £5.50. The National Westminster Bank on the opposite corner drowsed in slanting sunlight. Gulls wheeled, harassing the blue sky above The Salad Bowl on the sea front. A red-faced woman with a shopping-trolley said to a fresh-looking eighteen-year-old girl in tennis whites: "I had *no* time for a tea-break be'ind that counter all day, what with one thing and then four others. I were fair embattled."

It's no good trying to admire churches in Sandown, as one might in Shorwell or Niton. The earliest place of worship might be Christ Church (1845), but this undistinguished pile by William Woodman underwent many additions and restorations in the course of time and the hamlet-cum-barracks continued to remain backwaters of island life until Dr Henry Maund praised the local air in 1867, five years after the railway had reached Shanklin and two years after Shanklin Esplanade transformed the little place. Then guest-houses began to proliferate, until in 1878 the pier opened and Sandown life began as we know it today. The pier was elongated in 1895, then a pavilion was provided and a steamer landing-stage made it a port of call from the mainland and other island ports. C.L. Luck was responsible for St John the Evangelist in St. John's Road, which does not invite a closer look, having earlier completed St Paul's on Regent St., Shanklin (1875-6).

Desperate for a building to like, I found the spacious Ocean Hotel, with well-kept gardens between the beach and High Street; it belongs to the leisurely days of the 1850s, with discreet modernisation instead of revamping, and a 'Colonial Bar' which you might well think altogether too nostalgic.

The enlarged pier pavilion opened in 1934, a slightly flailing attempt to keep up with the Shanklins and Ventnors. Noisier amusements impede your progress to the pierhead nowadays, when fishermen – as in fresh water, a race apart – silently bait lines and wait forever, or for bass and mullet: they are the fatalists of sport, extra time built into every match.

You somehow do not connect the peeling faces and the

gaudy buckets of Sandown with the major novelist Edward Upward born in 1903, who not only lives here, but makes no secret of his passion for the magic of Sandown, and in particular of his house at 3 Hill Street bought by his grandfather more than a century ago. His wife and Upward both resigned from the Communist Party of Great Britain in 1948 because they disagreed with its newly adopted unLeninist theory that the establishment of socialism in Britain could begin before capitalism had been deprived of state power. Edward Upward, whose autobiographical fictional trilogy *The Spiral Ascent* (1962-77) must be placed beside the better-known works of his contemporaries and friends, Isherwood and Auden, spent nearly thirty years as a schoolmaster, at Alleyn's in Dulwich, where he headed the English department. This career seemed the least uncongenial to him after his education at Repton and Corpus Christi College, Cambridge. He has published little, but pondered a lot.

"I should have realised much earlier than I did," he admitted later, "that Stalin's so-called socialism was nationalistic to the point of being Fascist." I felt as schizophrenic reading Upward's soul-searching Marxist fiction in Sandown as I had felt reading William Saroyan's comic stories in Moscow. The humorous, sensitive man's latest stories, *The Night Walk* (1987), offer the same bizarre, fascinating disjointing of experience: obsessive Marxism with realistic fantasy, as if George Orwell had an *alter ego* capable of regarding the Communist Manifesto as gospel truth.

The Rivoli Cinema on Station Road sang out its jazzy 1920s art deco features, but it has been ambushed in later times by the plague of bingo, infecting all it touches like bubonic plague. Emerging from the station (the 22.23 had just arrived before its last seven-minute leg to Lake and Shanklin), a pasty-faced city girl was silvered by the light of a sliver of the waning moon. Her countenance, after prolonged exposure to the fashionable sun, would swell and crinkle like puff pastry, peeling off in flakes and be cured only by prolonged exposure to the dark of winter. "You do love me more than Sharon, donchoo?" she pleaded with a youth in sweatshirt and jeans. He, terribly in the silence of the cracked night, said nothing: he did not even turn towards her.

She snivelled quietly from the shallowness of her discontented heart. Her whining would never stop, but only suffer interruption, by a casual disco, or a boring job, and be called ever back in regression to a spoilt infancy as a weapon whenever all else had failed, and make her more hated by a resentful husband. "There", I felt like calling out from the other side of the street, left behind them and ignored like an oak which two little dogs had passed, "wipe the little bits of skin off your nose and have a good blow."

Next morning, children were skipping and shrieking on the beach below the esplanade as if nothing had happened. And had it? Surely not: the beach may always be subtly different, day by day, and generation after generation, but in its own way it remains reassuringly eternal, like the sea itself. Man-made piers and breakwaters may crack and be swept away, but the endless voyaging of the waves lures not only our eyes but our imagination, to Conrad and Melville, to the pulsating violence of Turner's sea-tempests and shipwrecks. The tang of the sea in my nostrils, the grit of sand between my toes, the taste of salt in my tongue: life pulsed back through my veins as if I were gripping the planks on a plunging raft, gripping with whitened knuckles to stay alive.

I stood third in line for a tin of Coca Cola from a small white-coated man – a sparrow-headed surgeon dipping his hand into the entrails of his refrigerated cart, an entrepreneur subverting the height of summer with the depth of ice. The two sisters in front of me both asked for "two cokes, plays", though they probably wanted only one apiece. "Is it cold?", asked the more freckled. The iceman looked doubtful, and touched one or two near the top. "Many are cold", he replied, "but few are frozen".

I didn't see any British visitors on Cape Cod. Likewise, throughout the whole of the Isle of Wight, though I was taking note of denizens like a cormorant on a ship's prow, I found only one American. The Island is not on the trail that entices Yanks from London through Cambridge and Stratford to York and Edinburgh.

My sole catch made up for all the rest however, like the Iranian mullah who once harangued me in Mashhad about the fatal evils of apostasy.

in rising ground' and occupation of the beautiful district is testified by flint implements used by Palaeolithic man 75,000 years ago, Roman coins of sixteen hundred years ago, and account rolls showing payment to a reeve who was 'bailiff of Shanklin' in 1272. Because of the fear of French invasions, there will always have been local residents or lookout men to fire the beacons on St Martin's Down as on Bonchurch Down and St Boniface Down farther south.

The population of Shanklin did not exceed 105 in 1801, and thereafter it rose gradually to 355 in 1851 and 479 in 1861. With the arrival of the railway, however, the appeal of Shanklin increased, the number of inhabitants soaring to 2,740 in 1881 and 4,533 by 1900. The mere six hotels in 1851 had risen to 43 in 1871, and house-building had spread from the ribbon between East Cliff and Daish's on one side, to Chine House, the Crab Inn and the Rectory on the other.

A lift was built by Sir George Newnes at a cost of £4,000 and completed in 1892, remaining open daily from 8 a.m., the fares being 1d per passenger, per dog and per item of luggage, 2d per pram, mailcart, wheelbarrow, bicycle or tricycle with attendant, and 3d per bathchair with attendant. This old lift was replaced in 1956.

I browsed in Shanklin Health Store at 25 High Street: for nuts, dried fruits and healthy drinks, recalling the half-forgotten discovery in 1676, by the royal physician Dr Fraser, that the chalybeate waters were as potent here as in Scarborough to treat anaemia, eczema, rheumatism, et varia. One spring was found at the Chine head, another at Small Hope, and a third below Osborne Steps. It was not, however, until the 1870s that the Royal Spa Hotel snaffled the last of these springs, using it as a private grotto. Foreign royalty arrived to take these waters, piped into new baths built in 1900 adjacent to the hotel, with separate entrances for visitors from outside the hotel. The town made great play of enjoying three microclimates: the seaside esplanade, the bracing clifftop, and the rural downs.

Hoteliers and other seaside promoters, whose medical friends could be economical with the truth for a consideration, made the seaside not so much a diversion as a religion. Dr Russell, and his successor Dr Relhan, had schemed to turn

New Shanklin. Theatre

Brighton into a veritable health paradise, with a chalybeate spring (as at Tunbridge Wells) but also that sea water, that blessed ozone, that freedom from "the insalutary vapours of running or stagnant waters": everything conduced to perfection. Even fertility seemed to be guaranteed, if your wife sat barren and disconsolate, chafing in her silent nursery. "The extraordinary fecundity of the sheep which drink this water," Relhan could write of Brighton's mineral springs, "gives the shepherds of this place an opportunity of extolling its prolific power."

So we need not be too gullible in accepting claims for Shanklin or Ventnor. It is a great shame, indeed, that Jane Austen never completed her sketch for *Sanditon*, which satirised over-expansive claims for resorts such as Eastbourne or Sandown. Mr Parker, pressing the claims of a new seaside resort, "was convinced that the advantage of a medical man at hand would very materially promote the rise and prosperity of the Place – would in fact tend to bring a prodigious influx; nothing else was wanting." He expatiates, like all cranks, to anyone and everyone, on his theme of the seaside as a universal panacea, a cure-all, much like Dulcamara's elixir in Donizetti's opera. "No person could be really well, no person – however upheld for the present by fortuitous aids of exercise and spirits in a semblance of health – could be really in a state of secure and permanent health without spending at least six weeks by the sea every year. The sea air and sea bathing together were nearly infallible, one or other of them being a match for every disorder, of the stomach, the lungs, or the blood. They were anti-spasmodic, anti-pulmonary, anti-septic, anti-bilious, and anti-rheumatic. Nobody could catch cold by the sea, nobody wanted appetite by the sea, nobody wanted spirits, nobody wanted strength."

It is a truth universally acknowledged, dear Jane implies, that a single man in possession of a good fortune must be in want of a seaside resort to develop.

While the nobs and toffs took the waters, the silent gentlemen of the night sped unobtrusively about their business, depriving the Customs and Excise of their lawful revenue. Between 1780 and 1840 it has been estimated that two of every three seafaring Shanklin men took part in smuggling from Barfleur such exotica as cognac and lace, silk, perfume, watches and jewellery. It is the excise officers to whom we owe the marvellous views on prowling cliff walks such as Eastcliffe Promenade, allowing wide-angled views of the shore and waters from their quarters first in Jessamine Cottage, then at the Watch House.

The pier pavilion was destroyed by fire in 1918, and the pier itself fell victim to the great storm of October 1987, when many fine old trees languished and died. Now the chine looks almost restored, after sensitive replanting, and a heritage centre delineates Shanklin's past for the curious. The esplanade's most interesting building is a former sea-plane hangar from Bembridge, brought here as a cimema in 1923, but given over to the garish rumpus of fruit machines. Outside, a raddled youth of 24 sneered at a slightly younger model, with fully mature blackheads and earwax, "I'm gunna wavver gudty im", and shambled off with shoulders hunched. The Shanklin Conservative Club in Cross Street, an old building with a new exterior, proclaimed itself true blue next door to

Acorn Records (Fine Young Cannibals, Roy Orbison, Kim Wilde and Fleetwood Mac), then the Regal Cinema deceives, in gold and green early 1930s splendour, for the epitaph is up: Regal Cinema RIP, 1932-1986. A small Liberal Club in Landguard Road is equally deceptive, for the Isle of Wight County Council was at the time of my last visit controlled by the SLD/SDP/Liberal alliance, even though South Wight Borough Council was Conservative-controlled.

In The Good Companion, 'Old Books', in Kensloe Street, a quiet pensioner nursed a toy poodle seventeen years old. "He looks a bit weary", I offered. "Looks 'armless, don't ee?" chortled the OAP, "but 'ee watch 'im: he rewls two Weimaraners wi' a rod vyon." A Michelle, chewing gum, spike-heeled into the hairdresser's nearby: dry cut £2.20; wet cut £2.60; wash and cut £4.50. I smiled brightly, and stood ajar, as if making up my mind between dry and wet.

"Anyway," mumbled Michelle through her gumwad, "I spoke to 'im for more than an hour over that lager and lime."

"Was he all right?"

"That was the amazing coincidence. I mean, all that time and we found we had absolutely *noth*ing at all in common!"

I riffled through postcards in Vectis Stationers.

A triangular matron in brown edged in. "Er you ga Coun'y Press from las' week?" "Now I doan bleeve we yav. You can get it at the County Press office."

A mildly local lady from Gatten allowed her eyes to roam lazily between the liquorice allsorts and the pile of new *TV Times*. "Twenty-eight Barton Road," she ruminated to a fringe companion holding *Woman's Weekly* as if hoping to recognise Lobby Lud, "that's the 'ouse that Bill's in." The bright cosy lady behind the counter called out to a departing lady with a wart "I think they didn't give out rain on the radio."

Up the hill, holidaymakers from Sheffield, Halifax and Bradford were arriving by the excursion coach at Daish's, where Queen Victoria used to stay. The staircase walls are adorned with show business stars who have stayed at Daish's, an imposing three-storey construction of solid Victorian virtue, as if it were made of mahogany and Gladstone. In the absence of Jeanne and David Wilson, Samantha showed me the gardens and the tasteful dining-room. I found Cyril Hoyle, my friend the retired coach-driver from Nottingham. "The food is very good," he told me, "and the lassies are very nice. The shopkeepers are very nice here. In Nottingham you've to go into the shop and call out, 'Is there anyone there?' but in Shanklin they can't do enough for you. There's cabaret every night, and tours organised every day, like Newport market day and Godshill."

Back in the 1950s, when I visited Shanklin for the first time, I bought a postcard of Shanklin's 'Beauty Spots' which showed ten sites: Rylstone Gardens, Appley Cliffs, Shanklin Head from Keats Green, Old Village, the lift, the pier, the cliff path, Small Hope beach, Keats Green itself, and (stretching a point) Luccombe Chine. A more hardy walker might take an hour's hike through St Blasius' churchyard, over the stile, and up the hill keeping to the right of the down, to Wroxall. A four-mile walk to Luccombe and back might start in the Old Village, taking the coastal path to Nansen Hill viewpoint car park on the A3055 to Ventnor, continuing to Luccombe Farm, 'The Lynch', Cowleaze, to Upper Chine School for Girls (boarding between 7 and 18, daygirls accepted) and St Blasius'.

St Blasius' has small Flemish panels of the 1520s on the pulpit, but otherwise dates from a rebuilding of 1859. The church is opened on Sundays and at certain other times, but you are equally likely to find a depressing note: 'We regret that you have found our church closed. Theft and vandalism have forced us to open only with supervision. Any queries to Rev. Kenneth Parkinson, St. Blasius' Rectory.' My query would be: 'Why is there more vandalism here than anywhere else on the island, like Shorwell or Godshill, where the wondrous village churches are left open at all times?'

Nearby, the Manor House was a farmhouse until about 1880, but it was rebuilt by the enlightened Lord of the Manor, Francis White Popham, in 1883. Until then, his main residence had been at Wootton Lodge, with a marine retreat at Eastcliff, Shanklin. An able magistrate and far-sighted landlord, White Popham shrewdly issued only conditional building leases, requiring from each new home-owner that only a detached or semi-detached building be put up, and that every property must have a garden or lawn. He died in 1894, but the

Manor House was occupied by his widow until 1929. Now the Manor House is a hotel run by the McLindens to high standards, with neat walled gardens and the crack of willow on ball on Sundays and Wednesdays next door during the Shanklin Cricket Club season. In the Bevin Bar (where Ernest Bevin once played Father Christmas), I found only a scattering of residents and visitors.

I listened to (couldn't help overhearing, I suppose I might say, but I always try to overhear) a West Indian doctor in a neat pinstripe explaining the intricacies of an unusual case to an interested young lady, clearly enamoured, and puckering her lips to lines rehearsed that morning in her mirror. After a while, a bleary-eyed man of ex-military demeanour faltered firmly in the direction of the West Indian's table, propping himself on the polished brown table-top with both index fingers. The young lady in a white blouse and navy skirt didn't look up, but the West Indian smile politely. One index finger waggled. "I must say", interposed the military person, "I think you people are very good at sport." And after a moment's silence for this kindly opinion to sink in, "Viv Richards, you know, et cetera." I fled.

Poor Shanklin! Who could honeymoon here, wandering on the sands in disconsolate grief, after reading *Our Mutual Friend*, and the forlorn hopes of Alfred and Sophronia Lammle, adventurer and adventuress, caught and lost in each other's snare? Two weeks after their wedding, we find them in the Isle of Wight.

"Mr and Mrs Lammle have walked for some time on the Shanklin sands, and one may see by their footprints that they have not walked arm in arm, and that they have not walked in a straight track, and that they have walked in a moody humour; for the lady has prodded little spirting holes in the damp sand before her with a parasol, and the gentleman has trailed his stick after him. As if he were of the Mephistopheles family indeed, and had walked with a drooping tail.

'Do you mean to tell me, then, Sophronia — '

Thus he begins, after a long silence, when Sophronia flashes fiercely, and turns upon him.

'Don't put it upon *me*, sir. I ask you, do *you* mean to tell me?' ..."

78

The sea lapped unobtrusively thirty or forty feet off, like a kitten quite happily playing on its own, before suddenly nipping at your toes with pinprick teeth. Two men in white shirts with the sleeves rolled up above the elbows, and trousers rolled up above the knees, were reminiscing with the comfort of ancient mariners knowing they cannot bore each other: they have seen too much together.

"I reckon", said the one I instinctively considered Stan, 'there's no better sound than Staveley Works Band playing Forty-Second Street on a sunny July afternoon."

"Phil the Fluter's Ball", responded Alf.

"Oh aye," smiled Stan, with a slight chuckle. "'appen tha's right. Fiddle the Fluter's Ball."

On Hope Road, in the Channel View Hotel's sing-along Phoenix Bar, the live music was tuning up at 7.55.

"Ey", said a bricklayer from Birmingham with a check shirt, "did you know that ten years ago in this country we didn't eat no kiwi fruit, and last year we ate thirty five million?" "Not me, mate", answered a short-back-and-sides from Telford, "I've never tried that foreign crap." "And another thing," pursued the Brummie, "they say we eat five million miles of spaghetti in 1988." "You and 'oo else?" parried the Telfie, and his blonde girl-friend in jeans with a ring on each fat finger sniggered dutifully. "Comin down the 'musements?" announced the Telfie, placing his bitter exactly on the stain its predecessor had made on the table, half in question, half in command. "Ff", replied the blonde, suggesting agreement. At the same instant they reared up from behind the round table, and padded heavily towards the door, puffing with newfound exertion. "Ponce", sniffed the Brummie in contempt, and looked around for another to harangue.

Shanklin Chine might be a reminiscence of the Turkish mountains near the Cilician Gates or summer in the Czech Tatras, were it not for the interested naturelovers with binoculars and sensible walking-shoes. Two ballerinas from the corps at English National Ballet were talking loudly about Peter Schaufuss and the new production of *Napoli*, involving dramatic gesticulation, very loud enunciation of French terms, and stage laughter more commonly associated with Victorian melodrama.

You always feel sorry for men married to dancers, whose necessary obsession with their feet and their diet might make any man nervous unto divorce. I think any judge should be persuaded to grant such a martyr instant balimony on request without further proof of hardship. "Yes," he would nod, "if she wears out one more carpet with the 32 fouettes from *La Bayadère*, you get custody of the *tutus* and never have to listen to another score by Minkus under duress."

Stage effects are not alien to the Chine: floodlights nowadays pick out greenery and cascades as if one needed a torch to distinguish the tuppence coloured from the plain. 'Chine' is defined by the OED as 'an open fissure or crack in a surface; a cleft, crack, chink or leak' and supposed obsolete, as though nobody from Oxford had ever bothered to find out, in the Island, how very current and even common the term is here, along the eastern and southern coastline, snagged and bitten as the sandstone has always been by insistent waterfalls. There's a small admission charge to Shanklin Chine, and Englishness might be defined by this downward amble, or upward scramble, among forty thousand shades of green, which quiver and change as you observe them.

During World War II, Shanklin Chine was taken over and used by commandos based at Upper Chine School as a commando course. Lord Mountbatten planned to supply Allied invasion forces with petrol by means of two pipelines under the ocean (acronymically PLUTO) which would fork out from Sandown and Shanklin, providing 56,000 gallons a day across the Channel to Cherbourg.

At its mouth, the Chine expands to a hundred yards or so, fanlike from the top. In the Victorian Tea Garden, waitresses in Victorian raiment purvey cream teas, morning coffees, ice-creams and lunches. I found a secluded spot right next to two heavy-jowled prize-fighting ladies with handbags obviously weighted against the slightest hint of an outrage.

"Even when she's all done up in a ball-gown," snorted the one with four rings on fingers with bitten nails and a whitlow, "you can tell that her parents were gypsies and she goes to bed in a hairnet and pink rollers."

"I've no patience with any one of them", retorted the other, whose mascara had smudged beyond recall.

Shanklin Undercliff, between Chine and Lift

One year I spent a week at the delightfully-positioned Adelaide Private Hotel on Shanklin Esplanade, advertising a '5-course dinner, with quality and quantity to satisfy a holiday appetite'. The glassed-in terrace provided shelter from cold gusts but, as usual, I was drawn more to the characters I found there than to the rows of deckchairs and footprinted sands.

A ginger-haired man with a sheepish smile spent the week trying to mollify his petulant wife, Vera. He was called from the terrace one day to the phone while Vera was upstairs.

"Vera?"

"Wotizi?"

"It's cousin Ron. He says his wife's died."

"You can get a funeral wreath at Allsop's when we get back. They do Interflora. And eh!"

"Wossa?"

"While you're out remember to get that Stergene from Boot's. Does he want me to come?"

"It'll do no good."

Another exchange between Jack and Vera concerned an outing to Blackgang for the illuminations.

"Did the taxi-driver say when he'd come to pick us up?"

"Right."

"Well?"

"He said he'd come to pick us up at seven or eight, whichever's soonest."

'Well that's all right then. Or, if you don't ask, you don't know where you are." Jack managed to slip 'to be quite honest' or 'to be quite truthful with you' into each sentence somewhere, as if perpetually accused of lying.

Not far from the Adelaide, Waverley Court is a tasteful new brick development; on an upper storey a seafaring gentleman in shorts was training binoculars on a vessel. *"There* she blows!" I imagined him called out to a bored wife drudging over the stove as though still at home in Ealing.

The Longshoreman Free House was one of those pubs inviting men whose brightest hours are always spent in pubs, and are tempted to play rugger for stops on the way home, or to think of as a place to interrupt walks with Rover.

The bar-stools were lined with similarities to Arthur English, Arthur Lowe, Arthur Daley, the mythical English characters merging with the slightly real, acting out their zigzag destinies in wide tie and tweeds, assumed accents and bursts of guffaw, cigar-smoke and questionable mo'or chat ("knocked off, is it?"), watching the threatening outside world with the quizzical half-lost impudence of an Ascot pickpocket, a smart operator dahn the Old Kent Road, avoiding the slightest interest in, or understanding of, foreigners who – some say – might not even exist, a mere invention of the suspect media to keep their mind off strikes an' 'at, and the dole, litter and muggings, graffiti and four-letter-words that speckle the air and the walls like ineradicable measles.

2 Bonchurch and the South

Luccombe

Luccombe on the outskirts of Shanklin was once idyllic, like Bonchurch, but in January 1988 a terrible landslip destroyed four houses and put another twelve or so in imminent jeopardy. South Wight Borough Council officially stated that it had no money to help, and even in July 1989 there was no report from the Department of the Environment on whether Luccombe could be saved. Frances Longman, chairwoman of the Residents' Association, believes that Luccombe's problems are soluble. "I think it's just sewage seeping out and rainwater draining off National Trust land, pushing the stratum on top of the blue slipper clay." She wants the DoE to save Luccombe, but the costs of stabilising the whole area may be too high; the action too late; the district too perennially vulnerable.

Luccombe Farm is owned by the National Trust; the whole rural area is a paradise for walkers. I arrived downhill at Rosecliff Lodge, leading to Smuggler's Cottage, and chatted at the gate with a man from Peckham staying in a caravan at Bembridge but visiting his sister-in-law here, where blossoming hydrangeas nearly met across the road in a fraternal petal-shake. "Cor, lumme, it's great dahn 'ere," enthused the Londoner, "you can really get away from the old petrol fumes dahn 'ere. Course, it's murder on the old 'ay fever", as he sneezed and clutched at the gate to stay upright with the force of the explosion, "but once you've wiped yer sore eyes, wo' a sight for 'em, eh?"

I had to agree: a red squirrel skipped out of sight behind a tree-trunk on the path down to the Chine, but a 'danger' notice stopped me in my tracks, and I retraced my steps: the agile squirrel had shimmied away to another safe branch, well out of eyeshot.

Wroxall is a sleepy village that seems an odd place (but

Map of the Isle of Wight, South

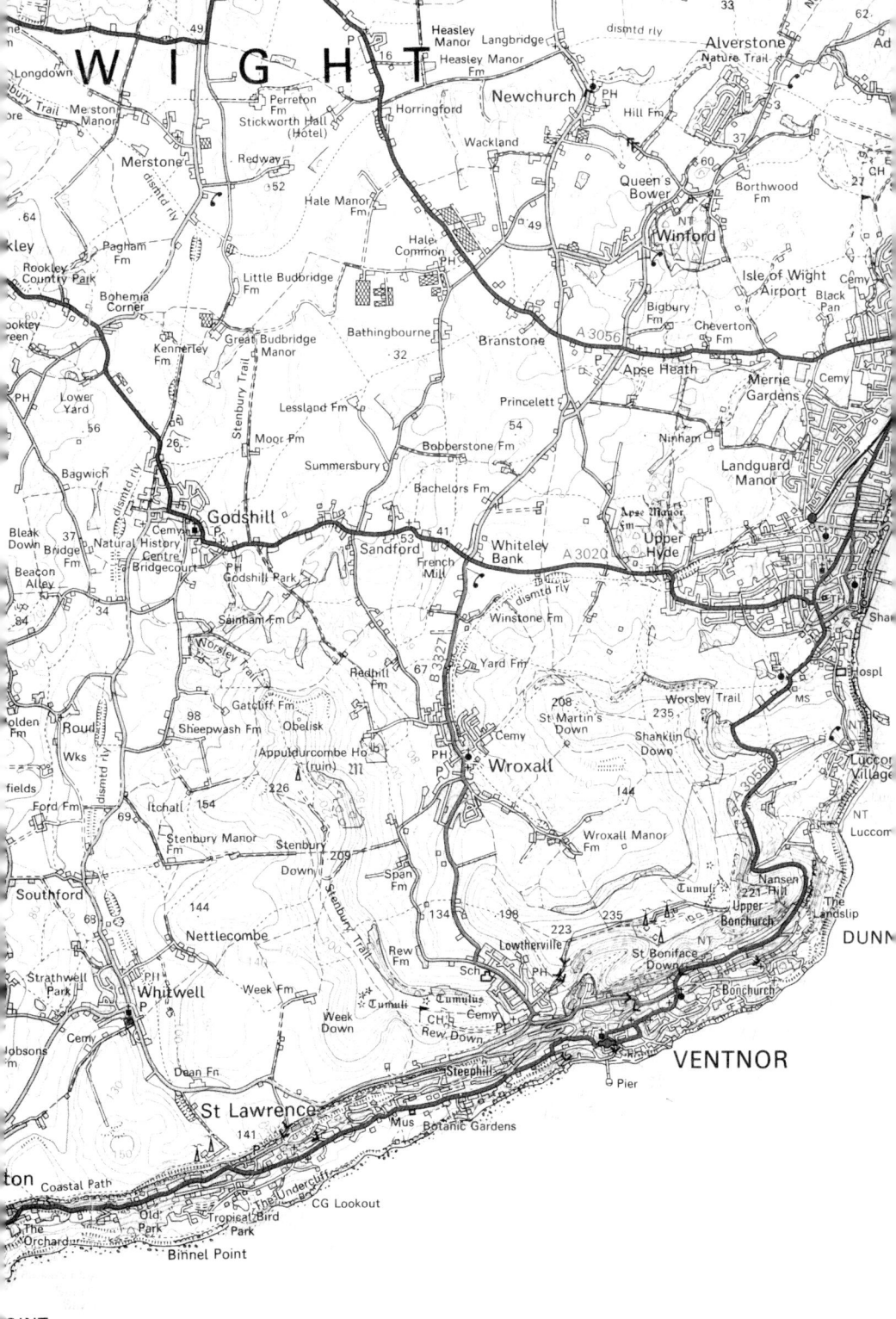

Wroxall. Wallis Close

then, any place would be odd) to bury a nuclear shelter thirty feet below the chalk down of St Boniface, first dug during World War II but recently updated and still an option for those with access, in the event that anyone would have time to get down there, following a polite warning from an enemy. Three minutes to get below the earth, gentlemen. Two minutes. One minute. Time. Time, gentlemen, please, we're closing the door on human history, and *we don't know when it will be safe for us to come out.*

Appuldurcombe

Such nightmares seem entirely remote from the rural car-park welcoming visitors to Appuldurcombe Park, in the centre of which rises the shell of a once glorious home, created on the site of a demolished Tudor mansion by Sir Robert Worsley in the decade from 1701. The architect was not a 'minor provincial', as strangely mooted by Pevsner, but as Arthur Oswald opined, "he must certainly have been a London man. The building is in the grand manner... and it has a sophistication which would be absent from a provincial architect's work." It was in fact the work of John James (1672-1746), joint Clerk of the Works at Greenwich with the great Nicholas Hawksmoor, and after Appuldurcombe he worked on St Paul's Cathedral, Assistant Surveyor under Wren in 1715, and Surveyor in 1723. His is St George's Church in London's Hanover Square.

Appuldurcombe today is lip-curling Vanbrugh explored by Dr Watson. "Good God, Holmes, someone has stolen the entire contents of the house." "And the roof, too, Watson, with every pane of glass from the windows. There's only one man in England capable of such awe-inspiring sleight-of-hand." "You mean?" "Yes, Watson, Father Time." It was actually a land-mine that exploded close by.

Locally pronounced "*Appl*ercombe', the grand house – in the sense of Grand Tour – was never finished in Sir Robert's time. His sons died before him, and it was not until Sir Richard's return from his own Grand Tour in 1772 that the house was completed – nay 'added to' and 'much improved' in his own vainglorious words, sparing no expense by hiring Chippendale for his furniture, 'Capability' Brown for his land-scaped garden, and Wyatt as architectural consultant. However, in 1855 the estate was sold to a company planning a hotel, but this grandiose scheme never achieved fruition and the noble pile was turned into England's most unlikely pre-paratory school: Dr Pound's Academy for Young Gentlemen, an enterprise doomed from the start and foreclosed in 1884. We have seen at Quarr how the monks of Appuldurcombe had tried to raise the funds to buy the house but failed and left for resurrected Quarr. During World War II an exploding land-mine finished the demolition that billeted troops had started in World War I, and it is due only to the foresight of Lord Mottistone that the house was not pulled down, but left in its open glory to incarnate on the Island those spacious 18th-century days of Watteau and Fragonard, Boucher and Canaletto, when the Englishman's home was more com-monly than nowadays a castle, and the Corinthian capital held sway above a world holding its breath in the years before Revolution.

English Heritage has tactfully repaired and consolidated the crumbling edifice, and in 1986 re-roofed the Great Hall, Draw-

Appuldurcombe. Audrey Ward

ing Room and Dining Parlour, greatly to the approval of pigeons spending the winter at Appuldurcombe. Each elevation presents a picture of stately grace and classical harmony. The south-east pavilion containing a drawing-room is especially notable, when seen across the fountain and pool of the Yarborough period (1805-55). The equally impressive northeast pavilion contained the dining-room. L.O.J. Boynton suggests that the practice of stressing the wings instead of the centre of the façade derived from Louis le Vau's chateau at Vaux-le-Vicomte. I stood in the porte-cochère, visualising the rattle of carriage wheels and the *whoa-up!* of the driver, bustle of footmen and maids, deference of the butler, and flutter of chambermaids.

Back in the porter's lodge, now a ticket-office and museum, I learned of the Worsley scandal, when Sir Richard separated from his wife, Seymour Dorothy Fleming, in 1782, seven years after their marriage for the bride's 'love' noted the acidly gleeful Gibbon, 'and £80,000'. His wife admitted twenty-seven lovers, only the last of whom was cited by Sir Richard in an action for £20,000 damages, of which he was awarded 'one shilling' because of his connivance. Reynolds' enchanting portrait of the erring Seymour once at Appuldurcombe, now has a place of honour in the gallery at Harewood. What happened to the amorous Seymour? She married a Frenchman, caught syphilis, and died at sixty, a real cautionary tale for the times, when the trial transcript sold to a public avid as ever for skeletons in aristocratic cupboards.

Godshill

Godshill stands for the Isle of Wight in many a scrapbook, because of thatched cottages and tea-rooms, with a homely pub, the Griffin, where in truth you are likely to find more overners than locals beneath its barge-boarded gables. Shops catering mainly to the tourist trade offer gems, lace, herbs and herbal products, copper, brass, ceramics and glass, cider, wood and ironwork. The Bat's Wing Restaurant has a crafts shop, and the Natural History Museum contains an aquarium. A conversation between two ladies in cotton prints circled round the daughter-in-law of the taller, with a wart on her nose the cynosure of most eyes.

"If she was here now she'd be making those comments, what are they called?"

"Tart?"

"Snide. She gets at me all ways. One week it's anorexia, next is bulimia. I don't know which is worst."

"I think Bulimia's worst, in my uncle's opinion. He's been all over South America, and he'd rather be in Peru any day."

Few can resist taking photographs of the delightful thatched cottages near All Saints' Church. Generally only smaller homes were thatched, exceptions being the large farmhouses at West Billingham, near Chillerton (now tiled), and The Bays, Rookley (now slated), which were obviously once thatched. The commonest roofing material all over England until the thirteenth century, thatch retained its popularity well into Tudor times. Nowadays, the best places to see thatched houses are Suffolk and Norfolk in the East of England, and Devon to West Sussex in the South. If I'd wanted to buy a two-bedroomed detached bungalow in Godshill, with a tiled roof, 1 Ternal Mead was on offer in 1989 for £85,000 freehold.

The Island has a new commercial deer farm, the Sainham at Godshill, with in its second year seventy hinds producing 35 stag calves for venison and 35 hind calves for breeding in 1989. The day of the deerburger is at hand.

Maureen Beisly runs a weekly canework and rushwork furniture restoration class from her thatched cottage in Godshill, and she invited me to see a Friday workshop, with upholstery and other materials typically costing no more than £12, and £12 a day at the class, which includes a home-made lunch. Her own thatched roof is maintained by a man from Freshwater.

The church perches on a steep hill, with magnificent views, but one legend of several tells us how workmen originally tried to build it on the plain, in a field subsequently known as the Devil's Acre, for the fairy folk decided to move it from their meadow to the hill, out of their way. The workmen were astonished, arriving next morning, to find the walls removed to the hill, but stubbornly brought the materials back down. After the fairies had thwarted all their efforts for a third night running, the builders gave up and treated the meadow as diabolical ground, and the hill as divine. These rolling downs are, of course, just the place for elfin dance and hollow tree, dryad and naiad. Witchcraft will never have died down round Godshill.

Which makes the church of All Saints (Pevsner calls it St Lawrence) exceptionally vibrant: a crucifix held aloft among warlocks. Another legend says that the church was built on the site of a pagan shrine, a practice, common among the early Christian missionaries, to induce local people to return to their former places of worship, which I have noted all over Latin America, for example. Pope Gregory the Great, who sent St Augustine to England, specifically recommended his envoy to use familiar ground when building churches for the heathen *gens Anglorum*. There is no remnant of the early Saxon church mentioned by Sir John Oglander as dating from the "rayne of King Edward the Confessor", that is 1042-66, but the first Norman church has left one mark: a capital now visible at the east end, between the two altars. Of the early 14th century are the chancel east window, the south chapel windows, the lower parts of the west tower (the upper parts

Godshill. Churchgate Cottage and Church

being 16th century) and the transepts. Revenues from Godshill owned by the Abbey of Lyre near Evreux in Normandy after the Conquest were the highest in the island, and were sometimes channelled elsewhere. Edward I used them to help his Scottish wars, claiming in 1304 massive quantities of wheat, barley, oats, beans and peas. In the 15th century, the Norman abbey – who had sent armed monks against a newly-appointed rector in 1308 – effectively lost control of Godshill, which now belonged to Appuldurcombe House, two miles off, once also under another Norman abbey – that of Montebourg, near Valognes (south of Cherbourg) and subsequently under the Nuns of Aldgate, who let it to Sir John Leigh, at that time reputed the island's richest man.

Sir John, who died in 1529, is commemorated by one of those passionless alabaster effigies that call to mind 'the stiff upper lip'. Even more remarkable is the toy-soldier-like figure of Sir James Worsley, his red-robed wife a decorous distance behind him. Sir James was the son-in-law of Sir John, and took the onus of 'whipping-boy' to Henry VIII, who of course could not be beaten as a naughty boy, being a prince of the blood royal. Sir James, who died in 1538, gave All Saints at Godshill his "beste tawyne velvit gowne to be made in a vestyment." His son Richard it was who, in the reign of Henry VIII, strengthened the island with castles at West Cowes, East Cowes, Sandown and Yarmouth. Richard too is buried at Godshill, and recollected in a standing monument erected at the expense of his brother and successor, John. Other Worsleys clutter up All Saints' with their worldly vainglory: Sir Robert, who rebuilt Appuldurcombe House in 1710 and died in 1747, and a thirty-ton sarcophagus on lions' claws commemorating another Richard, who to his credit collected Greek sculpture and died in 1805. It must have been an enormous relief to him to survey pure classical proportions after the dumpy realism of Sir James and Lady Anne, who might have stepped out of an amateur production of a Shakespeare history play.

I do not know what I love best in Godshill church: the angels, the bellcote outside the south transept, or the triple-padlocked parish chest common throughout England since that mistrustful year of 1611, in the reign of James I? No, it must be the Lily Cross, a restored painting of about 1450 depicting Jesus' Crucifixion from three boughs of a bush now in full leaf. Like all such, it was limewashed during the Reformation, and emerged to the light of day here only in the nineteenth century. Christ's head hangs to the right, and two angels can be discerned above. Much is made of the Lily Cross's rarity, but others such are known on the Continent, and even in England who knows how many more mediaeval murals might be uncovered by removing layers of lime?

That view to Appuldurcombe and the downs should not divert you from Godshill churchyard, with its 15th-century churchyard cross, lopped and now topped with an 18th-century sundial. Look for the oldest grave, of the 13th or 14th century, with a cross raised in relief (halfway up the path from the cottages to the church on the south side). The third stone down from the churchyard cross is in memory of Ann Loader (1775), showing the Book of Judgement with an arm holding aloft her coffin lid and an angel blowing a trumpet. The Resurrection was always in the mind of these Godshill folk, as in the case of Richard Gard who decreed that the lid of his coffin be split open and his grave be dug no more than two feet

Godshill. View southward from the churchyard

below ground, to facilitate early springing at the Last Trump. A notorious cattle-rustler and horse-thief, according to the memoirs of Sir John Oglander, Gard had a fulsome memorial recommending him to posterity as someone "whom virtue cloth'd with fame." Pshaw!

You might think that God would look after his own, but York Minster suffered enormously in recent years, and Godshill's destiny-defying hilltop position has brought several lightning strikes: 1778, when parts of the clock melted; 1897, and 1904.

The church's six bells alone are well worth a visit to Godshill, which is best seen on a wintry day – if you are lucky – when nobody is there but you, the winds bite like vultures, and the gray sky mimics dull aluminium before dusk. I can, possibly, discern among the clamour of the bells the fourth one, inscribed for wedlock, "When female virtue weds with manly worth, We catch the rapture and we speed it forth." Rooks desperate for crumbs remind you of the Worsley motto: I swoop to soar once more, *ut sursum desuper*. As I descended to my car, I passed a rook that flew up, hastily read the proofs of its roughly drafted nest, made up one or two author's corrections in black, then provisionally passed its roundel for press.

I met the Barfields, man and wife from Bexhill, who had come up to Godshill to see where her parents were married, in 1925. "She always said I must come and see it". "And so we have." They sanctified the sunlight in their enduring harmony. A man and a woman, making a marriage work.

Bonchurch
I drove the winding cliff road to Upper Bonchurch which, given the treachery of the blue slipper, could sooner or later become wreckage at Lower Bonchurch, or washed altogether out to sea, in a tide of oblivion. From Luccombe and the aptly-named Landslip by Dunnose to Blackgang Chine we risk our lives in the knowledge that geology is against us. Within the last couple of centuries (mere nothings in geological aeons) the Greensand has slipped from Bordwood Ledge and thus seven miles of Undercliff have been contorted and deformed by cataracts, landfalls, blocked streams. It is territory for smugglers and seafaring men, with small bays and tiny inlets accessible only with the latest local knowledge.

The National Trust's 570 acres of down and farmland, with St Boniface Down at 764 feet the highest point on the Island, is named for a saint to whom was dedicated the first church of Bonchurch. It is the 13th-century Old St Boniface, though some Norman masonry was reused in that reconstruction. A wall-painting on the northern nave wall might represent St Christopher; a black oak rococo cross is from Flanders. Here the poet Algernon Charles Swinburne (1837-1909) was baptised, though he had been born in London, but he was to be buried in the new St Boniface (1847-8), designed by Benjamin Ferrey. An atheist rebelling against the High Church tendencies of his parents Admiral Charles Henry and Lady Jane Henrietta Swinburne, he earlier came to worship the sea from his home at East Dene in Bonchurch, where he dwelt from 1839 to 1865. Just as Sandown expands like a palm, Bonchurch grips like a fist, tight and dark, jagged grey stone and twining hawthorn. Keats found Bonchurch coyly 'romantic', its cottages "covered with creepers and honeysuckles, with roses and eglantines peeping at the windows. Fit abodes for the people I guess live in them: romantic old maids fond of novels, or soldiers' widows with a pretty jointure." Pretty indeed, with a quarter of a million pounds no longer rarely found in the local property price-range. Bonchurch writers were afflicted with feyness and that parochial nationalism which all too often replaces breadth of vision and depth of sympathy among provincials: Alfred Noyes wrote his *Drake* (1908), an epic poem glorifying a bloodthirsty pirate; and H. de Vere Stacpoole was responsible for a series of forgettable popular novels such as *The Blue Lagoon* (1908) and *The Pools of Silence* (1909). In Bonchurch I felt unnervingly cut off, by the height of the Undercliff rearing above me, the close proximity of trees and walled villas, and the sharply dropping road with hairpin bends that demand the most attentive driving.

Swinburne's imposing old home, stunning oak panels and gracious lounges, cane chairs and wooded enclosure, was a magnificent holiday home of the Workers' Travel Association when my wife stayed there in 1961. Nowadays, the time of

Bonchurch. Swinburne's House, East Dene

young Alice Meynell and Carlyle's encounter with Dickens long past, East Dene is a study centre, where some visitors pardonably mistake the Victorian lodge for the mansion itself. Even now, one can easily understand why Bonchurch had been only slowly, stubbornly overtaken by that *parvenu* Ventnor, which it secretly despised, before Ventnor grew in the mid-nineteenth century and – truth to tell – still does. Yet Domesday showed Bonchurch with enough arable land to support half a plough, while eleventh-century Gatcombe could find work for seven, and Calbourne for twenty-five, at a time when Newport was merely a rustic appendage to the hill fort of Carisbrooke. And if you're juggling figures to compare the fluctuating fortunes of villages on Wight, Mottistone in 1334 counted sixty taxpayers, and Carisbrooke a mere 29.

Elizabeth Missing Sewell (later called Ashcliff) lived with her brother William at Sea View from 1844 and became friendly with the Swinburnes. Now long forgotten, she wrote popular history, travel and novels, many with religious themes, such as *Amy Herbert* and *Gertrude*. The latter caught the Oxford Movement controversy, which was then inducing young women to visit the sick, poor and needy, concentrating on good works, attending church services daily and neglecting their filial duties, much to their parents' consternation. Miss Sewell's *Autobiography* (1907) is essential reading for Bonchurch addicts, explaining how the new church came to be built and paid for (it is bigger than you would expect). The parish school and teacher's house were built to a large extent with money provided by fees and royalties from writings by Elizabeth, her brother, a major figure in the Oxford Movement and Warden of Radley College, Oxford, and William Adams. Elizabeth Sewell described Bonchurch as "two rows of thatch-roofed cottages, lovely to look at, but very uncomfortable to live in"; the larger houses at the lower level included Undermount, Winterbourne, and East Dene, with Cliff Dene halfway up (in Brannon's engraving of 1843), and Ribbands' Hotel on the upper level, where most visitors stayed. Now Bonchurch Manor Hotel welcomes you with grace and elegance, the Lake Hotel relaxes you in two acres on Shore Road, and the Highfield Hotel on Leeson Road has sheltered, brilliant gardens. Upper Bonchurch offers the Leconfield Hotel, on the bus route to Shanklin rail station and Ryde ferry; on Bonchurch beach the Horseshoe Bay Hotel must be a good choice for children and 'well-behaved dogs are welcome'.

In his mid-seventies, the man sat staring into the sea, into low clouds, into the sea, searching for a sign, then dropping his tense shoulders and conveying to anyone who would feel the unspeakable grief of a man married for forty years to a woman he neither likes nor ever hopes or desires to understand. She chatted on harmlessly, endlessly, winding the interminable wordstrands on to her skein, off again, and back on.

"You're not listening," she said at odd pauses, the only interruption to her discourse, and I believe she was correct.

The proprietors at Madeira Hall Country House Hotel, on Trinity Road, before Ventnor High Street, might well lure harassed writers with their recommendation from Lord Macaulay, who wrote in 1850, as he worked in Madeira Hall – spasmodically – on the third volume of *The History of England* (1855): "I look out on one side to the crags and myrtles of the Undercliff, against which my house is built. On the other side I have a view of the sea, which is at this moment as blue as the sky, and as calm as the Serpentine. My little garden is charming." If you cannot spend a night in Bonchurch, try a cream tea at the Smugglers' Haven Tea Gardens on Leeson Road.

Two married couples, dreading each other's company like ill-assorted fish chucked into an aquarium, weighing the others up to judge if there are cannibals about, indulged in the kind of desperate polite conversation that gives small-talk a bad name. The women were, as usual, making the best of an almost intolerable job, but the men were hot and irritable, and saw no reason to like each other. Bernard, the fat one whose collar had a life of its own, mostly homicidal judging from the purple colour of Bernard's face, tried again.

"I hope Middlesex don't win the Benson and Hedges again this year," he suggested to Robin. "Why's that?", answered Robin, politely.

"Well, it's creepy coming seventh to a county that doesn't exist any more. It's a bit like losing at croquet to the ghost of Jacob Marley."

Bonchurch. Joan Wolfenden at Yaffles

The National Gardens Scheme is one of those subtle British compromises that allow you to visit people in their own environment without being invited. So when the chance to visit Joan Wolfenden at Yaffles in Bonchurch arises, twice a year, pop in and chat with this exhilarating lady in a good charitable cause.

Joan exemplifies the indomitable spirit of Englishwomen: Hester Stanhope, Jane Digby, Lesley Blanch. An artist, embroiderer, gardener, and *cordon bleu* chef, she founded the Peacock Vane publishing company to produce her charmingly-illustrated books, and runs the Bonchurch Bookshop in Ventnor, which is always worth a visit. She runs a house and garden with help only three hours a week, and what an extraordinary garden, clambering down rock hewn into fantastic pits by quarrymen, and overlooking the churchyard, the Peacock Vane hotel which she sold a few years back on retirement, as well as the azure sea.

"To move forty tons of earth", she told me, "you shift six wheelbarrow loads a day, and it's done before you know it. I put six pebbles in my pocket before I start, and cast one away every time I tip out a barrow." Her son John is the Island chairman of the Council for the Protection of Rural England, and lives in the house below, the coach-house and stables of Peacock Vane. Joan is of Walloon extraction, and brought continental cuisine to Peacock Vane, creating a reputation second to none. A green woodpecker flitted across the gladiolas, laughing in the way that earned the birds their dialect nickname 'yaffles', after which Joan's part of the Stacpoole house is named. Joan has Stacpoole's best bedroom, morning-room and billiard-room, while the bulk of the novelist's home, Cliff Dene, has other owners.

Before ten, Joan answers her post, she gardens 10-12, and at midday takes a bath, changes and makes lunch. Painting absorbs 2-4, she runs up to the bookshop from 4-5, and spends the evening on needlework and writing.

I found Joan wielding a mean mattock, and as she rested she showed me her garlic crop, mimosa, one of the finest fuchsia beds I have seen, and a wondrous passion flower. "Weeding," she told me, "is a form of meditation. I can do it without thinking about it, leaving my mind free to wander at will over the day or the infinite."

She will show you her herb garden, but scrutinise odd corners and you will find the mild or pungent scents of oregano and mint, lovage and tarragon, sage and parsley, all prospering in carefully composted soil. I found wild balsam – she has none of the snobbery of traditionally thoughtless weed-detesters – and a limpid blue agapanthus. "Everyone complains of moles," she said, "but if you plant a euphorbia latifolia, that's this caper spurge, moles will disappear soon enough." *The Year at Yaffles*, on this garden, is a colourful treasury of garden lore.

Beside the pillar-box on the slope outside Yaffles a red-faced man in a maroon pullover and highly polished brown shoes was pacing around his Vauxhall Astra in the distracted manner of Alain Prost at a pitstop while a new engine is found at Hockenheim.

I fear that I had to intervene.

"May I help at all?"

"No, I'm waiting for the postman."

"Special delivery?"

"I hope so. I only came down the Pitts to post a letter. Ended up by hanging on to the letter and posting the car-keys. Now I've got to wait for the postman to open up so I can drive home in time for 'Gardeners' Question-Time'."

"Alan Titchmarsh?" I enquired.

"Are you?" he said in some surprise. "My name's Dougie Donaldson."

While the gentlefolk of Bonchurch, the Sewells and the Swinburnes, slept away their peaceful nights, little casks of cognac were being carried to the cliff-cave known as Old Jack, J.L. Whitehead explains in *The Undercliff of the Isle of Wight* (1911), "in which five hundred gallons of smuggled spirits and other illicit goods are known to have been stowed away at one time. The origin of the numerous ghost and other like stories, so rife in the village, may be traced to the nefarious operations carried on by gangs of smugglers, for the mysterious noises often heard during the night were intentionally added to with the object of frightening away the more curious sightseers. At certain seasons, the lower road was thought to be haunted by a 'Phantom' as it was called, on horseback. This apparition created a great scare and for a time it was a terror to the neighbourhood. It was a clever device of the smugglers, who made use of the horse for a twofold purpose, to carry away the tubs of spirits up to the little coombe at the rear of St Boniface House, and to frighten away the timid villagers. To deaden the noise, and at the same time to frighten the uninitiated, the hoofs of the horse were padded, and the application of a little phosphorus to man and beast produced a very startling effect."

Dickens spent some time at Winterbourne, on the opposite side of Old St Boniface's Church from Swinburne's East Dene, and both these very different authors would have cherished their proximity to the venerable church, named for a Devon-born missionary saint (680-755) who spent much of his life in Germany and was martyred in Friesland, now a part of the Netherlands. After St Lawrence's old church, St Boniface's is the smallest church on the island, a quality itself appealing in isolated Bonchurch. You can hear a rivulet pass on its scurry down to the sea, and the sub-tropical languor of moss and fern, heavy dews and soft air makes one yawn and want to stretch out on grass among the box tombs and tilting head-stones. Try to visit the church if you can for the service on the saint's day, 5 June.

It was in Bonchurch's Lake Hotel that I saw her, on a garden chair overlooking the sloping lawn.

She was fifty-four, I suppose, a woman of stunning compos-ure and natural beauty, on whom make-up would have seemed unthinkably vulgar, so she troubled with Oil of Ulay only, a light cleansing lotion, the merest touch of lipstick, her beautiful grey hair unfussily permed with unpretentious eleg-ance. Wrinkles around her eyes were undisguised: they attested her maternity, her wifely concern, as tree-rings dig-nify a mature tree. She had loved and been loved; she wel-comed children with beckoning arms like the Madonna's in Leonardo's Cartoon, she dignified the mean world about her with a smile both gracious and sympathetic. She would always be terribly vulnerable, so must never be wounded. She would expect to be taken for granted, so must never be taken for granted.

She sat alone.

Ventnor

If you can tug yourself away from Bonchurch's charming pond, and its ever-changing views, there is a lovely stroll of about 1½ miles above Horseshoe Bay to Ventnor. Like Shanklin, Ventnor was an invention of the 19th century, with only a few mansions and cottages by the sea until James Clark's *The Influence of Climate in the Prevention and Cure of Chronic Diseases* (1829 and later editions) persuaded the ailing rich to try out the temperament of Ventnor for themselves, measuring the rainfall, the temperature, prevailing winds, protection by surrounding hills, and relative humidity. The message was: if your chest or lungs can improve anywhere, they will at Ventnor.

The Crab and Lobster Inn on Grove Road afforded sustenance to travellers for centuries (Charles I had visited it in 1648), but few travellers came, with no stage-coach or even post-chaise in this corner of the island. The bay was left alone, with its handful of farmers and fishermen not averse to the odd night's smuggling, keeping their illicit catch in plentiful caves in the Undercliff. James Sanderson had built a mansion call Steephill Castle for a certain John Hambrough in 1828 (it was demolished in 1964); it was Hambrough who paid for St Catherine's (1837; chancel, 1849), and in 1836 a Congregational Church (now the church hall) went up in the High Street.

In the graveyard at St Catherine's I found the headstone of 'Mary Chessell Noble, d. March 12 1868 aged 181 years, with Christ which is far better'. The pink Country House Tea Rooms next to the Natwest Bank on High Street disgorged four fat ladies who had partaken heavily of the confectionery: the Wightish word for them is 'pundles'.

A sudden wave of visitors, valetudinarians or genuine sufferers, turned Ventnor into a health resort without planning regulations, where cottages, villas, "mean rows of squalid dwellings" (to quote a contemporary), and hotels, shops and services shot up quarried terraces which the Incas themselves might have found challengingly steep. Amenities and sanitary facilities lost out in the race to fill the available theatre where the daily spectacle of scudding clouds, ever-changing seas, mists, dawn and dusk would compensate for the absence of city amenities. After all, had not Queen Victoria herself made the Island her home? A road to Bonchurch was completed in 1843 and an Esplanade in 1848.

At a hotel I shall not name on Ventnor's esplanade, I chose the fish. So, at the next table, did a sprightly curtly-spoken military gentleman with gold cufflinks and a handkerchief triangularly tucked into the breast pocket of his slightly shining blazer. His long-term wife, stunned, pained, moving her linen serviette until stared at, avoided his glassy eyes.

"What," said the aggrieved major to a waitress with bangly earrings, "is this so-called fish?"

"Plaice, Major."

"So-called plaice."

"Plaice, Major."

"Pah. So-called."

It occurred to me then, as it still does, that none of it was anybody's fault.

Ventnor Cascade Gardens contain a model Isle of Wight on which kids can play while muddling up their north and south. Ventnor pier, deliberately cut in half during World War II to delay enemy landings, suffered recent accidental damage by a fire which demolished the amusement arcades.

Many of the kids are happily not too bothered by the elimination of those arcades: they still paddle, build sandcastles, sit for a while on deck chairs then run off irresistibly, looking back to see if Mum and Dad are watching. They still find jellyfish, throw sticks for mongrels ever eager for a scamper, beg for ice-lollies, and bury their parents up to the neck in wet sand.

"Look, mum, a jellyfish!" squealed little Sandra, and Darren made as if to stamp on the creature near the breakwater. The scolding scream mews in my ear to this day like a seagull's cry.

The fine King Charles I Hotel in Grove Road, built about 1850 but badly damaged by fire in December 1988, gave the style to mid-Victorian spaciousness in Ventnor, once the town woke up to a preference for the wealthier invalid. Charles Turner designed the Gothic school building on Albert Street and in 1862 the Holy Trinity Church, now a capsule of its time, apart from the 1912 screen, proclaimed the ecclesiastical majesty of Ventnor. Visitors complained how difficult access was by land, so the town fathers resolved on a wooden pier, where a promontory would be smashed away. Since it was the promontory which had kept the high tides and high winds away from the shore, it is no surprise that the pier was torn away in a gale, the esplanade was pounded by the sea, and the land began to subside into the water. Chastened, man hastened to repair the damage he had done, and the promontory was built up again. Steephill Road acquired in 1871 the Royal National Hospital for Diseases of the Chest, with stained glass of 1873 by William Morris and jarring Art Nouveau glass of 1892 by Sir William Reynolds. The Roman Catholic Church of the B.V.M. and St Wilfrid (1871) was enlarged in the 20th century, but all through Ventnor names such as Albert Hall in Victoria Street and heavy and spacious style where space allows evoke antimacassar and aspidistra, patriotic and patrician, from the pier to the discreet affluence of the suburban village that replaced Steephill Castle. Myrtle, magenta hydrangea and heliotrope stun the senses: soft air

Ventnor. Winter seas from the Wroxall Road

wafts like cumulus, and cricket is played by Englishmen with the intensity that Russians reserve for chess or Basques apply to pelota.

The gardens were created by an imaginative borough engineer from a tract of waste land called the Triangle. I loved the 1930s Art Deco Winter Gardens, run down though they may be, with beery men slopping pints and singing to stop themselves thinking. Ventnor had been shell-shocked early in World War II by an attack on the radar base which missed and hit Burt's 1840 brewery instead. The kids were evacuated from school to Steephill Castle, and must have been bemused by mediaeval-style battlements, sullen to learn in later life that the 'castle' was just a peacetime folly. These kids are now middle-aged men in the Hole in the Wall, formerly coachmen's quarters in the Central Hotel. The Royal Victoria Pier was smashed by the people to prevent enemy landings in the War, then again by gales in recent years; the Town Hall is a mere façade which is planned to front a sheltered housing development for 27 elderly people; the last trains left long ago from Ventnor Town station where Steephill Road meets Castle Road, and from Ventnor Station where Grove Road meets Newport Road.

The Rex Cinema in which I first saw *Brief Encounter* has become a noisy amusements arcade where adolescents delay the learning of social arts and graces.

Despite the rigours of hurricanes and the transience of dreams, the sands still bring out children with their buckets and spades, grown-ups with their picnic bags and beachballs, deckchair attendants with their keen eye for the scarpering defaulter.

"Be'n Sourfen enni'?" called a Cockney on the sands, his beach shorts cluttered with sails, clouds and the legend MIAMI in shades of green and orange. I hovered around his windbreak, hoping like a fox that he or his curly-haired brunette would let slip the chicken of a letter 't' that I could hungrily snatch away. Nothing doing for fourteen minutes of absent-minded prowling, like an amateurish pickpocket on his day off (no pockets). Then she opened a flask. Could this be the moment? "Wanna dring?" she asked, pouring a decidedly brown liquid into a white cup. "Cor ye," he gasped from under the yellow towel over his head, "I cudoo wivva cuppa cha." I slunk off with my tail between my legs to seek more promising prey.

Two plump ladies in bright spotted dresses had drawn their deckchairs close enough to dig each other in the elbows at the height of a good yarn. "And then she said, I'll never forget, she said, you'll never credit this, she said, she told me straight out, she said 'I was the thirteenth baby', she said, 'my parents had lucky loins'." "She never did!" "The right baggage". "That was Shirley Bassington all over."

Denizens of the deckchairs are suffering one and all from the condition known as human. They complain about it, sometimes bitterly, until the moment of their arriving death, and then they bitterly retract thoughts of their misery, and swear to like it just a little bit at least if they could be granted one more day. How wondrous is every hour that we spend with both palms pressing our doors against the swollen floodwaters of our annihilation! A rat's life is royal: how should ours be less than heavenly?

"Did you bring your flask?" "I would have, but I forgot." "'Ave some o' mine." "Don't mind if I do, if it's sugared." "It's not sugared." "That man over there is the dead image of our Rhoda's Charlie." "I don't like the way 'is knees stick out the front." "He's got his nose."

Our attitudes to the seaside have changed, decade by decade, generation by generation, more or less, but I still see the same anxious little faces peering into rock pools as though sneering lobsters will leap out and make a sudden fatal grab at onlookers. There are still arguments about how far each child should be allowed to paddle out into the sea, with which garments rolled up to what height. "It's cold", says the fearful child. "Go on in", encourages Dad. "Come back out", admonishes Mum. As though the waves won't do it for them. At certain times of the middle of a summer's day the piercing brightness of the sun scatters the apprehensive indoors: light has scarred their confidence; they invent symptoms of hunger, thirst, clinging to routine mealtimes as if they were appointments with a specialist. Their clothes are always crumpled, even after an hour on the beach, as if they had been slept in. Sweat is the great leveller.

A girl from the Prudential showed me over a three-bedroomed terraced cottage, 53 Dudley Road, on offer at £87,500 to include fitted carpets.

The Winter Gardens advertised a Steam Railway Film Show – if you can't ride them, watch them – and Brian Lee's Children's Showtime at 8 p.m., admission £1.50. Ventnor Carnival would take place from 14 to 19 August.

At the Royal Tavern in Belgrave Road I enjoyed a game of darts (Hare and Hounds) with excellent players from the pub's team, and listened to desultory chat about E.E.C. plans to support a new high-tech, all-weather 'facility' to attract 300,000 visitors a year. "Then," murmured one cloth-cap to a maroon cable-stitch pullover, "mebbe we wouldn't have to see any one of 'em." Next morning I dawdled to Ventnor Heritage Centre, which stresses its troubled wartime, vanished railways, and early drawings and photographs.

Tuberculosis is conquered, so the old Chest Hospital closed in 1964 and a car park conceals its footings. The Botanic Gardens, next to Ventnor Cricket Ground, tempt one to use the old sobriquet 'the English Madeira', hackneyed though it is. Loquats and pomegranates flourish as in southern China; eager ladies just back from the Chelsea Flower Show tell each other the names of the flowers: "*lovely!*", "how *marv*lous!", "Adèle do come and see these fuchsia, darling!", "*divine!*" I could imagine each one 'coming out' at a deb's ball all those years ago, during the season, with their cream dress and coiffure immortalised in the *Tatler*'s decorous monochrome.

Ranges of underground vaults within Ventnor's Botanic Gardens have been transformed into a Museum of Smuggling History – the undercliff of the Island's economy, which more innocently claimed prosperity from agriculture and the sea. Seven centuries of evading customs and excise officers are neatly depicted in gosh-mum tableaux, where methods of concealing and transporting commodities of value are at last brought out to public gaze. First it was tea, silks and brandy, then gold, diamonds and watches, then drugs... But it is all over now. Isn't it?

Near the Garden Tavern, set among rose gardens, two conspiratorial shop assistants were tucking into a café's cream teas.

"She's real bossy, that new madam with the Liberty scarf wrapped round her pigtail."

"How d'you mean?"

"She gets in thirty seconds early then watches the clock as you sidle past, with 'er smile like a cobra waiting to digest a good feed."

"I know the sort. They only write in capitals with thick felt pens and have boyfriends called Pablo."

"Or Paolo. If there's no quiche in the canteen they're not interested."

"They've got the latest Germaine Greer on their bedside table renewed from the library to swipe their boyfriends if they wake in the middle of the night."

"If Melvyn Bragg isn't on they feel jilted."

"She'll eat no bread but the flat stuff like a frisbee that's been through a mangle to get all the flavour rolled out."

"Any'ow, I s'pose she's all right once you get to know 'er."

It looks eternal, yet the geology of Ventnor's landslips is as sharply up to date as this morning's unopened newspaper. You put the kettle on to boil, and in the next instant a thousand tons of rock have submerged you to oblivion; it must be like engulfing by volcanic lava.

Walking along Wheelers Bay Road I felt as vulnerable as when I hiked to Randazzo on the slopes of Mount Etna. But nobody thinks of that during the Great Ventnor Smuggling Pageant in the middle of June, with Ventnorians defiantly costumed like their forefathers the smugglers, and 'officers of the law' waving to bemused visitors, who are never sure what is now and what is then. The week ends with the trial of the seized offenders, as the 'hanging' Judge Jeffreys blusters and rants at evildoers brought to justice. It is all thoroughly confusing and English, especially when you look up at the sign on 66 High Street, fresh from watching Julie Walters, Celia Imrie and the gang from the Victoria Wood show, and there it is again: 'Acorn Antiques', life imitating show business.

St Lawrence

St Lawrence corresponds to Bonchurch and Ventnor in possessing an upper village and a steep Undercliff, with a beach below. On the road to Niton, St Lawrence is a compulsory stop for the delightful 13th-century church of the same name, once only twenty-five feet long by eleven wide, but provided with a chancel in 1842 by Lord Yarborough of Appuldurcombe, who should have known better: to leave well alone and, as at Bonchurch, to build afresh if he wanted to build larger. Lower down the hill Sir Giles Gilbert Scott did know better, and in 1878 completed the larger and less interesting St Lawrence, which is distinguished really only for its Pre-Raphaelite stained glass rescued from the chapel of the Royal National Hospital for Diseases of the Chest in Ventnor.

About half a mile southwest of the new church is the 17th-century stone Woolverton Manor, with a 14th-century ruin once thought to be a chapel but plausibly a two-storey house named by Sir John Oglander as 'Woolverton-under-Cliff'.

Old Park in St Lawrence was the subject of a hawking charter as early as 1309, and we know that hunting here was legalised in 1340. While the Undercliff cracked, split and slipped downward, into the sea itself or cramming new boulders into old cavities, Old Park and surroundings changed their conformation until the ramshackle area came under the sway in 1791 of Sir Richard Worsley, Governor of the Island. The Victorian wing was added by General Sir John Cheape in 1865, ten years before his death: he was the uncle of Walt Disney and is buried in Old St Lawrence.

Now Old Park is a hotel with sixteen acres of Undercliff stretching to the sea, offering not only a heated swimming pool, sauna and solarium but even its own assault course for the commando in you. The complex incorporates Isle of Wight Glass, founded in 1973 by the glass artist Michael Harris: this is not to be confused with ordinary commercial glassworks, but offers dazzling unique pieces of great merit. For the romantically inclined, a woodland walk in the semi-tropical south-facing Undercliff is always a joy. For the quick talkback of cockatoo or a toucan, try the Tropical Bird Park, and the flamingoes, spoonbills and ibis of the Woodland Trail, Little remains of Wilhelm Spindler's dream to turn Old Park into a Portofino, with promenades and a new housing estate, for Spindler died in 1899, before he could realise his plans. But you can still see fragments of the esplanade, abandoned to the buffeting of wind and waves.

Whitwell

David Franks, the Island's only mushroom grower, started his business in Whitwell in 1983, and now produces anything up to 1½ tons weekly for wholesaling thoughout the Island and retailing at the tunnel entrance.

"It was a terrible problem putting in heat, electricity and dehumidifiers", explained Mr Franks. "Then again, I've got to bring in ready-made compost from the mainland once a fortnight. The costs always go up, but the price of mushrooms barely goes up at all, so it's always a struggle. You can get a crop spoilt by spores from other fungi getting in the tunnel, so we've to check each one of eight different crops separated by polythene walls. These walls help to keep humidity and heat constant while we're pre-cropping and cropping." It takes six weeks for a crop to appear on the compost, and he can obtain mushrooms from that compost over the next ten weeks, when he has to sterilise the area and start all over again. "I suppose," I asked, "it's a bit like creating the world, seeing it decay, destroying it again, and then creating it again from scratch." "Um," he said, "I suppose you could see it like that. A bit of the old starting from scratch". "A woman's work is never done," waved Cynthia Gallop from her low stool, dropping mushrooms in a basket.

Niton

Niton I should really ignore, like Taroudant or Jaisalmer, Kufra or Kashgar. The magic is of the Jack and the Beanstalk variety, when you suddenly rise or descend and the world seems to change completely at that moment. It is a village for illicit assignations, improper suggestions, daydreams of the unattainable suddenly within reach, Borges and Calvino. Whether you stay at Puckaster Lodge on St Catherine's Road, or the Georgian country house called Southcliff, the Pine Ridge or the Springvale, you don't want to tell anyone about Niton, for fear they should turn it into another Needles Pleasure Park. Niton sprang up after 1807, when a Newport surgeon called Waterworth found yet another splendid chalybeate spring; an 18th-century cottage was transformed into a new Sandrock Hotel, Royal after Victoria's visit.

Clive Lucas at the White Lion will tell you how Niton has disintegrated over the last century or so, with an estimated hundred thousand tons of rock collapsing from Windy Corner on 23 July 1928; fifty years later the earth moved again, cottages cracked and fell, and the sea slurped appreciatively as soil rushed into its gigantic gaping mouth. An old-timer licked the froth from his beer with calm intensity. He was a pawky little feller with hairy nostrils and a mongrel face who persisted in a smoker's cough that puttered away like a second-hand outboard motor throughout the forty minutes I stayed there listening. I tell you frankly, like him I'm not one who prefers chasing up and over St Catherine's Down in a howling gale to reading Ludwig Lewisohn's *The Strange Case of Mr Crump* or any other headlong gallop of words. I have a consuming passion for the great indoors and nightly muesli with hot tea.

St John the Baptist is just as romantic as the rest of rearing, tipping Niton. It is darkened by surrounding yews, immeasurably old even if one's yardstick is the Domesday Book of 1086, and of such significance that it was one of six churches donated by William the Conqueror to the Norman Abbey foundation of Lyre, near Evreux. The old village green is now enclosed within the churchyard and the public library pioneer Edward Edwards, who died here in 1886, is commemorated by a memorial given by his biographer Thomas Greenwood inscribed *Cinis non finis*, which one might longwindedly paraphrase 'his ashes are buried, but his lifework survives'. Better laconic Latin.

I love the embattled 16th-century Perpendicular west tower with its snugly recessed spire, the 12th-century north aisle and the 13th-century south aisle: and the great wooden door. The aspect to cliffs and sea might strike awe into most visitors' but luckily not into Sister Annunziata, who wrote in the visitors' book on 27 September 1988, "very nice". We probably have very few of the stones from Edward the Confessor's church, which was then known as St Michael, and the hectic restoration of 1864 is one to draw a hasty veil across, but nothing can destroy Niton's aesthetic appeal within its landscape, with a thatched cottage across Pan Lane. The Rectors' List is known from 1228, one Johannes Gaignard, to the pres-

Niton. St John the Baptist's churchyard

ent incumbent, Terence E. Louden.

The charming lady sacristan sat with me and spoke of her life and ambitions, her family and her faith. "About half the congregation is elderly", she regretted, in a soft sweet voice that rang with love of simple things, enduring things. "A lot of them come back to the Island when they are old, especially to the village. Grandparents retire here when they've done." Then mildly to me: "You are to do with the church, aren't you?" What could I say, a mere bumbling atheist in the face of so much serene confidence?

"In a way," I replied. After all, I have seen more churches, temples, mosques and synagogues than most men in a lifetime's travel. I am as much to do with the church as with the stage...

"We started offering tea and coffee in the north aisle seven years ago", continued the sacristan, placing one palm gently on the other. "We keep hoping to attract more of the young people, but they don't want to come. There are new people from Newport, 'Born Again' I think they call it, and we have Methodists in Niton, some Baptists, and people who meet in a private house and call themselves 'the Believers'. Do you think they are all right?"

"Oh yes," I said, reassuringly. "I should think everything will be all right. After all, the church has been here for over nine hundred years: what can go wrong now, providing the land holds stiff?"

"That's right," she said, and her clear blue eyes lost their troubled stare. "Everything will be all right."

I sat alone, with my thoughts, welcoming grey dusk and broadening shadows.

Why ever do people join a congregation if prayer is supposed to provide conversation with the Divine? How could you speak with Him or Her if little Gary is putting his tongue out at little Sharon, or Mrs Sturdy is wondering in the neighbouring pew whether she has enough Ariel Automatic for tomorrow's laundry? Where, pray, is the sublimity? In solitude, where fools and angels may rush in, shocking your conventional expectations with the rustle of wings and ethereal song: *Spem in alium, Beatus Vir...*

I toasted the eighty-fifth birthday of Margaret Parkes in Niton's White Lion under the benevolent eye of Clive Lucas, and nursed my cider as she recited one of her poems.

A man of thirty-three or so who may have been a student, as someone once put it, of Radar, or a health freak exercising lips and vocal chords, or an honest mad Jack, was sitting on a stool repeating time and time again, with a long-drawn out vowel, "Glue, glue, glue..."

"Have you noticed," whispered a folded granny with paper-white hair as tight as a twirly snail-shell, "that sometimes you can't tell whether some of these boys these days are girls or what?"

"Tsry", nodded her Tweedlefriend.

"You should do. I said to that oddment walking off there in tight jeans one day, I said, 'What's your name then, duckie?' He said 'Pisov'. I said 'That's not a name, that's a town in Russia.' "

No corner of Niton should be missed, from Mount Cleves of 1829, with a spire presumably intended as a shipping aid, to Bowl Barrow at the head of Bury Lane on an even earlier Neolithic site, and the Buddle Inn down the Undercliff, which

Niton. The Buddle Inn

is the only pub where I heard the dialect-word 'buffle-headed' used to mean 'stupid'. Part of the fascination of the place is the tingling sensation caused by the connotations of 'smuggling', where every farmer farms the seas, and every fisherman does the same, but smuggling is comparatively recent of course, dating from the time of tariffs and duties. Try the Gore Cliff coastal path from Niton to Blackgang, or the parallel motor road abandoned after the terrible landslide of 1927.

St Catherine's Down
St Catherine's Down, like the Hill a National Trust estate, comprises the southernmost point of the island yet this is no sub-tropical protected paradise like the Undercliff. It rises and falls like Catherine Linton's Haworth Moor, with black raging seas as an additional threat in the profundity of shrill winter.

In the Undercliff's shallow theatre it soars at the west end as St Boniface rises at the east: one is astonished that such a tiny Island can contain both the close-knit intimacy of Old Shanklin and the fleecy, nebulous, racing clouds way above St Catherine's.

So why is it that the breathless walker, striding up from Blackgang, should encounter an octagonal 14th-century lighthouse, buttressed like a stone Sputnik on its first hopeful launch, with a pyramidal roof?

Percy Stone, in *The Architectural Antiquities of the Isle of Wight* (1891), relates the sequence of events following the foundation of an oratory or hermitage here in the early 14th century, an episode revealed only by excavation long past and dull blemishes on the grass:

> "Three years after the foundation of this isolated chapel a circumstance occurred... explaining very clearly the *raison d'être* of the still-existing lighthouse. One stormy night in the winter of 1314, a vessel – one of a fleet chartered by sundry merchants of the King's Duchy of Aquitaine to convey a large consignment of white wine to England – drove ashore on Atherfield Ledge. The sailors escaped... and sold the cargo to the Island folk – 174 casks of wine, each worth five marks. The merchants took proceedings against the receivers of the stolen cargo, for it clearly did not belong to the sailors who were, however, apparently not deemed worth prosecuting, even if they could have been traced. One Island landowner, Walter de Godeton, was found guilty of receiving 53 casks, and had to pay 227½ marks. But another party besides the merchants had to be reckoned with, namely the Church, for the wine, it appeared, belonged to the religious community of Livers, in Picardy, who had lodged a complaint against de Godeton in the Roman Court. This resulted in the culprit's having to build, on the Down above the scene of the disaster, a lighthouse to warn ships, and to found an oratory for a priest to say masses for the souls of those lost at sea, and to trim the light. De Godeton, before 1328, did as he was required, and the existing ruin, repaired at the end of the 18th century, is the relic of his work."

Of course the Reformation put an end to the priest's solitary endeavours; interestingly, however, nobody thought to substitute another light, so for almost three hundred years ships continued to lose their way in fog and dark, their cargo and their crew and passengers, until a new light was begun in 1785 but abandoned shortly afterwards because treacherous mists rendered it virtually useless. The Back of the Wight has seen more than a hundred and fifty shipwrecks since 1750. Another lighthouse was erected to a height of 120 feet in 1840 but that too appeared almost invisible in the worst of fogs and in 1875 its height was reduced to 86 feet.

A mile's walk from the lighthouse northward along the breezy down will bring you to the seventy-two-foot tall Hoy's Monument, a column sometimes called the Alexandrian Pillar, which one Michael Hoy, who had grown wealthy by trade with Russia, erected "in commemoration of the visit of his Imperial Majesty Alexander I, Emperor of all the Russias, in the year 1814", to which in 1857 Lieutenant Dawes added a tablet to the memory of British soldiers who fell in the Crimean War against the "Emperor of all the Russias". Such ironies will not be lost on those alive today, who fought on the same side as the U.S.S.R. in World War II, and have been told by those who know about such things that we are currently fighting a Cold War against the same power.

A hermit of St Catherine's Oratory cursed 'The Giant of Chale' in shivering, shuddering invective which reverberates with all its ancient venom, as the cliffs slide and slip, dying and finally crashing, into the foaming seas below:

I curse the hell and I curse the strand,
I curse the ground whereon I stand.
Nor flowers nor fruit this earth shall bear,
But all shall be dark, and waste, and bare;
Nor shall the earth give footing dry,
But a poisonous stream shall run to the sea
Bitter to taste and bloody to see.
And the earth it shall crumble, and crumble away,
And crumble on till the judgement day.

Blackgang

Perhaps the streams were never poisoned, though peregrine falcons seeking their last refuge on the Niton cliffs are believed to have been exterminated by residual poisoning from pesticides. But crumbling has been a way of life at Blackgang throughout geological time, persisting till today and certainly tomorrow. Chale Common, once a cricket pitch, cracked open and pitched into the sea: one last googly before we say goodbye. Westerly winds and rains pound and sap away at the Upper Greensand and gault clays, eroding the cliffs at the rate of a metre every two years. When soft rocks disappear, they may leave a ledge, like Atherfield Ledge, exposed at high tide and dangerously concealed at high tide. A devastating landslide in 1978 robbed Blackgang of several houses.

I asked Simon Dabell, of the Dabell dynasty at Blackgang, about present danger levels.

"My ancestor Alexander (1808-98) had a bungalow at the top and bottom of the Chine, but the lower one was demolished in 1908. In 1911 the last path to the beach fell away, and in 1928 a cliff-fall swept away the road to Ventnor, after which a new main road was completed over the downs behind Blackgang. A land movement in late 1985 threatened the only road left, and a projection shows that the present large car park, landscaped in 1986, will be overtaken by slippage shortly after the year 2010."

Blackgang village consisted of thirty-odd houses in the 1950s, but nowadays there are only a dozen, most of them owned by the Blackgang Chine Theme Park or related companies, and many of them summer holiday cottages, or short-lease premises provided by South Wight Borough Council for homeless families. The Borough Council has been especially helpful to Blackgang, which is recognised as an area of outstanding natural beauty and an official Site of Special Scientific Interest. Alexander Dabell arrived in the island from Nottingham with his father, a master lacemaker, and the rest of his Huguenot family. Having served his apprenticeship in Newport, and enjoyed a taste of the wide world in London, he returned to Newport High Street to start his own gift shop about 1830, expanding to Sandown and Shanklin before deciding to lease Blackgang Chine from a hotelier and publican already established there. This was in 1842, when he bought a whale stranded off the Needles and displayed the skeleton in a hut next door to a gift bazaar run by his wife Amelia. Dabell landscaped the gardens, and they would have looked much as Shanklin Chine looks today until the 1950s, when the model village and Smugglers' Cave were set up. Nowadays, such theme parks have to gallop with the times, and to 'keep up turnover' an attraction has opened at the rate of one a year throughout the eighties and nineties, with a sawmill, St Catherine's Quay, Adventureland resited, a flight simulator, a Weather Wizard, gold-panning (with gold from the Welsh mine at Clogau) and the landscaping of a 'lost valley': a chine hitherto unexplored and revealed only by landslips. Children played happily in most areas, and seemed to enjoy most the maze, the Fort Buffalo assault course, and the model ship, 'The Jolly Smuggler'.

"Christopher!" remonstrated one chickenpecked mother hen, "stop hitting Helen so hard!"

Down by the Tyrannosaurus Rex, a lost woman had given up the chase for her brood, and was consoling herself with a fag and intensive gossip. "Take my word for it", she said, "I *saw* her doing it with these two eyes of mine! From that day on I'll never trust a woman capable of putting unused paper napkins back in the polythene bag."

On 'The Jolly Smuggler', overlooking the Lower Chine, infants yelled "Daddy!" "Maam!" and a host of names like "Michael!" and "Susie!", cries taken up by their anxious parents, running helter-skelter like a perpetual orgy of Seeing Children's Buff. "Daaad, I wanna go in the 'Smugglers' Rest' again!" An over-excited boy of nine howled "'ow can we get *froo*?" in tones of near hysteria. I forebore to complicate matters by offering answers. 'ow indeed, I mused, *can* we get *froo*, beyond all this fiddle? This rushing and noise, our interminable desire to be somewhere else, to see something new, as though the already familiar is in some way inferior to the yet unknown?

Whale Chine
Westward along the coast from Blackgang, Whale Chine was getting ready for twilight, with a slightly perceptible drift up to the cars.

A lad of seven was urging his sophisticated ten-year-old sister to secure his castle against the encroaching tide.

"You've got to help me!" he shouted at her, as she dreamily dragged wet heaps back into a sucked, sloping height, about to drift helplessly away again, wet and relentless as quicksand.

"We'll come an' build another one tomorrow", she replied,

having seen it all before. She vaguely remembered having made the same urgent appeal to her father a few years back, when little Paul had been too young to bother.

"It's not the *same!*" cried her brother, on the slip-edge of tears. "You've got to save it now!"

That summer of 1989 heat hung around all day, long into the evening. A beautiful girl of twenty-three lay Seychelleasy on the beach. I passed close by, to admire her classic lines. With transparent pearls of perspiration on her tanned forehead, she smelt of fried bacon, and I turned away from planned seduction with a sigh of relief that might well have been taken for its opposite.

Chale and Chale Green

Chale Green is one of those halfway villages of England which hang on to a general stores as a meeting-place and communications centre. If you run the shop, you must relay gossip, phone for the ambulance, put up notices, remember when you last saw Cheryl, and work long after closing time to deal with all the stock-orders, reminders, bills, there's never an end to it

Chale Green. General Stores

all. A BP petrol pump ensures that you are never stuck in Chale Green, and "With every 2 videos hired, one free glass or sundae dish", there will never be any need to relapse into conversation, that old-fashioned interruption to *Neighbours* and *Richmond Hill*. A box of dates costing 98 pence here could be found for 75 pence in Newport. A notice invited "All Ladies of Chale Chit-Chat every Wednesday 2.30-4.00 at W.I. Bring crochet, knitting, mending."

Like many before me, at Chale I took a respite in the bar at the Clarendon Hotel, where mine host, the jolly bearded John Bradshaw, regaled me with tales of his nineteen years as a travelling salesman, and his wife Jean from Adelaide presided over the kitchen. Three-quarters of their hotel guests come from the Home Counties, Dorset and Wiltshire, averaging ten days in summer, but taking odd breaks throughout the rest of the year. Local fishing, riding and clay-pigeon shooting is well-renowned, and views extend to Tennyson Down and the Needles, or over St Catherine's Down. The bar was crowded, and it was hard to make out more than 2% of the conversations, which ranged from the weather to meals long past.

"Did you know", insisted a little bald anorak with a bulbous red nose glaring like a belisha beacon, "that every single dog in the world was born with toxicariasis?" He spoke, to a rat-faced wall-eyed herbert, with the missionary zeal of a born-again wally who has just discovered that God should have been a vet.

John Bradshaw encourages singing guitarists and the odd jazz trio, but he has banned discos, preferring a traditional sing-song.

Under oak beams rescued in 1836 from the three-masteed sailing ship, *The Clarendon*, I listened to soccer tactics from the kind of earnest pundit who models his beard on Jimmy Hill's and refers to winning as "doing the business".

The *Clarendon* lost all but three of her eleven crew and fourteen passengers, and most of those lost in the disaster off Blackgang were buried in the churchyard of St Andrew's close by. Celebrated visitors to the *Clarendon*, originally a 17th-century coaching inn, included the Mountbattens, Alexander Fleming, Moiseiwitsch, Lord Beaverbrook and Edward Heath.

A woman from East London was discussing the fads and

foibles of her absent husband to a sympathetic if restive friend, whose eyes roamed about as if in search of something mildly interesting. "No," stated the speaker, "'e takes no pleasure at all in the wireless since Wilfred Pickles wen' off the air."

John Bradshaw showed me his vast collection of malt whiskies from the Highlands and Islands, Islay, the Lowlands and Campbeltown. "Look at that," he said, "an Australian whisky, a Japanese whisky, even one from the Isle of Man. Our local connoisseur Norman Fisher has a preference for this Bruichladdich, from Islay; Jean and I love this one, Old Pulteney from Wick.

I tried the Fisherman's Platter: a delicious selection of prawns, crab, cockles, mussels and battered clams on a bed of salad, with brown roll and butter, followed by an oriental ginger ice-cream from Minghella.

Sheep and daffodils dotted the spring meadows at the back of the Wight Mouse Inn, but before exploring the church I sauntered round the new Church of England primary school next door to 'Chale Parochial Schools, 1843' in weathered gray stone. A pimpled youth with a Sony Walkman and glazed eyes passed me without glancing to left or right, up or down, radiant birdsong shut resolutely out.

A two-bedroom detached bungalow with large gardens and garage was being offered at Chale for £93,500 in mid-1989, but the second most interesting house in Chale, now called Lower House, called Jobson's since 1613, was originally a farmhouse which would have been supported by several acres, and looks remarkably how it must have seemed three and half centuries ago, with coursed rubble providing room for two storeys on an attic on a heavy stone plinth capped with coping stones. Chale's most interesting house is the former Chale Abbey, with an early 14th-century hall positioned south-north and, nearby, a buttressed barn.

Chale Abbey, according to Percy Stone's *Architectural Antiquities of the Isle of Wight* (1891), was built by John de Langford, Warden of the Island, about 1330. Langford is recorded as being responsible to one Thomas Chyke of Mottistone in 1340 for the defence of much of West Wight, and Mr Hilton Cheek, a descendant, resided at Chale Abbey in the

1980s. Langford's original home stayed more or less intact until 1562, when Richard Worsley of Appuldurcombe bought it, and added an open fireplace, which involved taking out the stairs and filling in the ogee windows. Its strongly ecclesiastical appearance, exemplified by the pointed northern window and walls three feet thick, led to the mansion's being widely known as an abbey, but there is no record of its ever having been so used.

The glory of Chale is St Andrew's Church, at first a chapel dedicated by the Bishop of Winchester in 1114, then enlarged by a new Manor Chapel and Walpan Chapel near 1200. However, the Perpendicular tower is a 15th-century addition, embattled to proclaim its defensive rôle during times of sudden French invasion. This is the time when the south and north porches were added, the latter now used as vestry and sacristy. The rectors list begins in the 13th century with Richard Hamilton and provisionally terminates with the appointment in 1981 of Terence Edmund Louden, whose rectory is in Niton. Of the six bells, one dates to 1314 and another to 1896.

Chale. St Andrew's

Turner visited the Isle of Wight in August-September 1795 as a youth of twenty, but his sketchbook of topographical drawings and sailing boats barely hints at the mastery and originality of his seascapes of the 1830s and 1840s and the subtlety of his views of Venice, which he arranged to disappear in mist. He drew Chale at this period and, on his return to the Island in 1827, when he stayed with John Nash at East Cowes Castle. He drew the castle itself, and painted directly on to canvas both the castle and views of the regatta, with shipping, sea and sky off the headland.

In his *History of the Isle of Wight* (1781), Sir Richard Worsley wrote of Chale Bay: "Some years ago, it was discovered that the sand under the cliffs was mixed with gold-dust: this for a while engaged the country people to wash it in bowls and pans, as is practised in Africa and South America; but from a number of dollars occasionally found there, it appears likely that both were the contents of some Spanish ship wrecked in this dangerous bay, and in stormy weather thrown up by the violence of the waves."

Domestic serenity seems almost at odds with Chale, the thunderous breakers in the bay lashing at the cliffs daring one to come outside like John Fowles' *French Lieutenant's Woman*, and face the fury of the waters and the howling of the wind on a dark day fraught with hostility, when a hot toddy seems the best cure for most potential ills. To the west of Chale, Atherfield Ledge claimed a century of sailing ships in the century from 1750, no fewer than fourteen occurring in one Night of Terror during 1757.

Atherfield Bay

Two adjoining deckchairs sagged, generously overflowing, at Atherfield Bay holiday centre.

"D'you still have trouble with insomnia, Rhoda?"

"Not since I've been on one of those alarm clocks that sends you to sleep".

"?"

"You can choose pelting rain, or leaping waterfalls, or ocean waves if you're not easily upset by seasickness."

"D'you use the waterfalls?"

"Not any more. I'm better with the ocean waves, if I take a Dramamine around nine-thirty."

"I had trouble getting out of bed in the morning till our Cynthia bought me one of them clocks that wakes you up by shaking and poking at the back of my 'ead without making any racket at all. That way I can get dressed in the dark without 'im noticing me veins."

"Our Gary's got an alarm that chants 'Ere we go, 'ere we go, 'ere we go', so 'e's got time to pray to John Lukic for a clean sheet before 'e brushes 'is teeth."

"I bought our Steve the one with the built-in boxing-glove. Once you set the alarm it punches you on the side of the 'ead and you wake up with a cauliflower ear. Never fails if he sleeps close enough to the edge of the bunk bed."

"Does 'e like it?"

"Does 'e stonacrows! If you're a milkman what is there to like?"

3 Freshwater and the West

Chillerton

"I'm never going to that church fête again, over by Totland," confided a sapphire-and-white striped lady in the bus shelter at Chillerton, its window boxes yellow and red with daffodils and hyacinths. I read 'This public shelter was provided by the Isle of Wight Rural District Council and the Isle of Wight County Council, March 1956', with a plaque to Lt. Col. Sir Vere Hobart who improved highways *Sat cito si sat tuto* (fast enough if safe enough), and a bill announcing 'Brownies Coffee every Wednesday, 6.30-8.00 Chillerton Village Hall.'

"So, 'Would you care for tea or coffee?', she said. I said 'No thanks,' I said, 'I don't want my innards coated with tannin or caffeine,' I said. So she picked up a bottle of this orange squash at me. She said, 'Would you like your innards coated with tartrazine, citric acid, potassium sorbate and sodium metabisulphate,' she said."

"Well!"

"I thought, I'll never darken your tent again, you rude goose."

The bus sighed to a halt, and we joined a party of ramblers in lurid badges, pop socks and khaki rucksacks. "I'm just beginning to enjoy this," said a mournful youth of seventeen, "nits time to go back home."

"I want a job", murmured a nineteen-year-old girl, a word-processor operator from Chelmsford, "that pays more than the dole and leaves me free to look at stars even when I can't see them".

Gatcombe

I alighted from the bus at Bowcombe to walk into Gatcombe valley, and larks headed away, luring me aloft into the empyrean. Swinburne, Tennyson, and the powerful David Gascoyne of Northwood are the poetic spirits of the Island. I

Map of *the* Isle of Wight, *West*

could imagine few other writers happily adapting to these Samuel Palmerish glades, idyllic downs, lively copses, redolent with bracken. The *Artorius* of John Heath-Stubbs would have been impatient with the quiet men. Those Roman legionaries, Welsh soldiers, Celtic fighters who intermingle in the intimate epics of David Jones would never have settled in Gatcombe. This is neither Dylan Thomas country nor Sorley Maclean territory, much less the hesitating, half-secular, half-reverent district rented by Philip Larkin or the apocalyptic city-desert landscape auctioned off to Eliot, the only bidder for *The Waste Land*.

Gatcombe's tiny world has only a few ships at perpetual anchor: cottages here and there, Sir Edward Worsley's three-storey manor house of 1850, and the reassuring presence of St Olave's, a thirteenth-century parish church which seems to have lost its parishioners, scattered very far, very wide; it was obviously built for the private prayers of the Lords of the Manor, the de Estur or Fitzstur, of Norman stock. They would have replaced a humbler wooden Saxon edifice, but the original de Estur church has been replaced in later centuries by confident restorers, often over-confident, and all we see nowadays that is decidedly original is the little font, poor as Jesus, simple, upright, easily overlooked.

A visitors' book invited comments. Lucy Allen noted 'lovely kneelers', referring to the embroidery covers contributed by members of the congregation, a folk art well worth exploring. Gisele Dobson added 'perfect serenity', a feature central to St Olave's, and Kathryn Dalton concluded 'nice stained glass'. The 15th-century glass, in the south windows of the nave, depicts angels conquering the haphazardness of human fate by the intervention of the Lord. The east window's pre-Raphaelite glass from 1865-6 is a magnificent collaboration. Rossetti's is the Crucifixion, Ford Madox Brown's the Entombment, the Baptism is by Burne-Jones, and the rest, by William Morris himself, comprise the Last Supper, the Marys at the Sepulchre, and the Ascension, realised with a clarity of vision inspired by the precepts of Cennini's *Libro dell' Arte* of 1390, that is to say wholly 'pre-Raphaelite'.

I found the Rector of Gatcombe and asked him whether, in these days of diminishing congregations, there was more doubt in his parish than in the previous generation. "To be honest", replied the Vicar, smiling in a swathe of perplexity, 'I think that there may be more doubt than there used to be. Although there may not." The Roll of Honour paid tribute to the local fallen men: 5 Kerleys, Groveses, Mustchins, 4 Hendys and Salters, 3 Westmores and Tosdevins.

When I turned around again, she stood there, as if she had always been there, in a white dress with a black leather belt and black court shoes. Strange men would have gulped at her when she reached fourteen; would have tried to catch her eye when she was eighteen; devised methods of escorting her when she was twenty; proposed impulsively to her in St James' Park at twenty-two and frequently thereafter. Her blossoming vitality lured men into her penumbra. As a bride she bewitched the photographer, who would have cut out her bridegroom's face and kept the remnant on his mantlepiece. When pregnant,e exuded a perfume of serenity; dimpling with each of her babies she would cause preoccupied businessmen to forget their schedules, stopped, stalling, in their working tracks like tractors aground on high furrows. When forty, she bloomed again, with a zing in her stride that other women would copy for a few steps. In her fifties she radiated sympathy and comfort, a bewildering competence in her late career as though she had never interrupted it, combining it easily with a neat home and glittering garden achieved with the minimum of travail. She would be the first to whom her friends would come for solace in times of illness, divorce, despair. She was eighty-two.

She showed me the oaken figure of a crusader probably of early 14th-century date, with his feet touching a faithful oaken hound, and a protective angel just left of his head. The chancel by contrast dates from 1865, and the southern porch with timbers from the *Thunderer*, a vessel of Trafalgar wrecked in 1910.

Sir Charles Seely, founder of the County Library and other excellent institutions, bought Gatcombe in 1890 and commissioned from Sir Thomas Brock the movingly dignified figure of his eldest son, killed at Gaza in 1917: the white marble resounds in lustre and purity to the solemn tones of Britten's *War Requiem*, the haunting poetry of Wilfred Owen, the dur-

Gatcombe. Manor House

able prose of Siegfried Sassoon.

Close by, Gatcombe Manor House of the Worsleys and then the Seelys is the latest replacement for one of the three original Saxon manor houses, the others being Sheat and Great Whitcombe. Gatcombe was created in emulation of Appuldurcombe, Sir Richard Worsley's eminent mansion erected to proclaim the grandeur of the senior branch of the Worsleys. Involved perpetually in controversy, the Worsleys have always made rich pickings for Island gossip, from the refusal of John Worsley to pay Sir John Oglander ship money tax in 1637 to his royalist son's determination to set Charles free from Carisbrooke. But we have only a tantalising start to Gatcombe, for the capital H-plan of the first design was never finished: and we have merely the fully-achieved front part. There was the intention to create a lake, but this was never carried out, despite the existence of a painting showing a yacht on the water. The final effect is of muted, neoclassical splendour, in a wide open space of 34 acres quite unlike anywhere else on the Island, the copse and woodland heightening an air of rural isolation. The season for visiting Gatcombe, since it was opened first by the Thornton family and then by the Scott family in the 1980s, is March to October: apart from the house and grounds themselves, one may enjoy an adventure playground, nature trail, greenhouses, the Brannon Island topographical engravings, a Carriage and Bicycle Museum, and a Costume Museum from the Monte Carlo Opera House.

Sheat

From Gatcombe to Rookley one passes the manor of Sheat, the Anglo-Saxon name denoting a part of a manor, in this case of Gatcombe: there are others in Carisbrooke and Brighstone. Sheat Manor is a beautiful Jacobean manor house, with later additions, including a priest-hole in the east wing lending some authority to the supposition that the Urrys of Sheat were secret Roman Catholics, holding Mass at Sheat and protecting priests. In 1960 an underground passage leading towards Gatcombe House was discovered, but it had fallen in and been shut off.

From the distant gateway I gaped, like two cyclists who had propped their tandem up beside a tree.

The girl was brushing her long blonde hair back vigorously; the much older man, his cycle-clips pinching like footcuffs, bent his head suddenly at the weight of existence, with the troubled, hangdog air of a Scottish studio audience sitting through yet another rendition of Andy Stewart's "Donald, where's yoor troosers?"

Brighstone

Brighstone Tea Gardens is a welcome oasis for thirsty walkers, but there was a petition against its longer evening opening hours to be signed in a cottage opposite. These transient feuds melted above in the pure light of St Mary the Virgin. Outside, I had responded with irrational affection to the plaque "In Loving Memory of Margaret Mary Lover, July 22 1830 – September 8 1928, beloved wife, mother and grandmother" – what incalculable resonance such names possess: the antithesis of Ebenezer Grimes. The parish *Newsletter* recorded an evening of graphology, a daffodil stroll through seven local gardens, and a bingo evening in aid of the Red Cross. A leaflet from Mrs Gerrie Stride of 32 Ashley Way, Brighstone, membership secretary of the Isle of Wight Cat Association told us: 'members meet five times a year at the Friends' Meeting House, Crocker St., Newport'.

Prayers in the busy, massive church had been written in a book for all to share. "Dear God, My little rabbit is very ill. Please find it in your heart to spare his tiny life. I ask this in Jesus' name. Your faithful friend." "Please pray that Julie will not have to wear faun virgin socks." "Dear God, Help me safely back across the water to my house and help me get a boyfriend." "Dear God, Thank you for making me happy last night, but where's the £2?" The preoccupations of 1989 blared out for all to read.

The Ward Lock *Red Guide* calls the stone cottage village 'Brixton', to the amusement of anyone familiar with the London streets of SW2 between Stockwell and Brockwell. The grey stone church has stood here, changing or unchanged according to the mood of the time, for more than eight hundred years. Its ponderous light, boiling in angry grains of slanting sunshine, seems redolent of the majestic fervour of the church's reverend bishops. The hymn-writer Thomas Ken (1666-70 at Brighstone), later Bishop of Bath and Wells and author of *The Practice of Divine Love*, was jailed in the Tower for refusing to read James II's Declaration of Indulgence from his principled pulpit. 'Soapy Sam' Wilberforce spent the 1830s at Brighstone Rectory, pursuing his vendetta against the Bible Christians as Rector – and would become Bishop of Oxford. George Moberly (1866-9 at Brighstone) delivered while there and before his elevation to the See at Salisbury the Bampton Lectures entitled *The Administration of the Spirit in the Body of Christ*, yet another proof if it were needed of the Victorian Rector's confidence in his own theological certainties, and hearty rejection of everyone else's.

But 'Egbert's Town' – for the manor was conferred by that king on the See of Winchester in 826 – has also enjoyed its secular moments, with the uproarious annual Brighstone Fair, when a hundred years ago farmers and their labourers would make merry with inviting young ladies, and seek out scraps in such a manner as to invite the saying "Drunken Shorwell, Fighting Brighstone, Runaway Brook."

There is something reassuringly, paradoxically English about the great Norman arches and pillars on the north side of the nave. Could it be that the strength of British society lies in its absorption of Celtic, Saxon, Norman and other strains, and its weakness in single strands unfortified by other wefts? The Celtic perimeter of Ireland and Cornwall, Wales and Scotland, despite noble and persistent efforts to bolster their finances and provide new rural industries, seems to revolve in a poverty cycle, while the multi-racial societies of the South, Midlands and North of England prosper in proportion to their ability to adapt to new blood, and diverse attitudes.

The first course of the tower dates to the 14th century; and others a little later. The 15th-century Limerstone Chapel forms the western part of the new south aisle, and Wayte's Court Chapel extended the south aisle eastward in the 16th century. The nave roof has oak timbers renewed in the 1950s following the ravages of death-watch beetle in its predecessor. The six-bell peal is one of the village's great assets, adding one in 1960 to the five that existed in 1740. Another proud boast of this community barely twelve hundred strong is that in 1860 it was the first Wight village to volunteer as lifeboat crew, losing two men in the disaster of 9 March 1888, when the lifeboat *Worcester Cadet* capsized on its first journey to the American barque *Syrenia*, wrecked on Atherfield Ledge; but she made two more forays that night, and the lifeboat offered sterling service until 1915, when the station was disbanded.

Brighstone Forest has a well-marked rambling trail beginning from the National Trust car park at the trivium (be careful not to slay an old man here: he might be your father) leading north to Calbourne, west to Mottistone and east to Brighstone, near a disused limepit. You can take the Tennyson Trail westward above Mottistone Down, then passing tumuli on your left in woodland, or start immediately through a Corsican pine and beech plantation set in 1950. The best times to come are spring, when banks of bluebell lure your eye, and autumn, when thrushes and blackbirds attack berries of the wayfaring tree. Yellowhammers nest in gorse, and green woodpeckers prey on ants. At the top of the hill, you can try to make out Hurst Point on the mainland, with a lighthouse marking the area near Hurst Castle, whither Charles I was taken from Carisbrooke; to the east look for St Catherine's Hill and oratory; westward lie Swanage Cliffs on the mainland and closer, on the Island, the forty-foot high granite cross commemorating Lord Tennyson.

Shorwell

Neighbouring Shorwell possesses in St. Peter's a fine church to rival Brighstone's, but must be enjoyed slowly, one cottage at a time, to the climax of Wolverton Manor, halfway to Yafford Water Mill and Farm Park. The village separates two wondrous manor houses: North Court of the Leighs, and West Court of the Lisles. It seems a shame to spend ten hours a day sizzling on a beach at Sandown, when one might discover the progress of history on the human scale at Domesday's Sorwelle and Ulvredestune, to give Shorwell and Wolverton their historic names.

'Sorwelle' means the 'spring rising under the steep hill', presumably the spring in the gardens of North Court. John Leigh, born at Arreton Manor, married Elizabeth Dingley of Wolverton Manor and lived at West Court, being knighted by James I in 1606. He and Sir John Oglander of Nunwell were the only two Justices of the Peace in the Island for many years. Leigh demolished the old manor house on the North Court site in 1615 and started to build anew, creating a vast pile to reflect his knightly status. He died in 1629, very near the time of death of his grandson who died at nine months: they are buried together in St Peter's, the knight in armour gazing west, like the little alabaster child behind him, both kneeling. Barnabas Leigh, who had waited long for his inheritance, found himself burying his son as well as his father, as the inscription says:

'Innate in graue he took his grandchild heire,
Whose soule did hast to make to him repair,
And so to heauen along as little page
With him did poast to wait upon his age.'

It was a case of 'Our grandfather which art in heaven': a solemn thought that a child of nine months might 'enjoy' eternity waiting as page on a man he was never old enough to recognise.

Barnabas and his family haunt Shorwell with a desperate longing to be remembered. His first wife Elizabeth died in 1615, having borne fifteen children; his second wife Gartrude died childless, but equally honoured in her epitaph, four years later. Churches are loaded down with epitaphs and plaques to famous men, but women are less rarely honoured, and I gleefully transcribe the generous sentiments of Barnabas Leigh:

'Since neither penne, nor pencill can set forth
Of these two matchles wiues the matchles worth
Ware forc't to couer in this silent tomb
The praises of a chast and fruitful wombe
And with death's sable vaile in darkness hide
The ritch rare virtues of a barren bride.
Sweet saintlike paire of Soules in whom did shine
Such modells of perfection faeminine
Such Pietie, loue zeale That though we sinners
Their liues have lost, yet still themselves are winners
For they secure heauens happines inherit,
Whilst we lament their losse, admire their merit.'

Other monuments relate to denizens of North Court and West Court: Leighs, Bulls and Bennets. Bibles are displayed, the Breeches of 1579 and the Vinegar of 1717 (with 'vineyard' misprinted). The famous 'Last Supper' of 1834 by the Icelandic painter Ofeigur Jonsson has however found its way back to Thingvellir, and a replica is shown instead.

Another of Shorwell's surprises is a small Netherlandish Early Renaissance tablet showing Christ contorted during a vigorous Flagellation. The original 15th-century stone pulpit gathers the congregation around it, instead of keeping at a lofty distance. Don't miss the carved stone corbels supporting the chancel roof beam: Sin, I fear, did not put the wind up me, for it looks like someone watching TV from the floor, supporting head on elbows; but Death is a vacant horror that left me properly aquake.

Shorwell. St Peter's

Shorwell's chief glory is the mural painting of the Christ-bearer dated around 1440. Left, St. Christopher accompanies the Devil, then renounces that service on observing a Tannhäuser-like blossoming of his staff. A colossal central figure of the Christ-bearer proceeds across a river towards a hermitage and the night's refuge. On the right, Christopher is attacked with arrows, while the Emperor Gaius Messius Decius looks on, and the sword that eventually killed him is prepared in the hands of an executioner.

Shorwell's vestry was originally the Tudor gun-chamber, housing one of the cannon kept by decree in each Island parish.

I passed the time of day in Shorwell St Peter's with a beaming old lady who might have been a direct descendant of the Leighs.

Her mouth appeared to be filled with discarded piano keys, some off-white, some black, and some tilted alarmingly like Mottistone's Long Stone. Any dentist would have resigned in favour of a piano-tuning mountaineer.

Doves whirred and scooted at the Crown Inn (Licensee: M. Grace). Two nineteen-year-old lads in multi-coloured shorts were taking tea together, their bikes outside nudging each other for consolation.

"Eh, Darren," said the first, "did you know a newborn mole only weighs as much as a sugar lump?"

"Well, just put the milk in mine then. I don't take newborn moles."

A brown dog called Monty romped, whimpering when nobody took any notice, then bounded into the road below the sign pointing to Newport 5¼, Chale 4½ and Brooke 4½, Freshwater 9¼, as though Shorwell was intent on proving itself roughly the centre of the known universe. One spring I was leaving St Peter's when a sixty-year-old man walking a spaniel saw me watching the late primroses wondering when to wither. "They've had the good sense not to mow the primroses down this year," he called, "now we'll get more next year." and raised his woollen cap, presumably at a lady out of my view.

I caught him up. "Sorry to bother you," I said, "but I'm an overner stunted in the rural arts, and wonder if you could spare the time to point out some of the local flora." "Well, you comalong o' me," nodded the old feller, wimble and wight. And his stick aimed accurately at houndstongue and vervaine, red bartsia and eyebright. I thanked him profusely for his trouble, envying his friendly familiarity with the colours and characters of peaceful hedgerow and chalk hill. He smiled at them as one might at an old school photograph: some faces immediately recognisable, others fading in the memory, yet others barely a name. My ignorance bit at my ankles. I bade him farewell, but he had already forgotten about a man so distant from the earth he trod on as to be a virtual Martian.

Like Balaam's ass, I stood undecided about whether to seek out North Court, from St Peter's, or West Court, in the opposite direction. It was George Brannon who decided me, writing in his *Sketches of the Isle of Wight* (1832) that "North Court boasts of an uncommon, picturesque beauty. The mansion is a spacious and venerable pile of the age of James I, most substantially constructed with a durable kind of freestone, procured in the vicinity of Shorwell and, being of light gray tint, affords a fine contrast to the luxuriant ivy which mantles its lofty walls."

The old house of 1615 having been altered first in 1837, after Brannon's time, and then in 1905, you might think that some of the glory had gone, but no, it has lost only some of its ivy. Indeed, it was no less a figure than Sir Edwin Lutyens who connected the main house to the domestic wing, adding two more storeys to the latter in gratifying harmony.

The Leighs sold North Court in the 1790s to the man of sensibility Richard Bull, a friend of Horace Walpole and collector of engraved portraits; he was succeeded by his daughter Elizabeth, and she by her half-brother R.H.A. Bennet the younger; thence by marriage the estate passed to General Sir James Willoughby Gordon (1772-1851), Quarter-Master General to the Duke of York in the Peninsular War (1812). It was Willoughby who invited Turner to North Court.

Gordon's granddaughter Mary became friendly with Swinburne, to whom she was related by marriage, and in North Court's library Swinburne wrote parts of his verse drama *Atalanta in Calydon* (1865), published when he was twenty-eight. It seems likely from the abundant written and published evidence on Swinburne's side that he fell in love with Mary but never dared to declare it. On her side, she married General Robert William Disney Leith, but cannot have been oblivious to the insinuations of the world, for she felt obliged to pen a denial in her book about her cousin, *The Boyhood of Algernon Charles Swinburne* (1917):

"I am anxious to say once and for all that there was never, in all our years of friendship, an ounce of sentiment between us. Any idea of the kind would have been an insult to our brother-and-sister footing, and would have destroyed at once and for ever our unfettered intercourse and happy intimacy, which Algernon himself has so beautifully described in the "Dedication" to me of his tragedy *Rosamund, Queen of the Lombards*:

'Scarce less in love than brother and sister born,
Even all save brother and sister sealed at birth.'

Even if Mary genuinely thought this, Swinburne must have

been just as genuinely devastated by her marriage to Disney Leith at St Peter's Shorwell, in 1865. If you are there on that wedding anniversary, June the fourteenth, say a compassionate word for the lovelorn poet who, in 'The Triumph of Time' would write of Mary's relationship to the two men as:

'Flesh of his flesh, but heart of my heart;
And deep in me is the bitter root,
And sweet for him is the lifelong flower',

disguising his pain by publishing for the world to see the impersonal 'one' for 'him' in the last line and for 'me' in the last but one. Shorwell, to Swinburne, would always be remembered for the golden days of North Court, and the tragic loss that June day in St Peter's.

Since 1963, North Court has been the home of three branches of the Harrison family, who with determination and self-sacrifice have restored the crumbling structure and made the proud mansion habitable: all eighty rooms, including the fabulous library and the main oak staircase carved by Grinling Gibbons.

To West Court, south of Shorwell, Pevsner allots only 3½ vague lines, but as always one can rely on *The Manor Houses of the Isle of Wight* (1987) by Ron Winter for authoritative text and Michael Rainey's outstanding photographs. The Tudor east end is of 1519, with a contemporary stone barn; it was built by Sir John Lisle, a descendant of that John de Lisle recorded as owning West Court in 1279. The main part of the house, enlarging the old mansion, dates from 1579, but there is a further Jacobean extension. West Court is owned by the Russell family, who farm 250 acres, and keep the place as attractive to their generation as it must have been to the Lisles'.

Wolverton Manor is yet another example of how a determined family, in this case the Pattersons, can modernise a great manor house so effectively and unobtrusively that posterity benefits. The king's tenant farmer, one Ralph of Wolverton, built the first manor house in the 11th century, after which his descendants lived there until the Dingleys from Kent acquired the property in the 14th century.

John Dingley, Deputy Governor of the Isle of Wight, began the present completed Wolverton Manor in about 1630. His daughter and her husband John Leigh of Arreton Manor lived at West Court for some years before leaving to rebuild North Court on the other side of Shorwell. The private chapel, once a barn, is now a woodshed; the first house's moat can still be seen at the northeast, and it has been suggested that the two-storey porch may survive from that time. A secret stone chamber under the hearth of a first-floor room looks as though it might be a priest hole, but in this area rife with smuggling who can say what might not have been stored in such a capacious 'little room'?

From West Court you might climb to the head of Limerstone Down, where the Quinn-Smith Monument indicates the direction and distance to Cherbourg or John O'Groats; even better is the view, whether clear or misty with Wightish phantoms, elvishly elusive. I shivered to be alone there one dusk, as invisible birds far off called for me to return home to my nest.

Yafford
Another day I visited Yafford's eighteenth-century water-mill, watching seals calleer and cavort in mid-morning sunshine. I felt as envious as at Philip Wayre's otter sanctuary, or at Tampere's dolphinarium. Old farm machinery and tools would have meant more to Hardy's Tess then they did to me. But by the streams I closed my eyes for four minutes and pressed my memory back in time and place to the dramatic wilderness of the Chinese scholar-painters, whose ability to live as hermit-scholars in the stupendous mountains extends the frontiers of our own potential, at least in the imagination.

Mottistone
Every Wednesday afternoon in summer, Mottistone Manor opens its grounds and you should try to be there.

Sir John Nicholson, Lord Lieutenant of the Isle of Wight until succeeded by his half-brother Lord Mottistone in 1986, lives with Lady Nicholson in this most exquisite of historic homes as a tenant of the National Trust, who accepted his brother's bequest in 1963. The rest of the manor house is

Mottistone. Foliage in June

occupied by the Trust agent. Nothing has been done to the fabric since 1984, when the chimney was rebuilt after a fire, but Lady Nicholson has continued to tend the gardens, over the last quarter of a century, with superb views at every level, leafy, knolled, rose-scented, encircled by thick woodland tended by the Forestry Commission.

She spoke not as a febrile, clever violin, first or second in an argumentative quartet, but as a mellow conciliatory viola, affirming rather than asserting, moderate in tone and passion: an example of tested equilibrium. A pole-star.

Sir John sat pensively watched by his dog Tomo, in the Long Room, and pointed out hangings by Brian Thomas painted in 1953 for the second Lord Mottistone with subjects from *The Pilgrim's Progress* by Bunyan. "Are these not slightly odd scenes for a secular Long Room?" I asked Sir John. "Not at all," he replied, "I've never thought them odd. Both Jack and his partner Paul Paget, son of the Bishop of Chester, were firm Christians." In Sir John's study he showed me two fine Morland oils of smuggling scenes. "Bit of a scoundrel, Morland." The dining-room is used only for parties. In this oldest part of the house, Sir John pointed out a portrait of his stepfather on a horse called 'Warrior' in World War I.

I asked him about his work as first chairman of the Isle of Wight Development Board, and how he reconciles the need for change with conservation of the Island heritage.

"There's no doubt that we need to change with the times, for the Island is relatively poor, with a GDP among the lowest in the country. It was our job to reduce the high unemployment rate, and to moderate the drift of old people in and young people out. We risked becoming a geriatric backwater: another Worthing. It's no good depending on Westland and Plessey when diversification is the secret to success, because both are vulnerable. Wight is the only offshore island that doesn't benefit from government grants, and we're making some headway towards obtaining central government aid, but not enough, as yet. The average unemployment rate in the South-East is 5%, for the country as a whole $7\frac{1}{2}$%, but here it's 10%. We must get more help with roads, for one thing. All in all, I think we've achieved a balance between a headlong dive into progress and a wilful retraction of a tortoise's head into

Mottistone. Sir John and Lady Nicholson, with Tomo

its shell. But only the future will tell if we've got it right."

"Quite frankly, it's bad for an island to be too dependent on a few large employers, and of course we're all anxious over Plessey's radar plant future in Cowes. Too many people rely on seasonal leisure and tourism industries, so we should make more facilities all-year-round, and expand the small to medium industrial sector. The new business park at Westridge is a step in the direction we should be travelling."

Sir John gazed ahead of him, a cross between Wilfred Thesiger and Mountbatten of Burma, authoritative, commanding: a natural leader of men though withdrawn and contemplative, at home equally in the field or in the boardroom. He is of the calibre who built an Empire, sustained it, and then withdrew with dignity at a time judged right.

There is something Poohish about Mottistone (do you remember Cottleston Pie?), something so quintessentially English that no stranger to these shores could ever quite penetrate, something like the essential France of Chartres, the essential Italy of Pienza, the essential Bali of Ubud. Church and State, England and Anglican, manor house and parish church: such a warp and weft cannot be separated without destroying the fabric, and in Mottistone the tale is no less true for being repetitious. Brian de Insula, who owned Mottistone Manor in the 12th century, established the first church of St Peter and Paul for his tenants, and it was enlarged by the Cheke family, who possessed Mottistone from 1300 to 1621. The Dillingtons followed the Chekes, the last of the line to live there, Frances Dillington (buried in the church) passing away in 1703. Tenant farmers lived in the dilapidated premises, which suffered a landslide in 1706 burying almost all the rear wall of the east wing. It was sold to John Leigh, who used it still as little more than a farmhouse. In 1861 the Manor and estate were acquired by a Nottinghamshire coalmine-owner, Charles Seely, who actually lived at Brook House, but cherished Mottistone. His son, later Sir Charles, is immortalised in the Isle of Wight County Seely Library Service, and his son General Jack became a lifelong lifeboatman from the age of 17 in an island service that his father Sir Charles had helped to found. Sir Jack was amazed to find, on removing the 1400

Mottistone. Manor House

tons of soil from the east wing in 1926, that the great rear wall had survived the landslide of two hundred and twenty years earlier, and he restored it once again to habitation. General Jack's son John became an architect and pursued his aim to make the pre-Elizabethan manor house a place of beauty and resonance in which to live. When General Jack, Lord Lieutenant of Hampshire and the Isle of Wight, died in 1947, he was succeeded by John, whose splendid gesture of bequeathing Mottistone Manor to the National Trust on his death in 1963 has not only guaranteed beneficent maintenance of an English architectural gem, but also preserved Mottistone Down, the village (an island Lacock), farmland and woodland alike.

Like the ineffable, timeless Pooh, I made up a hum as I headed for the church of Ss Peter and Paul, wearing its battlemented tower like a small, squat crown, with a dunce's cap peering out, much too low in proportion to the church's length.

> Niton, Newtown,
> Sheat and Shide,
> Alverstone, Hulverstone,
> Rookley and Ryde.
> Which is your favourite
> place of them all?
> Mottistone Manor
> with Peter and Paul.

"A devoted husband and loving father," runs the inscription, "John Edward Bernard Seely, 1st Baron Mottistone of Mottistone, a man of steadfast faith in Christ, whose ashes lie at the altar steps." Umm, perhaps not quite grammatically as intended: I suppose the inscription, devised by the architect Sir John, meant that it was *his father's* ashes that lie at the altar steps...

Two ladies were dusting and polishing, flicking motes and beams into vagrant sunlight with swift abandon. "Oh look," she whispered to the tall lady, who had dressed in her best grey suit for the dusting, "the owner of that pair of gloves must have come and picked them up." To which a sepulchral hoarse female voice hidden behind a column confided to another unseen presence, "Dear soul, she thinks everyone is as honest as she is."

The Roll of Honour lists three Seelys, four D'Albiacs, five Emmetts, two Barneses, two Hookeys, a Desdames, two Siviers, two Wykehams and three Watsons, the old French families interspersed among the native English like hares above a rabbit warren.

The late twelfth century is represented only by the chancel arch base, the north arcade bases, and part of the font. In the fifteenth century the Chekes remanaged much of the church, rebuilding the nave and adding the chancel, the tower and the west end, and the manorial chapel. I love the cedar lining of the chancel roof: the cedar came from the wrecked barque *Cedrene*, foundering off Brighstone on its maiden voyage in 1862 with convicts from Bermuda who were able to scramble ashore without loss of life. Candles are still used for lighting at Evensong, an event not to be missed.

Hulverstone

Derek Chedgey poured my Strong's country bitter from the barrel at the Sun Inn, Hulverstone, and I sank my freshly-chipped tooth into one of his succulent crab sandwiches. My drinking companion I had rescued from a punctured bicycle as he was on his leisurely way (now made even more leisurely) from Freshwater to his holiday cottage at Godshill.

He cleared his throat ominously, like a true blue returning officer about to announce a Labour victory in the Vale of Glamorgan: "I once dropped my false teeth in the Manchester Ship Canal", he stated, "and I've never been back there since." Three locals exchanged glances, like a mafiotic Camberwick Green isosceles, each of them daring the others to ask how it happened, but chickening out at the last.

The Sun Inn, five centuries old, tempts you away from workaday concerns to the daydreams that led H.G. Wells' Alfred Polly to desert his wife and home for a trouble-free life at a country pub. In fact, on my first visit ten years ago, a loud man from Swindon was laughing at his own jokes to a sparse audience.

The Swindonian looked as though a sponsored team had tried to cram as many men as possible (and then more) into one suit, for the *Guinness Book of Records*. He was the kind of interferer who would buy his son Lego and then demonstrate with it discouragingly improbable cityscapes with working railways and wet rivers beside bonsai botanic gardens.

Brook
In a car park on Hanover Point you overlook Compton Bay, and hang-gliders hover from the ridge between East Afton Down and Compton Down. Low tides reveal a petrified pine raft: logs crushed on a river sand bank by a sudden flood about 110 million years ago, give or take a million years. Brook Bay and Brighstone continue the line of the Back of the Wight. On foot you walk the Tennyson Trail towards Brook Down; by car you can turn up from the Military Road (A 3055) and park in Brook village. Brook House (1792) stands on the site of a Tudor mansion which it is said once lodged King Henry VIII. Now of only two storeys, it once boasted three, and was owned by the father of General Jack, 1st Lord Mottistone, who in 1914 built an even more remote home on top of the hill, subsequently owned by the novelist and playwright J.B.

Brook. 'Brooklands', Brook Farm Close

Priestley, far from his native Yorkshire. St Mary's Church in Brook dates from 1864, ten years after Charles Seely had bought the manor. Garibaldi was at Brook House in 1864, planted an oak tree, shown nowadays as a sturdy survivor of more expansive days.

I chatted to a lady aromatherapist and yoga teacher from Shepperton who was gardening at "Brooklands", 3 Brook Farm Close, one of five in a group, one of which made £190,000 when last sold. Her husband David works for the National Trust at the Old Battery, the Needles. Rosemary Webber felt herself finally accepted by the villagers, though it took some time and some effort; hostility is latent, like love, and can be brought out by unconsidered words or actions.

Past General Jack's Brook Hill House, you can stroll through half a mile of attractive woodland in Brighstone Forest and a fine stretch of downland to the clearing with a megalith known laconically as the Long Stone, a thirteen-foot high sandstone cocking a snook at the centuries from its elevated position of a long burrow dug here about 2500 B.C. From here you pass again through woodland down to Mottistone, so called from this 'moot stone' where Saxons held their local 'moot' or meeting.

Thorley

Thorley Street is the village before you come to the street called Thorley. Of such violations of sense and meaning are foreigners' panics born.

St Swithin's, the little church at Thorley, dates from about 1270, but the village is known from the time of Edward the Confessor, when the 'thorny lea' belonged to Earl Tostig. Domesday says it belonged later to one Alsi, but it reverted to the Crown. One enormous rabbit warren, Thorley was left alone with undisturbed undergrowth according to a manorial survey of 1110, and in 1306 the prior and convent of Christchurch received rabbits in payment from the villagers, and the King was paid twopence per capita for an average yield of five hundred conies per annum.

The old St Swithin's was founded by Amicia, Countess of Devonshire, and it stands now behind the manor farm, truncated so that only south porch and bell-tower survive. But how sturdily its ancient body stands, a greybeard without a crutch! We know of no vicar earlier than John Draper (1537), then in 1712 the present William-and-Mary manor house was built, sensitively maintained by C.T. Muddiman today, and deserves stylistic comparison with its more august contemporary at Appuldurcombe. If you want to see similar manor houses of distinction, go to Freshwater and look at Kings Manor and Afton.

By the middle of the 19th century, the residents of Thorley Street outnumbered those of Thorley, and a new church was built on the Street in 1871. The bells of 1499 and the font were brought from Thorley, but otherwise the modern church is one of your worthy Victorian pieties. A lady cleaning the brass apologised for the absence of a guide: "only it was so long that Bob Adams and the others are having to cut it down to size." Outside on a lay-by, a coloured youngster on a motor-bike captured the sunlight on his dark glasses like Stevie Wonder. "Hey man!" he waved at his departing girl-friend in her flouncing skirt, "you nastify mah soul!" and roared off in a wave of granite chippings.

Yarmouth
Yarmouth is to mild and quiet West Wight what Ryde is to the rather noisier, more populous east coast. You cross from Lymington, passing Jack in the Basket, and end up in a seaport with a hinterland that tempts you away. As with Ryde you should delay succumbing to such a temptation.

Yarmouth has a personality of its own, with a yacht harbour second on the Island only to Cowes, and forts here and at Norton erected at the orders of Henry VIII, who commissioned others at East and West Cowes (1536) and Sandown following the victory over two thousand French invaders, who swarmed over the island in July 1545 after landing at Bonchurch, Shanklin, Bembridge and Seaview. Henry ordered that each parish was to keep a gun, a 'falconet of brass or iron' which usually ended up in the church or a hastily-built cabin adjoining it. We have no record that such guns were ever used.

The entrance to the little castle, opposite the King's Head, seems strangely low-key, but then the fort is closed from 1 October to 31 March, and relinquishes its secrets only from

Yarmouth. Harbour

9.30 to 1 and 2.00 to 6.30 during the summer, except on Sunday mornings, when visitors are silently exhorted to be at St James' Church.

In Adlard Coles' time – his classic appeared in 1933 – Yarmouth did not require the space for ferries and yachts needed today. Some thirty thousand vessels use the harbour in an average year, and 'harbour full' signs often go up nowadays. Mamie, Adlard Coles' widow, is sanguine about the future. "If we didn't foster yachting and boating in all ways, we'd be depriving the next generation of a marvellous recreation. I don't believe Adlard would have been sorry to see this massive increase in numbers."

On the square, walls had been painted long ago with fading legends: 'Phone 32. A. Cooper, High St., Freshwater, Charabanc Tours Daily. Also Saddle Horses for Hire. Funeral Equipment. Freshwater agent for L.S.W. Railway'. The Tourist Information Office advertised 'Yarmouth Crime Line. Weekly Post. Island Police 811999. Let's Keep the Island Safe'. The Apollo Players were putting on Shaw's *Pygmalion* at the Apollo Theatre, Newport. Wellow Institute were arranging a Jumble Sale. A seagull sardonically mewed at me, banking like a model aeroplane.

A Sealink ferry silently parted the waters from Lymington, while a queue of patient shiny cars waited methodically, calculating the minutes before docking. A hoarding advocated 1¾-hour cruise from Yarmouth harbour: 'See Colwell Bay, Totland Bay, Alum Bay, Needles Rocks and Lighthouses'. "It were luvly", panted one of the mountainous floral frocks disgorged from this trip. "It were *that* luvly", wheezed her fellow-inmate, "I could go back on again." Another explorer, fluffing her hair up against the disgrace of being seen with her lilac rinse out of perspective, was confiding in a small twinset with a coral brooch: I said to the doctor straight, 'So what do you reckon to my fallopian tubes?'." "That was straight talking." "So he said, 'Well I don't know Mrs Agshot, I don't know what to say'," "That was telling out." "He was never one to mince his words." "So what happened next, then?" "So he bunged me straight into the Queen Elizabeth at Welwyn without another word." "Well I never." "My Derrick said it was the funniest thing he'd seen since our gerbil came down with the whooping cough."

I took a light lunch in the Bugle Hotel, props. Rinaldo Perpetuini and Christopher H.R. Troup, without venturing to enquire whether with names like that they'd met in a vaudeville knockabout act in Cleethorpes. I sat opposite a lady who had crowded into her chair with the kind of imperturbability that gets seventeen undergraduates into a telephone kiosk, but she would give away very little about her background, so we talked about our daughters. After darting her eyes about in approved CIA secretiveness, she confided "My third one's a poster designer. She has this new radical vision of the nineties allied to a conspectus of the Art Deco fancy, with a dash of Charles Rennie Mackintosh in her stained glass vitrines. That's what they call shop windows in Cheltenham now: vitrines. She's persuaded the Athena people to keep everything brown." "Brown?" I inserted at a stern nod. "Brown lettering. Brown design." "Different shades of brown?" "Not really, apparently. Solid brown." I noticed, unnerved, that my lettuce had started to fade into pale khaki, her teeth were beige, and that my coffee, when it came, had assumed too chestnut a colour for my liking. I paid the bill at the bar after making rapid excuses, and headed for the pier.

Yarmouth Pier may have been built in 1876, but the craze for sponsoring everything from anorexia to amputees has spread to its planks. 'Doris White', one plank had been christened, 'Gladys Wallace and Jaspar Goddard' (half a shivered timber each?), 'Isabel Sneed' and 'Simon Farnsworth', It is an odd immortality, this lump of wood, precariously poised between air and water, leading to a tiny greeny wooden kiosk. A man and woman from Newport giving their names as Mr and Mrs Smith waxed alternately furious and explanatory over the disgraceful behaviour notorious on all sides. The traffic jams in Newport start at eight and go on till 9.30 and start again at 4, not relenting till after 6. "It says to keep the kiosk clean", remonstrated the fawn anorak and check scarf, "but *will* you look at that!"

Anglers, leaning avidly or nonchalantly over the bars, had draped their gear so that nobody could sit down out of the wind and sun. "No fish or bait on any seats", it says on the notice, complained the anorak's goodwife, accidentally kicking a bucket. "The dog-fouling is getting worse every year, and we've seen it all for sixty years." "Is that just in Newport?" I enquired, doing my concerned yet informal Kilroy-Silk expression. "There's skateboarding in the church precinct", blustered the anorak, "on the path from Ventnor to Puckaster there's dog-fouling all along." His wife interposed "They've appointed dog wardens, but they've not got eyes in the back of their heads a mile off, have they?" "No", I conceded. "Then there's that beach hut we rent at Puckpool. Do you think the messy dog-owners can clear up afterwards?" "Probably not", I

152

Yarmouth. Pier

guessed. "We've to get off the Island every few weeks, just to get away from it all."

Yarmouth is the 'Ermud' of Domesday, and became a town with its own charter in 1135. Though never large, it sent one or two members to Parliament from 1304, until disenfranchised as a 'rotten borough' by the Reform Act of 1832. Its charming town hall was rebuilt in 1832; the town's coat-of-arms is a three-masted ship, compared with the two-master of Newtown and the single-master of Newport. The reason is that Yarmouth was long the Governor's seat, and one Governor, Sir Robert Holmes, entertained Charles I here. Holmes was Captain of the Wight from 1667 to 1692 as reward for naval adventures off the coasts of Africa, America and in the Baltic Sea. Frankly a pirate, if we may speak of our compatriots in that cavalier manner, Holmes robbed gold from a Dutch vessel off the coast of Guinea giving rise to the minting from the trove of 'golden guineas', as Dryden affirms in his feeble 'Annus Mirabilis':

'And Holmes, whose name shall live in epic song
While music numbers, or while verse has feet,
Holmes, the Achates of the General's fight,
Who first bewitched our eyes with Guinea gold'.

Holmes, a feared duellist, also captured a French ship carrying a sculptor and his unfinished full-length statue of Louis XIV, who was to have sat for the head on the artist's arrival in Paris. Holmes compelled the hapless sculptor to model a likeness of Holmes' own head for this figure, which stands now, gloriously out of keeping in its chaste white marble, in a chapel south of the chancel in St James' Church. Thomas Pocock, in his account of Yarmouth in 1704, offers the rather less dashing explanation that the sculpture was washed up and fell to Holmes as his due, being Captain of the Wight. This is not the first church in Yarmouth; it has been suggested that the first St James lay under the remains of the castle, and a Church of St John may once have stood below the present cemetery. French incursions in 1377 smashed the little town, and caused the end of both churches: "utterly razed and defaced" according to one account. The present St James, with a square tower that seems to belong to a different edifice altogether, is recorded from 1614, and consecrated in 1626, but so many alterations were made in the nineteenth century that it has little of the charm of Godshill or Shalfleet.

The memorial to Edward Rushworth (1755-1817) commemorates a man who married a great-granddaughter of Sir Robert, and built Farringford House, later on the home of Tennyson.

A curiosity is the preacher's hourglass above the pulpit: the hourglass is over 250 years old, and the bracket holding it dates back to 1626. Others include five 17th-century paintings hung in front of the gallery, here on loan.

Holmes' house is now the George Hotel (formerly the Pier Hotel) on Quay Street, with a garden leading to the Solent Yachting Centre. To think about 17th-century Yarmouth, consider how in 1664 the marshes had been embanked to leave the little town high and dry from encroachment by the sea and the brook. A drawbridge could be lifted to keep the defence secure, and four gates allowed the inhabitants to sleep easily: Hither Gate, Inner Town Gate, Outer Town Gate, and Quay Gate, while landward a redoubt could keep watch southwest by Thorley Copse.

In the King's Head I was jotting down notes on the church, hoping to be unobserved, when "I once had an idea for a book," came from a man with a face speckled red and freckled brown, with a bulbous nose like a fat carrot. "Wuduv bina best-seller, that wud."

Moules marinières with crusty bread at the King's Head came with yachting talk centred on fuel tanks and flexible mountings, corrosion and paint. "The engine's lasted forty year: quite phenomenal really, till that trouble off the Needles."

The thriftless artist George Morland (1763-1804) found the men of Yarmouth as suspicious as they were in the days when Henry VIII warned them of spies, counterspies, and French agents. The boy Morland, having shown promise, was locked up in an attic by his father to paint and draw from casts and pictures, the copies being sold by his parent to dealers. The boy managed to contact some dealers direct, however, and produced for himself an income throughout increased labours. He painted quickly and brilliantly for most of his life, but by reaction sank into dissipation, spending on drink what he earned by his brush. Escaping from his father's apprenticeship, and refusing another period with the celebrated Romney before accepting the hospitality of a canny dealer, Morland spent beyond his means, and it was to escape his creditors and unpleasant drinking-cronies that he fled to the Isle of Wight in 1799, accepting the use of a Cowes cottage belonging to his London surgeon, a Mr Lynn. Morland's brother, happening to overhear talk of bailiffs and their mission to apprehend the painter at his retreat in Cowes, slipped away and warned George, who found refuge with the notorious smuggler George Cole in Yarmouth. There, according to George Dawe's sensational *Life of George Morland* (1807), "Morland, with his brother and man, had not been at this place many days before they were arrested by an order from General Don, commander of the district, as spies... He and his companions were accordingly marched to Newport, a distance of about twelve miles, where the bench of justices was sitting; though the day was extremely hot, and they had their port-folios to carry... They were dismissed, but not without a strong injunction having been laid upon Morland to make no more sketches."

Among Morland's works known to have been painted at Yarmouth were a 'View of Needles' and 'Freshwater Gate' (both 1799). The important landscape painter James Ward (1769-1859) became a pupil of Morland and married his sister. Morland married Ward's daughter, who separated from him, unable to stand his drunken ways. Cook's *Popular Handbook to the National Gallery* (1888), à propos of Morland's 'Inside of a Stable', notes that "after a life of dissipation, duns, and debts, he died in a spunging-house in Coldbath Fields." Morland painted Yarmouth Fort (1803), and as you walk round the snug Great Hall, the round powder magazine, and the master-gunner's quarters, it is pathetic to think back to those days of a feared French invasion, when Morland's drawing of a spaniel could be construed as a clever outline of the Isle of Wight.

My own best-loved artist's view of Yarmouth is the watercolour of about 1875 by William Gray the Elder of Ventnor, whose 'Culver Cliff from Luccombe Beach' is probably my favourite Island view of all: both are reproduced in colour by Robin McInnes in *The Isle of Wight Illustrated* (1989).

At a deal table in the Coffee House, on the corner of Quay Street and Yarmouth Square, I sipped a coffee as near as possible to two ladies in their mid-sixties for whom Gray's *Anatomy* must have been required bedside reading. They spoke of portions excised from their bodies which I had not realised they had. It was as though the surgeons had permed any two organs from four under the scalpel's fine threat. I paid the pallid, terrified teenage girl behind the counter and closed the door quietly behind me, to "I always felt sorry for Geoffrey." "Why's that?" "His St Bernard snored, and for another thing, he was the middle one of Siamese triplets."

Yarmouth's magic may effervesce even today, but one recalls with regret the passing of the rowdy annual fair on St James' Day, 25 July, when a pole with a stuffed glove at the end (to denote openhandedness) was pushed out from the town hall, and there was a license for drunkenness which the law did not choose to see. This fair apparently passed away in the 1870s when, across the water, Thomas Hardy was producing *Under the Greenwood Tree* (1872), *Far from the Madding Crowd* (1874) and *The Return of the Native* (1878).

Another quaint custom that the modern motorist would be forgiven for not knowing about, now he can drive direct along the A 3054 to Totland, was the ferry operating from Yarmouth across the Yar to Norton and the once-isolated Isle of Freshwater. A car blasts away mystery before it as a foglamp pierces through mist, and we are not always the richer for it. Smugglers and ferrymen made no bones about their opposition to the idea of a bridge across the Yar; they charged sixpence to ferry a toff, identified by his white collar, and a penny for a blue-collared workman. But in the name of speed and progress a causeway and drawbridge passed to Norton in 1863, and the ferry died. A pier was built 13 years later, and boatmen sculling passengers from ship to shore were put out of business.

Walking to Norton treats changing visions with proper deference: the car, elsewhere a proper device, like a battering-ram at a siege, here becomes an interloper, like a battering

Norton. Cottage called 'Norton Thatch'

ram at a picnic. Norton has Easter Bonnet Parades, with cottages out of Samuel Palmer given names of such definite romance as 'Norton Thatch'. Seaward through the village, Fort Victoria Country Park harks back to the nervy 1840s, when fifty-two guns protected Sconce Point, a battery built here in 1800, and modified in 1880. A railtrack brought fresh supplies from the jetty, now disused. If you amble from Sconce Point to Cliff End on a nature trail you will come to the nearest point on the Island to Hurst Castle: this is Fort Albert, with luxury flats so secure you would think it a refuge for a former President of the U.S.A. or a toppled African dictator fearful of popular vengeance. Nature thrusts evidence of its ingenuity towards you: a galaxy of colour and texture, scent and shape: wych elm and hazel, ancestral oak and fugitive wild rose, clematis and alder. You could be back at Ventnor's botanic gardens, but without the planner's intrusive hand.

I stayed till soft nightfall, when Lymington set out its coded lights for decipherment across the expanse of Pennington Marshes. Stars sparkled like serried diamonds on a jeweller's flatteringly dark blue velvet backcloth. My torch fleetingly illuminated the disarrayed clothes of a young Scouse girl and her paramour: "It's gonuthin to dowitha, ri'?" "Fie ge' married, it'll beefa berra or wares." "I'm windin' yerup, yer pillock!"

Totland

That evening, taking dinner at the Sentry Mead Hotel at the edge of the Turf Walk, on Madeira Road, Totland, a woman who believed in the curative value of mascara and lumpy anthracite earrings enquired of her angular companion, who seemed to have elbow-bones outside her flesh instead of inside, "How's Ron getting on with his cookery lessons?"

"Not bad", replied the speaking skeleton. "Lesson one was getting him to boil an egg without soaking the cooker and putting out the gas. He mastered that after a couple of goes."

"What's lesson two?"

"It was boiling two eggs at once. He seemed to get a bit of a rush to the head with excitement, but after I told him to put them both in the same pan at the same time he was off and flying."

Totland has retirement homes and nursing-homes the way Patpong Road in Bangkok has massage parlours. Old people find the resort quiet, relaxing, and healthy. At Bishop's, the estate agents, D.K. Burningham spoke of the excellent value offered by Totland compared with the mainland. At Parma Villas on Hurst Hill, near Alum Bay New Road, a three-bedroom brick semi-detached house was on offer at only £72,000 freehold, much lower than a similar property nearer London. Totland Broadway is as far removed from its New York namesake as one is likely to see in a lifetime's search. Vectis Products, Wool 'n' Things (cakes and sweets are the things to be found with the wool) opposite a 'qualified carpenter'; the Kingdom Hall of Jehovah's Witnesses up Granville Rise. The Kingdom to Come seems nearer at Totland than at most other villages because the average age must be 78 come Tuesday. The summerish Greensward House accommodates Abstract Computers Limited, a far cry from the thick woodland that once stretched from Totland to Freshwater. The older generation make do with Totland's pebbly beach, while their noisier offspring head for the sands of the eastern coast. Rambling is pleasant northward to Colwell Bay and southward and westward to Alum Bay, where the earth of England peters out to rocky Needles and the unfriendly ocean. The old *Red Guide* speaks of 'bathing machines' at Colwell Bay where now clanking, roaring 'amusement' machines have been carefully computerised to divide punters from their pocket-money by a good margin of bad fortune. I missed out Fort Warden Holiday Camp because my head is the wrong shape for funny hats. New defences against the sea's threat were constructed in 1966, but there has been no lifeboat here since 1924: the luckless have to wave instead of drowning till their boat comes in from distant Yarmouth.

Middle English's *toten*, to 'look about, look out', became to 'tout' and this sense of a watch-point is preserved in Totland's name, the land where the look-out would stand ready to light a beacon warning of intruders. I should make not for the prosaic new road to Alum Bay, but over Headon, where the ten-year-old W.H. Auden had inspected 'the Tumulus' (there are in fact more than one) and been turned away from an isolation camp where cerebro-spinal meningitis was being treated.

Alum Bay
The Needles Pleasure Park sounds a contrived trap for tourists, and such it is. Alum Bay Glass has a museum and workshop below the evitable salesroom, where a coach party from the East Midlands were buying small green frogs and T-shirts with such legends as 'It's hard to be humble when you're as great as I am.' Four Japanese touring in a Toyota were choosing high-quality postcards. A wooden pastryboard had been lettered 'Of all my relations, I like sex best'. The car-stickers ranged from 'Buckingham Palace – Parking Permit' to 'Act Natural, You're Stupid'. Off the car-park stands a mysterious edifice inscribed 'The Super X is a real simulator. Adult £1. Children 60p. Persons of a nervous disposition and those subject to heart disorders are asked to note that this simulator reproduces the stress of high-speed movement. In the interest of safety we regret that we are unable to admit persons less

Alum Bay

than 1 metre tall.' Signs nearby led to Amusements, Military Shop, D.I.Y. Sand Shop, Gift Shop, Kiddies' Fun Park, and Seafood & Popcorn. A chairlift is situated handily near a notice warning all and sundry, and presumably especially those of a weakly disposition, subject to leg disorders and below 1 metre tall: 'Beware: there are 234 steps to the beach'.

However, even those resolute against the rising tide of tourist mementoes might be persuaded to collect a phial of multi-coloured sands from the geological history of this tiny corner of the globe. Two thirds of the way down the steps a hut suggests 'fill you sand tubs here', a thought taken up by so many day-trippers over the decades that one is constantly amazed that any cliffs remain. An East Midlander who had puffed his portly way down the steps to this point without a word confided in a hoarse whisper to his tall, bald companion with maroon braces, "My wife's been much better since she started taking that kelp and oil of evening primrose".

The bald man in braces watched the holidaymakers with a doglike pathos, still saying nothing. He struck me as, like Joseph the father of Jesus, one of life's mute spectators, one of those bystanders who watch processions while *not comprehending what is going on.* Alum Bay's strata are the stuff of madness however, in the fantastic compression of millions of years in a few steps' width: Reading Beds, London Clay, Bagshot Sands, Barton Clays are the prosaic, heavily localized human names for these compacted environments from tropical aeons and subtropical millennia. The alum is a yellow visible in the clays which was worked here as early as 1561, and used for making materials fireproof, for sizing paper, dyeing and tawing skins. With the glory of geological evolution present to one's eye in a range of subtle colours and to one's imagination in a kaleidoscope of terrestrial time, it is wince-making to readjust to the horrid gnomes around the wishing well in the pleasure park above: 'Ring a Bell and Make a Wish' it says, and too many people do.

A boat trip to the Lighthouse and the Needles enables you to suffer humility before a vision of White Cliffs colonised by smug cormorants and menaced by wheeling seagulls. The Old Needles Battery (1861-3) was reopened by the National Trust in 1982 and makes a fascinating postscript to Portsmouth's maritime heritage displays across the water.

Freshwater

When overners in droves overwhelm the east coast, West Wight becomes the unsung home-from-home of islanders 'wanting to get away' for a summer weekend, and Freshwater Bay is an obvious choice. There's the usual wide range of accommodation. At one end of the scale, the Farringford home of Alfred, Lord Tennyson, is now a splendid hotel with croquet, swimming pool, hard tennis court, putting green, and indoor games room, with a nine-hole golf course in the grounds and an 18-hole course less than a mile off. At the other end, Blenheim House, Brookside Forge and Cambridge Lodge are quieter and much less expensive.

At the seventeenth-century country house hotel called Yarlands, I took breakfast with an excited resident who had come over to the Island to ride on Havenstreet stream railway and to find the oldest bus on Southern Vectis scheduled services: the 'Old Girl', as she is known: an open-top 1939 Bristol K type CDL 899, fifty years old, but running just 'as sweet as a nut', in the words of the enthusiast. A couple from Herne Bay had come to inspect a cottage-style town house in Freshwater: 1, London House on Queens Road, a two-bedroom Victorian home on offer for just under £70,000.

Another year, I spent some time at the Victorian South View Hotel on the Square, Freshwater Bay. Every evening a military gentleman with a nicely-tamed moustache would march off before dinner.

"Off to put on my best bib and tucker", explained the flushed major, to a bored audience of three elderly ladies, wary of their knitting as if it might suddenly bite.

The ladies preyed on single women, few of whom chose the South View, but on my last night the chance of a fourth at whist was offered by the arrival of a pretty forty-year-old who confided in me that she needed the break after a crisis in her office at Portsmouth.

"What I do best," she announced to put off the rest of the whist platoon, "is sleeping. Dreaming, sometimes, nightmares, mostly, but definitely sleeping."

One winter evening at a Freshwater pub, I was nursing a pint of Whitbread's best and waiting in vain for Felicity Lott to burst through the door dressed as the Marschallin in *Der*

Rosenkavalier.

"It's marvellous what they teach them in schools, nowadays," blurted out a bulky man in a hippo's anorak. He looked around for challenges with the air of someone who preferred argument to conversation.

A meditative postman, having finished his round, sipped a beer like a political prisoner expecting to be poisoned. He offered no challenge, allowing his maroon braces to rub more deeply into his rounded shoulders.

"I say, what with black holes and white nights, natural history is never what it was. Young Raymond comes 'ome and says you need immunity these days. He says you've to be careful of Auntie Bodice. I ask him who she is and 'e's off: no respect. I don't know where they get it from. In my day, one word of cheek, and you're lying on the floor with two teeth missing. I left school at sixteen straight into me first 'eavy goods ve'icle and now I'm taking two 'olidays a year instead of one. You'll not catch me with two G.C.S.E.s to rub together. What do you reckon?"

The postman, who had averted his gaze throughout the constant battery of interruptions, now brightened up and straightened his back. "Thanks", he grinned, "mine's another bitter."

Freshwater Bay's Albion Hotel was filled with men in suits chomping their way through a meat course. I riffled through the rack of holiday romances and sleazy fiction: Barbara Raskin's *Hot Flashes* and Jacqueline Briskin's *Dreams are not Enough*. You can tell a hotel's clients from the rack of books it sets out. Seagulls yelled their terrifying warnings to me over craggy rocks eroded by millions of years of patient waves. Ever since I learned the Greek word for eternity was *aei* I realise that seagulls have been practising the sound from prehistory, some stressing one syllable, some the third, some the second, some a mixture, until one day one will catch the right order, the right duration, the right stress, and be uplifted into the arms of Zeus or crash down to its doom into the arms of Poseidon, an Icarus with fated wings suddenly leaden.

A black mongrel dog leapt and pounced on imaginary pheasants amid the shingly sands. "Sam!", yelled an irate man with a red face who wanted to go home, "Sam! Sam!

Freshwater Bay

Sam! Sam!" I thought, "Why don't we all shout to put him out of his misery, or shoot the dog?" A prim King Charles spaniel pattered politely beside a proper gentlewoman in a deerstalker and lisle stockings. Didn't those go out years back? I bet the spaniel isn't called Sam. A Rotary Wishing Well opposite the Mermaid Café stood aloof with its litter of one-penny, two-penny, five-penny pieces tossed in thoughtlessly by passers-by. I walked off to Farringford Hotel while in the distance, an ever more desperate dogoholic yelled out "Sam! Sam! Sam!" (Perhaps it wasn't Sam at all.) And after a lingering pause: "Saaaaam!"

One year in the 1970s I stayed at the Farringford Hotel, and sometimes took afternoon tea in the Tennyson Lounge, over-looking the Downs.

Every day for a week they sat there: deaf aunt and vengeful

niece: seventy plaguing forty-eight with the incessant harping of old feuds and fresh malice. One day I smiled at them encouragingly, and sat in the shelter near enough to respond if spoken to, and far enough to allow them to keep their distance if so minded, the body language of a society terminally infected by embarrassment, like holidaymakers sitting together at a restaurant table watching each other avoid each other's eye as their palms sweat.

"Wossay?" screeched the aunt at her mithered wan-faced companion.

"I really *do* want to die", murmured the niece, out of ear-shot at twelve inches.

"You'll never learn to drive without a car", rasped the thin brown cardigan, as she plucked another piece of imaginary fluff from her tight lap.

Another afternoon, of the kind that drift like pincushions on a sloping sofa (they nod off, and only when you grab them do you come awake), I was taking a cream tea at the Fort Redoubt tea-rooms above Freshwater Bay, and watched as three little girls arrayed in fresh pink swimsuits rose like jills-in-the-boxes from the stubby waves at sea-edge, froth diminishing disappointingly like shaving foam before an advancing razor, their hair plastered seaweed-askew over eager brows.

Half-angels, half-sirens, they blared their shrill anxieties and ecstasies to the bored sky, which had seen it all so many times before.

I introduced myself to a divorced grandmother with blue-rinsed hair and a lisp whose makeup had been bravely, almost fatally, impastoed with the brazenry applied to harlot extras in *The Beggar's Opera*.

She denounced the litter, while genteelly avoiding any mention of the human beings who had put it there, with such conviction that I realised she must have said the same thing a hundred times before, with equal calm vehemence.

"We'll never be the country we ware again", she concluded, tapping her index finger on the table like a slender gavel.

"What is it?" I asked, "is it the lack of discipline in the home or the violence in the streets?"

"It's a multiplication of all sorts", she replied staccato,

shaking her head so her spectacles lurched down her nose like a greyhound on a leash.

The story of Tennyson, Poet Laureate from 1850, the year of his marriage and the publication of *In Memoriam*, is connected as intimately with the Isle of Wight as with his Lincolnshire birthplace. It was in the summer of 1853, while at Bonchurch, that Tennyson heard about Farringford, in Freshwater, an 18th-century mansion with a drawing-room added in the 1840s. He determined to quit the society of Twickenham and London, and crossed the Solent on a still November evening, with his wife Emily whom he had married only at the age of 41, when his prospects had been finally secured by the immense popularity of his poetry. To buy the house, originally leased, he wrote to his publisher Edward Moxon "to advance one thousand pounds, four hundred pounds he owes me, the odd six hundred to be paid if he will in March when I get my moneys in." He purchased the house outright with the huge income from *Maud* (1855). He and Emily lived at Farringford until 1867, then kept it on.

Anne Thackeray Ritchie, in her evocative *Records of Tennyson, Ruskin, Browing* (1892), allows us to share the flavour of those country years. She "walked with Tennyson along High Down, treading the turf, listening to his talk, while the gulls came sideways, flashing their white breasts against the edge of the cliffs and the Poet's cloak flapped in time to the gusts of the west wind. The house at Farringford itself seemed like a charmed palace, with green walls without, and speaking walls within. There hung Dante with his solemn nose and wreath; Italy gleamed over the doorways; friends' faces lined the passages, books filled the shelves, and a glow of crimson was everywhere; the oriel drawing-room window was full of green and golden leaves, of the sound of birds and of the distant sea."

Though Tennyson walked every day, the so-called Tennyson Trail blazed by the County Council from Alum Bay all the way to Carisbrooke is a fifteen-mile hike most of which the Poet would have skipped, especially after his national fame in later years, when strangers would rush up to him and disturb the very peace he had come to Freshwater to find. His son and biographer, Hallam, gave a site on which the Thatched

Church dedicated to St Agnes was constructed in 1908, absolutely charming, and as successful in its totally different way as Quarr Abbey's church of 1911-12 by Dom Paul Bellot.

Pilgrims to Tennyson (on whom Prince Albert himself had called, the villagers would confide in some awe) found themselves jolted by cart over rough tracks from Yarmouth, but would never complain, when in sight of the yellow-brick villa, for this was an Experience; their Man was the 'Jupiter of Farringford', the talk not only of Browning and Coleridge with Coventry Patmore, but also of theology and philosophy with Jowett and Maurice, politics with Gladstone, and geology with Charles Darwin. In the evenings his guests would listen to him recite – all, including Tennyson himself, with tears in their eyes. Edward Lear found it enough "to make you stand on your head". Anne Thackeray Ritchie said of these days that "everybody at Freshwater is either a genius, or a poet, or painter or peculiar in some way", a potentially mixed classification that readers can take at their own valuation.

The place that Tennyson held in Victorian society can never be recaptured in England; it is perhaps analogous to that of Pushkin in Russia. Tennyson always remained insecure of his own ability, and detractors could – by a line in a newspaper or a slur in a letter – put him off writing for days. But his admirers were mainly uncritical, identifying him with the spirit of Christian verse, in its moral fervour and high ideals, equating Victorian England with the antechamber to Heaven. Jenny Lind sang at Farringford, so the analogy is fairly apt.

Virginia Woolf satirised the grand community at Farringford in her play *Freshwater*, newly edited by Lucio P. Ruotolo (1976), and this amusing parody of the great, the good, and the merely climbing should be put on somewhere every summer in the Island to evoke, even at a legpull's length, the pomp and posturing at Farringford that drew thousands of sightseers then, as Bloomsbury itself was to do later.

Tennyson, that model of High Victorian seriousness in the key of Carlyle, Ruskin and Morris, inhabited a world aspiring to a chimerical certainty in church and state not yet undermined by Darwin, Freud, Marx and Einstein. We relativists who come after him tune our instruments to an ironic pitch not because we want to, in every case, but because we must.

The time is out of joint, and we must make the best of it, whether in the desperate length of Zukofsky's *A* and Pound's *Cantos*, or in the snatching brevities of Celan or Cummings. I can no longer read Tennyson, for he comes as if from antediluvian tradition, not only Before Christ but before Moses, with his flowing beard and declamatory stance. I know of no comtemporary poet who uses Tennyson as a father-figure or style-model, as he might use Robert Lowell, T.S. Eliot, Ginsberg or Berryman.

Mrs Julia Margaret Cameron arrived in Freshwater and in 1860 purchased two neighbouring cottages, named 'Dimbola' after the tea plantation in Ceylon which was the Camerons' chief source of income. While her husband was away there, she joined the two cottages together by erecting between them a mock-Elizabethan tower. Her motive in choosing Freshwater was to remain near to the man she idolised and pestered: Tennyson, who managed to resist her attempts to photograph him for three years, but eventually caved in before the cajolery, flattery and plain and simple bullying tactics of the detemined gruff-voiced lady, born in Calcutta, who was to become one of the most significant pioneers of photographic portraiture. In the end, Tennyson became – with G.F. Watts and Henry Taylor – one of her most frequent choices of male subject. Apart from his wife, Julia Margaret was the only woman Tennyson ever called by her forenames. I think the best story of her time at Freshwater is the episode of Garibaldi's visit to Farringford, when JMC fell to her knees before the great man to persuade him to sit for a portrait and was brushed aside, being taken for a beggarwoman.

Lewis Carroll's photography, mainly of pre-pubescent girls, was sharply-defined, clear, and brilliant. He wrote two satires on Julia Margaret's soft, misty photography, often of girls and young women (including the twenty-year-old Alice Liddell of *Alice in Wonderland* fame). 'A Photographer's Day Out' offers the ideal *dramatis personae* of portraiture: 'paterfamilias, materfamilias, two sons from school, a host of children from the nursery and the inevitable BABY'. In 'Photographer Extra-ordinary' he suggested that poetry should be transmuted directly into photography but, having tried out the method on verse from Byron, "the paper came out scorched and blistered all over by the fiery epithets produced." One only has to think of JMC's poetic renderings of May Prinsep as Beatrice Cenci (1870) and the Gretchen from Goethe's *Faust* of the same year to realise the justice of Carroll's barbs, even if one sympathises with her aesthetic.

The Camerons lived at Freshwater for fifteen years, and left for Ceylon in 1875 to be close to their sons, who were coffee-planters by this time, but they died soon afterwards, Julia Margaret in 1879 aged sixty-three, and her husband Charles Hay Cameron in 1880 aged eighty-five. Generous, eccentric, kindly, imperious, Julia Margaret made an indelible impression on all who knew her. Anne Thackeray Ritchie recalled seeing her for the first time as "a strange apparition in a flowing red velvet dress, although it was summer time, cordially welcoming us to a fine house and some belated meal, when the attendant butler was addressed by her as 'man' and was ordered to do many things for our benefit; to bring back the luncheon dishes and curries for which Mrs Cameron and her family had a speciality. When we left she came with us

Freshwater. Julia Margaret Cameron's house

bareheaded and trailing draperies, part of the way to the station, as was her kind habit."

The lefthand side of 'Dimbola' has retained its name, but has been diminished in appearance by the addition of a modern sunlounge. However, the interior is to a great extent untouched, with a good carved oak fireplace, 'Gothic' style door panels and a splendid staircase.

The right-hand side, still named 'Cameron House', has been converted into small holiday apartments of no distinction. The exterior is largely original, however. Now a property developer has acquired Cameron House and intends to demolish the garden, featured in so many of JMC's period photographs, and make it a carpark. The Island planning authority has asked the Department of the Environment to list Cameron House to prevent its demolition, but the rearguard action by Islandwatch and others to save the house and garden may yet not succeed.

At least Tennyson's Farringford has been saved, in the sense that it has been converted into a hotel, and the National Trust owns and safeguards Tennyson Down.

It was at the four-crown Farringford Hotel that I met up with an old actor-friend with whom I had been at school. Over the years, I had seen his name glide gracefully up the list of credits but stick roughly halfway, except for a leading part at the Comedy Theatre in a rôle that made him wince in retrospect. Dare one whisper that most actors and actresses are too intelligent for the parts they play or the audiences they reach, and spend their lives struggling for work, or being miscast if cast at all?

I gathered he was chaperoning a wealthy lady who had retired for the night with a mess of pottage and the appropriate Alka Seltzer. Our meeting was totally unrehearsed like a skate on a fishmonger's marble being poked with an umbrella-tip.

"The Commander's a bit of a lancepresado", whispered the retired actor, warily, behind his cupped palm.

"He's a what?" I enquired mystified.

"Lancepresado, y'know, an old skinflint. Never pays his round till everyone's gone home and he chalks it up."

Throughout the long evening, the actor – who shall be

nameless – characterised each member of the chorus, stars and all, by such outlandish descriptions from Marlowe and Jonson, Ford and Massinger. One was unforgettably a trailbaston: one who carried a stick; another transfigured from a hairy youth of the 'Look at me, I'm Jesus' generation to 'Pale Crinite': a blond hairy one. Yet a third I looked at with different eyes, when termed a palter-monger: one babbling senselessly to others, even when sober. I connected wimble with Lewis Carroll: "no," corrected my mentor, "Spenser wrote of one 'so wimble and so wight'," immediately recognisable of a puffy yuppie gambolling around a taunting crowd in the corner: nimble and valiant. It struck me that the fanciful thespian, in a brown leather-elbowed jacket stained with time and whisky, was enjoying life twice as much as someone with only half his wordcraft. It was as if, being a painter, he had invented twice the colours in any other artist's palette. I wish I had the wit to speak of a paltermongering lancepresado, but that is Edmund Kean territory, the uninhabited Antarctica of language, which only few explorers ever reach. The frostbite is in the overlong stay.

At the Farringford Hotel, I sat in the silent Tennyson Library, now a TV lounge. He built this when his upstairs study became too small to accommodate his basic library. I found the spiral staircase by which he could escape from unwelcome visitors when warned they were arriving up the front stairs. The poet's smoking-cap, cloak and scarf are protected in glass cases: how trivial these artefacts seem beside the intangibility of his speaking voice! His Old Testament prophet's head, recorded by JMC in her superb photograph, reminded me of the petulant remark by Jennens, librettist of *Saul*: "Mr Handel's head is more full of maggots than ever." A poet produces maggots by the basketful: what bait for readers!

One sunny evening I took lemon sole filled with crabmeat and fresh fruit at Tennyson's Restaurant on Gate Lane: the former Mrs Pink's. Dawn and John Ferriday came to Freshwater from Burnham Beeches in 1986 and had a terrible time getting started. Then they began home deliveries, taking meals to Mr Fox, Mr Fordham and a dozen others once a day on average, a valued service by the housebound not keen to rely on 'Meals on Wheels'.

It's a shame the old dialect is dying out, but in the remoter parts it can still be heard if you roam far enough and listen hard enough. This is how a West Wight wold feller told a story about an experience in the withybeds at Freshwater, as transcribed by W.H. Long, in *A Dictionary of the Isle of Wight Dialect* (1886).

"Aearly in the mornen, I zid a wold man lerruppen (thrashing) along the road, and every now and then stoppen and glaren all round as if a couldn't make out where a was got to. Predney a come up auverright (opposite) me, and makes a stop, and a zays, 'Hollo, mayet, what plaace do ye call this?' I thought a was about half sprung (cracked or tipsy), zo i zed too'n, 'This place is a withybed, as ver as I knows.' 'My eyes,' zays the wold feller, 'I can't maake noo fist (attempt) on't at all, that's the saame neyam as they calls it in the Isle o' Wight.' Hearen this maade *me* open my eyes pretty wide vor a minute. 'Well, drat (God rot) thee,' I zays too'n, 'Where dost think thee bist then?' 'Where I be?' a zed. 'Why, this es France, edden't it?' 'Why ye zoat (soft) wold man,' I zays, 'thee bist out on't all together, this is Freshwater.' "

4 Newtown and the North

Cowes

We first find the place named as "the Cowes, betwixt the Isle of Wight and England" in 1512, a designation perhaps of a local offshore sandbank, then applied to the land closest to the bank. The plural arises after Henry VIII had built a castle in 1539 on each side of the Medina. The reputation for shipbuilding that grew from 1588 spread to sailing with the visit of the Duke of Gloucester in 1811, and a club was founded next year by the Earl of Yarborough, then merely Mr Pelham. The Prince Regent permitted the use of the honorific Royal in the Yacht's Club name in 1917 and the club has been staunchly elitist ever since, as full of backbiting as a tank of electric eels.

The great William Daniell portrayed Cowes in 1824, as may be seen in *The Isle of Wight Illustrated* (1989) by Robin McInnes, a book indispensable to anyone fascinated by changing perceptions of the Island in art. George Brannon, whose *Vectis Scenery* so popularised the Island's magic in the 1820s, wrote about Cowes at this time. "The town covers the side of a steep hill and appears to its greatest advantage from the water, but it must be confessed that this favourable impression is weakened on first landing from the packet as the lower streets are close and irregular being occupied by tradesmen. The upper part of the town is altogether more pleasant, consisting of large respectable lodging houses (many sumptuously furnished) which enjoy uninterrupted and enlivening prospects of the Solent Sea. Besides there being three capital inns, several bathing machines are fully employed, also hot and tepid baths. The beach of small pebbles, having a good descent, admits excellent bathing at all states of the tide."

In *Memorials of the Royal Yacht Squadron* (1903), Guest and Boulton date the institution of modern yacht racing to 1826, when the Royal Yacht Club presented a Gold Cup of a hundred sovereigns to the winner of Cowes' first great races, to be held for members.

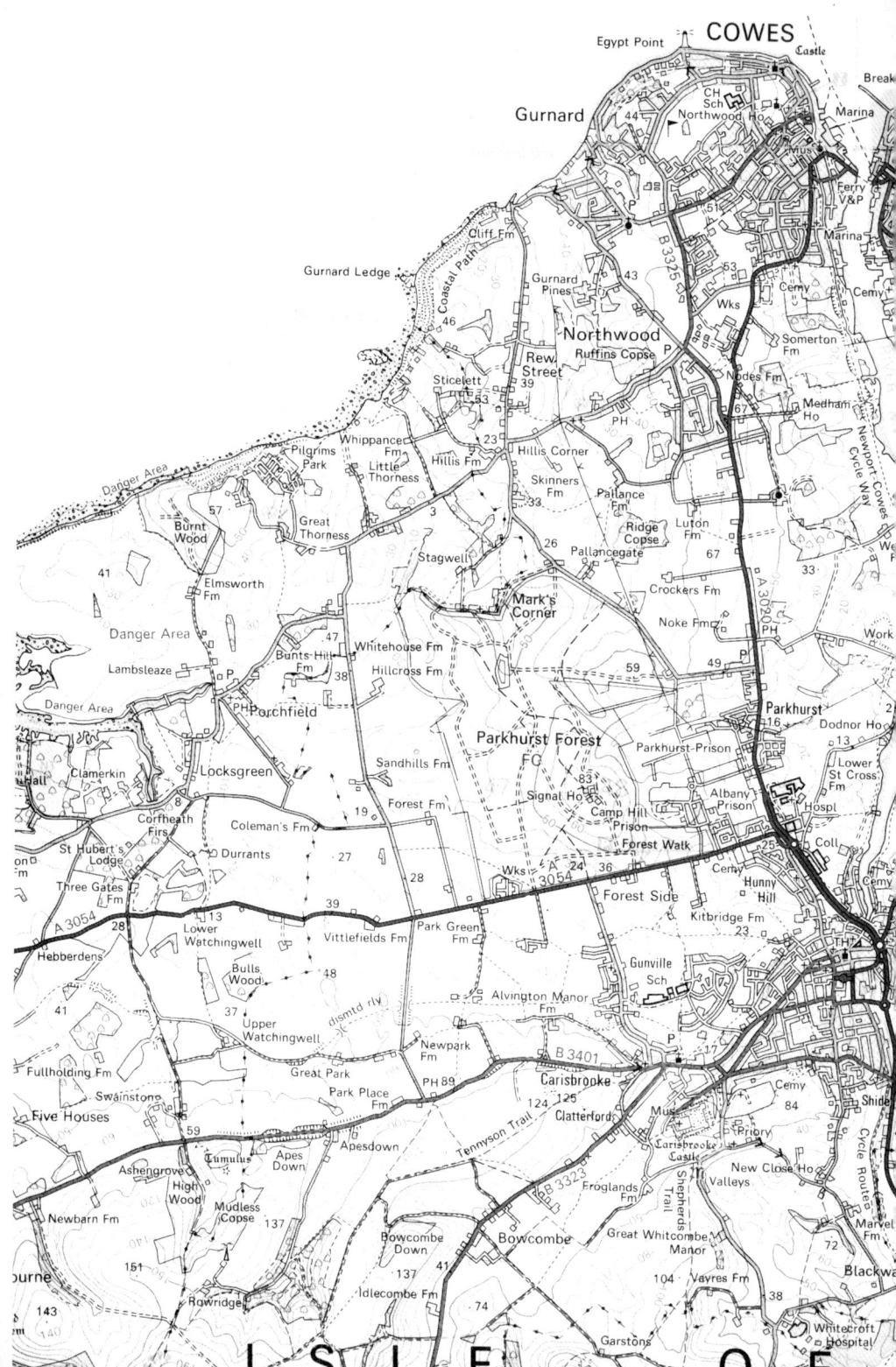

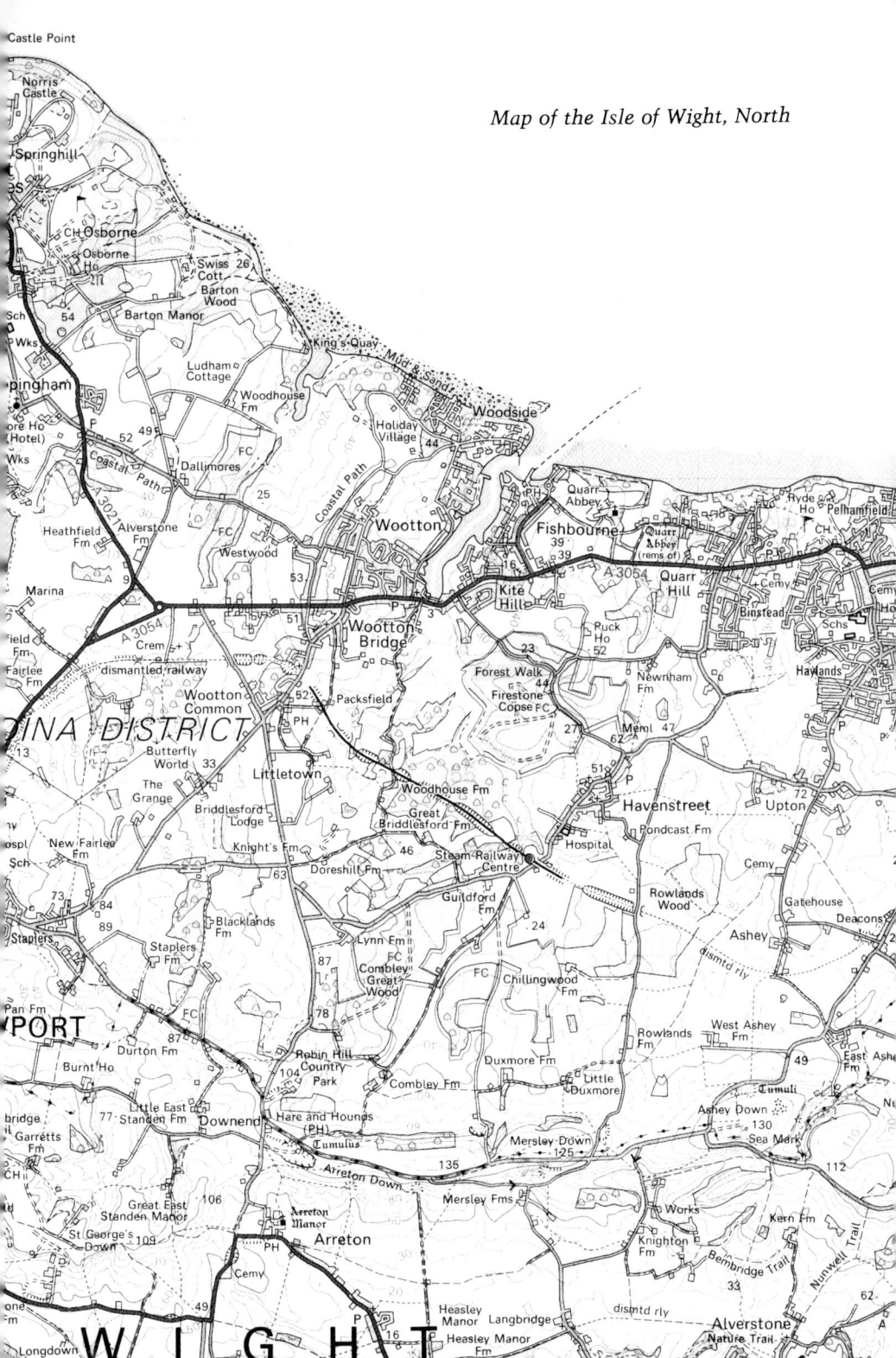

Map of the Isle of Wight, North

Since then Cowes has prospered, to the point where 1,813 yachts set out for the 1989 Round-the-Island Race on 17 June, the winner presented with the Gold Roman Bowl first won in 1930 by Tom Ratsey's fast cutter *Dolly Varden* in a time for the sixty-mile course of 5 hours and 51 minutes, 21 seconds, a time never surpassed by any monohull since. The staggered starts began with Round-the-World boats, then cruising multihulls, IOR yachts, Channel Handicap, finishing with non-rated cruising yachts. Freak weather conditions, hot and windless, becalmed every yacht in Freshwater Bay, producing an incredible sight which nobody at Freshwater that day will ever forget. The popular winner was Stephen Fein's trimaran *Full Pelt* (as in 1988), with crew of Fein, Jo Richards, Graham Deegan, Paul Stanbridge and Sports Minister Colin Moynihan. Jo – skipper, and co-designer with Ed Dubois – replaced the lower half of the main hull last winter, near his home on Newtown Creek, with an entirely new section, and a new and taller rig was added.

The 1989 Cowes Week featured over 800 craft in the nine-day season from 29 July to 6 August, with nearly two hundred races comprising 27 different classes. Cowes' population of 19,000 was bulked out by more than 8,000 competitors, families and friends.

Aquatogs in the High Street display chandlery, wellies, deck shoes and buoyancy aids. Edward Watts & Sons on Birmingham Road offer primers, undercoats, enamels, varnishes, antifoulings, thinners, abrasives and glues. Lynal's, the Joke Shop of Cowes, provides fancy dress, adult jokes and masks.

Cowes National Spiritualist Church advertised for next Sunday evening an address and clairvoyance, for the following Wednesday a video called 'Visions of Hope' and for Thursday evening, and matinée at 2.30, sessions of healing. In the pedestrian precinct Jolliffe maintained their est. 1853 prestige with stained glass. Beken & Son of Cowes, by appointment to H.R.H. the Duke of Edinburgh marine photographers, kept their windows immaculate, presumably in case of a sudden incognito royal visit. At 15 Bath Road their stocks of waterproof cameras stood expectantly.

"I don't like skimmed milk," said a laconically wafting beanpole in the grocer's to an acned adolescent draped across the till, 'I prefer cow's milk'.

Among the parade of designer T-shirts, I picked out one barrel-chested copperknob bearing the legend YACHTING and another, rakier specimen with long gorilla-like freckled arms who claimed to be a KNACKERED SKIPPER.

"Ao, Adrian!"

"Hullo!"

"Ao, I haven't seen him for absolutely yonks!" she piccoloed fortissima to her cringing girl-friends, waving arms and posterior in a ritual manner familiar to, amongst others, the great crested grebe.

I trod on a sticky beetle, a mammoth cockroach? I didn't dare look. Yes, I must, it is a necessary factor in the human condition that I force myself to look at little murders. Ah, I had killed nothing in Cowes yet: it was only dogmess. (Yesterday, in Shorwell churchyard, it had been a sticky beetle.)

A diminutive cottage called the Round House once acted as the estate tollgate for Debourne Manor, then the Ward estate. Along Baring Road towards the Egypt lighthouse you will see on the right 1841 walls hewn from Gurnard's Bembridge limestone.

The walk to Egypt Point is one of the charms of the Wight, for the vessels of the Western Solent — especially during Cowes week — glitter and glide in almost unobtrusive dance-formation, though if you glance away for a few moments their relationship has changed like characters in the next volume of the Forsyte Saga. At the foot of Egypt Hill stands Egypt House, a 19th-century home of the landowning Wards when they left Northwood House. George Henry Ward commissioned John Nash (shall we say 'and studio'?) to create a neo-classical mansion. This was begun early in the 19th century and enlarged in 1830-1 by William Cubitt, according to Prosser. The Greek Doric lodge echoes the Greek bell-tower of St Mary's in West Cowes, again designed by Nash for G.H. Ward, lord of the Manor of Debourne.

Northwood House has provided shelter for Benedictine nuns exiled from France in 1901, during World War I it became a hospital, and it has housed local government offices since 1929. St Mary's was originally West Cowes Chapel, intended as a sober place of worship — in 1657 — for solid citizens of the Protectorate, but that fashion consorted ill with the lighter souls who chose Cowes for recreation, and no longer does West Cowes so virulently engage in religious strife and dissidence as it did in that stone age launching the plethora of nonconformist chapels once teeming with pedantic nitpickers: Wesleyans, Free Wesleyans, Bible Christians, Primitive Methodists, with their Sunday school prizes for regular attendance and scripture knowledge. "A rich man shall hardly enter into the kingdom of heaven", Matthew quotes Jesus, "and again I say unto you, It is easier for a camel to go through the eye of a needle, than for a rich man to enter into the kingdom of God." So many rich folk: so many churches and chapels, like Mrs Heneage's yellow-brick Roman Catholic St Thomas of Canterbury (1796) on Terminus Road with – surprise! – two giant Doric pilasters; like the fashionable Holy Trinity on Queens Road, another yellow-brick construction, this time of 1832; like the pebble-dashed St Faith's (1909) on Newport Road, none of them worth valuable time except as dreadful warnings about the spread of religiosity before the Welfare State, the National Health Service and reductions in working hours allowed the hopeless and wretched to turn from the Vicar and the Lord of the Manor to social services, free doctors, and enough spare time for dignified leisure. The churchmen and landowners as a group did nothing to alleviate the lot of the poor; that was the achievement of post-War statesmen and politicians, encouraged at the polls by rising middle and working classes which determined to increase equality of opportunity.

Oh, of course Cowes still stands for desperately conspicuous consumption, but how exceptional it has become! There's nowhere like Cowes – apart from Ascot or Henley – for whooping it up with last year's May Ball partner, or this year's TV celebrity, like Annabel Croft with the yachtsman Mel Coleman. One night it's the Royal Yacht Squadron Ball, next night the Royal Corinthian Ball, a third the Royal London Yacht Club Ball, a fourth the Whitbread drinks party, a fifth the Mumm Champagne Ball at Northwood House, not to mention the luncheons and dinners, the receptions and barbecues, the royal sightings of Prince Edward and the Duke of Edinburgh.

Cowes. Sailing

Dragons racing from the South Basin do not compel the attention: sailing is the least engaging spectator sport since they started televising marathons. But that does not impede a press corps of five hundred from converging on this tiny town throughout Cowes Week, every August. Sailing has become so spectacularly expensive these days that individualism is almost a thing of the past, and sponsors have moved in for the Admiral's Cup (fifty per cent of boats are commercially funded) and for the Fastnet Race. About fifteen teams vie for the Cup, each with three boats and one or two support boats averaging I suppose a quarter of a million pounds each, or more than £16 million on view at any one time. It all seems disproportionate, inviting one of Howard Brenton's deeply caustic anit-plutocratic plays. Properties cost more in Cowes than in East Cowes as you might expect, though not drastically so. A detached 3-bedroom house in Cowes was priced at £87,500; a similar property was listed in East Cowes at £75,000, subject to offer.

It's speshully jolly good when the British win the Admiral's Cup, completed by the Fastnet Race to Plymouth. Princess Anne finished third in the Sigma 38 class, and Prince Philip a doughty seventh, having sustained three 'shunts' over the week. Crispin Lowe's fabulous new Ancasta Marina has suddenly revived the aspirations of Cowes to match the cachet of Monte Carlo. On the Parade, public relations girls picked for their Sloane accent and Daddy's background carefully avoid any mention of their tactics for the next party, and local girls with a good tan wait to be picked up by a yachtie. The Gloster Hotel was occupied by the Royal Yacht Squadron before they moved in 1858 to Cowes Castle, on the site of Henry's fortress, which had been constructed from Beaulieu Abbey's stone in order that, as Froude aptly suggested, the spoils of the church should furnish "the arms by which the Pope and the Pope's friends could be kept at bay."

It all finishes as the last fireworks swoosh and fall. Until next year. Cowes without Cowes Week, if not as dead as a doornail, is still as moribund as Aintree without the Grand National. Watch House Lane is named for the Customs house, whose excisemen were once led by William, father of Thomas Arnold, the great Rugby headmaster born in Cowes in 1795.

The Union Inn was converted from fishermen's cottages, and offers good food even for landlubbers like myself.

"Did she get that job at the otter refuge?", enquired a portly matron with upcurved sunglasses of her friend in a frock vertically shamed with unsuitable green stripes against crocus yellow. "No", answered the crocus field, "but she's applied to be Assistant Remembrancer in the Lord Mayor's Office in London. You get to meet Prince Andrew, she says". "That'd be very nice. When will she know?" "The shortlist is about Friday week, but she's keeping her hand in with those new porridge recipes I was telling you about. We're very close".

The Anchor Inn, claiming to have been a coaching inn during the 16th century, is known from the 18th century as the Three Trumpeters, its low-beamed ceilings comforting us with reassuring tradition in an age of quick change, like a yachtsman coming ashore for a binge after a hard day's stint. The stable and courtyard garden are all that remains of fifty acres once belonging in the 1770s to Lord Edgcombe, from the sea-front itself to 'The Orchard' and 'St Mary's Meadow.'

In *Pygmalion*, Shaw could conscientiously persuade us that Eliza Doolittle would achieve acceptance as a real lady, and not lidy, if she could enunciate roundly 'how now brown cow' and 'the rain in Spain falls mainly in the plain', as opposed to rine dropping in the pline. Professor Higgins, right then, would have been wrong now. For the cooing round Cowes, in the Isle of Wight, has become an oblong Kize in affected upper-class diction, and one daines dine at the hice these days. Arined the Yacht Club during Kize Week I carefully practise 'high nigh brine kigh' until it becomes if not second nature, at least third or fourth.

Rebecca, Samantha, and Sarah: Biblical names propping up girls indistinguishable from page three. The men escorting these charmers are Matthew, John and Mark; only the third evangelist has fallen into disfavour. They are penthouse and *Penthouse* oriented, intent on making their first half million before saddling their lifestyle with screaming babies and the nappy period. Hannah from Hampstead runs a busy personnel department in Southampton, but nothing would keep her and complex Simon, also 27, from Kizeweek. "Daddy's bug", she confessed. "He *would* take the boat ite every summer weekend, and of course we, Gillian my elder you know, we were hooked from about eight or nain. Well, Gilly was about eight. I was about six. I met Simon here, with a cride, usual thing you know. We got married last year and I'm *desperately* broody. We get three months full pay maternity, but I'll be missed so much I must just get back as soon as poss, otherwise I'll never catch up. Difficult abite a nanny but I'm sure we'll manage. After all, Gilly does, you know. I mean, *everybody* does in the end, yes?"

Cowes is surprisingly scanty in its hotel provision, but then of course one lives on one's boat as a rule doesn't one? A lobster salad is Jill's speciality at the Fountain in the High Street. "The lady on my shtarboard would like a gin and tonic", proclaimed a suitably rubicund admiral with dribble flecking chin and cheeks, "and I will take a shcotch and shoda." I forebore to suggest that he asked his lady fair to sit down.

From above the Cowes Corinthian Yacht Club, I watched a
Red Funnel car ferry leave East Cowes for Southampton. The
police station nearby was closed, but there was a telephone
number to call if you were being overpowered by three seven-
foot tall bank robbers. I found P.C. Game strolling on the
lookout for stray malefactors in the pedestrian precinct and,
in the best tradition of lookout men, kept him talking.
"Drunkenness and violence are about the only offences over
here," he told me. "Not many homicides. If there's any trouble, it's just a few lads getting rowdy in the holiday season.
We've nothing of the uproar that goes on over in Portsmouth
or Southampton. Quiet lot this side of the water. Oh, and
clear it with Inspector Arnold of the Isle of Wight Division in
Newport, won't you?"

Officially, Chief Constable John Hoddinott reported just
under five thousand crimes on the Island in 1988, a drop of
13½%, but offences related to drugs, drink and sex (the so-
called lax morality syndrome) all showed an increase, and
arson rose by 52%, half in motor vehicles. Drug abuse concerned mainly cannabis, sulphates and to a lesser degree
heroin.

The Job Centre too seemed quiet. Silver service waiting
staff were being sought in Freshwater district at £75 p.w. live
in; a clerical assistant was wanted for Totland at £2.20 p.h. A
pharmacy technician in Newport (37 hrs p.w.) would be earn-
ing £5,532 to £7,813 p.a. June's Florist was separated by an
ill-pink door from Corries Cabin headed (I tell no lie) Ye Olde
Fishe Shop. I restrained my impulse to explain that shop had
two peas and an ee.

Gurnard
West of Cowes, Prince's Esplanade leads to Shore Road, Worsley Road, Solent View Road and Rew Street. I dropped in to
visit Jan Peters, at Marsh Haven on Marsh Road, Gurnard,
since she is particularly active on the committee of Islandwatch, whose £1 *Guide to Development* is a priceless action
pack indicating how objectionable planning applications may
be opposed by concerned citizens, with sources of information, reasons for refusing applications, and names of council-
lors who might help to hold up distasteful, hasty over-

Gurnard. Creek

development. She showed me horrendous plans to swamp Wootton's Woodside Bay by which the Rotch Property Group would construct a new hotel complex, conference hall, time share units, concrete marina for 250 boats and an eighty-foot high glass sun dome, destroying Wootton's rural calm, devastating ancient woodlands, and threatening vital Sites of Special Scientific Interest. There are even plans to demolish Ryde's historic pavilion, and to extend Brown's Golf Course for another 'leisure development' at the expense of a river valley designated an area of outstanding natural beauty, but this plan has apparently already been passed by Sandown Town Council so all the opposition in the world is not likely to stop it. Like the lost fight for Bembridge's Royal Spithead Hotel, the damage has been done, despite energetic arguments from Islandwatch.

Luck Stream at Gurnard, now narrow and silted up, is believed to have been wider in mediaeval times, and navigable at least to Hart's Farm on Rew Street, where a mooring-ring has been unearthed during ploughing. At 2 Marsh Road I met a man from Tunbridge Wells who had immigrated to the Island nine years ago, and – unusually – admitted to regretting his decision. "I'd love to be in Tunbridge Wells right now", he sighed, gazing across to a boat called *Our Luck*.

At the Woodvale on Prince's Parade, Gurnard, two women were indulging in drinks before lunch.

"You've just no idea of the headaches I've got to persuade my Hazel and Rollo how to eat healthy food", stated a rotund fiftyish matron, with puce bags under her eyes, and a navy dress with coral beads. "I've the same trouble with my Newell", confided a perspiring beanpole at a rakish forty-five degrees, her spotted dress like a colony of measles. "My Newell thinks a balanced diet is holding up two beefburgers with extra chips in each hand."

On Gurnard beach, a labrador had been given its head within limits, bounding along a retractable line along a middle-aged man's wrist. It is the kind of conditional freedom we allow ourselves at weekends, on the beach, being drawn back to the office on Monday mornings by the uneasy, unspoken, invisible line attached to the boss's wrist.

East Cowes

The crossing between Cowes and East Cowes by floating bridge in 1989 cost 60p for a car and driver, 35p for motor-bike (misleadingly known as 'bike') and 10p for a bicycle (known as a 'bike'). Adult passengers paid 15p and children 5p.

The floating bridge is actually a chain ferry, making on average two hundred and twenty trips a day. The present ferry is the fifth, and operates by diesel-hydraulic motors driving wheels which drag themselves along enormous chains each weighing three and a half tonnes.

A perennial fascination of Cowes and East Cowes is the vibrant (if silent) clamour of class distinctions between the Royal Yacht Squadron Club House in Cowes Castle, and the ever-flowing clientele of the Ferry Boat Café (I nearly wrote 'caff') in York Avenue, East Cowes, handy for the bus stop.

The dignified Town Hall of East Cowes, now a Community Centre, dating from 1897, announced wrestling at the Town Hall, Ryde: top of the bill, Giant Haystacks v. Tony St. Clair. At the Ferry Boat 'all day breakfast' is available at £2.25: 3 rashers of bacon, egg, sausage and beans, toast and tea or coffee.

Two women faced each other over cups of tea, sparring for openings, one clutching at intervals her plaid shopping trolley, the other with a tight-fitting artificial fur cap, brown as the bear it imitated.

"I went in", stated the fur cap, "and got some rubber gloves, but the trouble is even the *tap* is too hot."

"You'll have to do something about that."

"It's not your hairdo this weekend is it?"

"No."

"It is?"

"No, it isn't."

"Oh yes."

"So anyway, she said to me, long time no see, and I thought to myself well you wouldn't if you cross over the street every time you see me."

"But they had some nice check jackets in there last year. Proper tartan, not like them Scotch jobs. Blazer types but checky. Maggie Thatcher wears a lot o' them nowadays."

"I like the way she dresses, trots a bit, my goodness she must have a lot of go in 'er."

"It's them electric plates in the bath. Covered in oil. Makes the skin go all young."

"She's a science graduate."

"Mmmm."

"Makes all the difference. I was going to get a swede yesterday, but I forgot all about it."

"A nice swede."

"I thought I'd go back to Taylor's, get some mince, baked beans, green beans and carrots."

"I tell you what I like: just the ordinary carrots."

"I usually get the tinned ones. They're supposed to be good for you."

"Not the tinned ones, are they?"

"No."

"I often eat the tinned ones."

"I do brains a lot."

"I put 'em in the oven the other day at seven o'clock. Forgot all about 'em. Gas mark three they were."

"I like them 1½ hours up the top on mark 3."

"Do you? That *is* surprising."

"Someone sent me a leaflet about new ones."

"Just a grill with a hot plate on."

"You can get these saucepans now can't you?"

"Are."

"These new electric ones. I think they're ideal, don't you?"

"Electricity was off Tuesday."

"Thursday?"

"And Thursday."

"In the old days we never had TV and you never cared about power cuts."

"That was a great boon. At least if you've got an electric kettle, that's all right. If there's no power cut."

"At least we can have a drink of soup."

"When I couldn't get out for Sandra's birthday I used that new 'Send-a-Bear' service. You send them the money and a bear goes out to the loved one of your choice."

From 19 Alfred Street, East Cowes, the view of terraced houses might be in Blackburn, were it not for the glittering strip of the Medina shivering under the azure sky, and the rise of West Cowes on the opposite bank.

Westland Aerospace has been expanding piecemeal in East Cowes for many years, so that it now sprawls over sixteen acres. The Aerostructures Division is to be consolidated on the Falcon Yard waterfront site, south of the Floating Bridge, and the Systems Division at the Osborne Works site. Plans are afoot to transform the area north of the Floating Bridge into Port Medina, with the Columbine Basin a new yacht marina. Residents of the nimby persuasion ('not in my backyard') have put up a sign on the Esplanade: "If you object to the

186

East Cowes. Alfred Street and the Medina

proposed marina development which will put a mass of housing on reclaimed land and thereby destroy our esplanade, then write now to the Planning Officer, 41 Sea St., Newport". In fact, the Shedden Esplanade itself has not been there very long: built by direct labour as a scheme for the relief of unemployment on land presented to the town by C. Shedden, it was opened as recently as 1924.

Nearby, the 'Old Castle Point Outfall' is a £7 million scheme to improve sewage treatment in Cowes. East Cowes Public Library in Clarence Road offered an open book for "Comments on the Port Medina Development", and I counted 29 in favour and 60 comments against, a proportion of roughly 1 to 2. D. Miles of 36 Old Road had urged "Yes, please. Do not delay. East Cowes needs this", while C. Nichols of 16 Albany Road reflected the majority view: "Plan very bad for East Cowes and its people. The plan is for the benefit of Yuppies and Yautsman and NOT the people who have lived here all their lives. It is a damnable rotten and crazy plan".

By Dover Road I wandered around the Car Ferry Terminal, passing Phoenix Travel of Yeovil and the Jade Garden, Chinese meals to take away.

Outside Gordon's the Chemist the road was disfigured by two of those zig-zag lines that seem to have been laid down by a road-painter significantly under the influence, and it petered out just in front of L. Smith, family butcher. It was amusing to reflect that dear old Cowes is twinned with sophisticated Deauville.

Osborne House

I first saw Osborne at the age of thirteen, when I rebelled against nature and art alike. Osborne House, I thought, would at least be a change from the seesaw of room and beach in Seaview. But 'the following regulations should be read by visitors before entering the Grounds of Osborne', I noted with increasing alarm and despondency, 'and should be carefully observed, for their enforcement as the public will readily understand is strictly necessary.' Necessary? I wondered about some of the 31 regulations. No. 7 decreed that 'No person shall ride or drive in the Grounds or bring in any bath-chair, perambulator, cycle or vehicle without the written authorisation of the Commissioners or the House Governor of Osborne House.' Who wants disabled people in Osborne anyway? No. 10 stipulated that 'No unauthorised person shall sell or offer for sale or hire in the Grounds any article commodity pamphlet programme or thing.' I wrestled with my conscience: was the *Illustrated Guide to Osborne* being sold at ninepence by a truly authorised person? Better not buy the pamphlet or thing, just to be on the safe side, and constantly bear in mind that 'No performance or representation, whether spoken or in dumb show or mechanically produced or reproduced shall be given in the Grounds', thus ruling out my impromptu mime of Queen Victoria. Rule 29 required that 'No person shall wash clothes or other things in any water in the Grounds or do any act likely to cause a pollution of the water in any drinking fountain in the Grounds', a fantasy assuming that people would bring along their laundry on a bike and auction off their sheets and blankets by dumb show.

My amazement continued within the House. The guide

reported a life-size portrait of Abbas Pasha late Khedive of Egypt in the corridor was painted in oils by H.J. Thaddeus, who assumed the name of Jones. For some reason, the Durbar Corridor, under the inspiration of Bhai Ram Singh, was entirely in Indian style and in the Durbar Corridor nine paintings by Rudolf Swoboda portrayed in oils Sarup Singh, Daulati, Ala Yar, Chutter Bhooj Kula, Sher Mohammed, Poorun Mishar, Bahar Shah, Shankergirr Fakir and Khazan Singh. Then came another nine, and another, as though the artist Swoboda could only paint in nines. In the eastern Durbar corridor I vaguely remember a wood, silver and ivory group representing the God of Wisdom and a Stag, presented in 1887 by the Emperor of Japan and looking as out of place in Wight as a flamingo at a pub crawl. Osborne also offered to general stupefaction a bouquet of tinsel flowers presented to Prince Alfred, Duke of Edinburgh by the Archbishop of Malta in 1858, a Maori canoe, and lifesize white marble figures of Plenty, being Princess Louise, Duchess of Argyll, and Peace, being Princess Helena. Or vice versa.

"Cor look, Leeny," cried out a fat lady from a charabanc, "there's Lord Muck", passing a portrait of the Crown Prince Frederick of Prussia, by Francis Xavier Winterhalter. Forty years later, I recollected this cheery dismissal of Winterhalter's unctuous composition at his National Portrait Gallery exhibition in London, and addressed a startled dowager in puce gloves and stabbing lorgnette, with those immortal words: "Cor look, Leeny, there's Lord Muck." "I do not see you sir," she replied levelly, with aplomb to the manor born. I felt thirteen again.

Osborne's Swiss Cottage had proverbs and quotations from the Psalms carved on the exterior in German. The Swiss Cottage Museum contained specimens of "various birds", according to the curator's hollow, official, voice which sounded as though it emanated from the rolling depths of his cavernous abdomen, "mostly shot by members of the royal family, also a small collection of butterflies". Had those, I wondered, also been shot by the royal family? If not, how did they come to be here? A kind of passionate lepidopterism, quite unlike Nabokov's later scientific enterprise, pervaded my soul and has never left it.

I suppose Osborne in reality is not so easily dismissed as it may be by a boy of thirteen. Its Italianate style may be distinctly out of place, but so is the infinitely superior Appuldurcombe, on the downs by Wroxall, or Newtown's marshgirt Town Hall. But whereas they have enough style to gather an aura around them, Osborne still worries the skyline with its fake clock tower and flag tower and clutters one's view in most rooms with too many columns and curtains, sofas and chairs, so that the drawing-room – for example – makes one long for the simplicity of Swainston chapel or the elegance of Gatcombe House. Now I have seen elaborate white marble Jain temples in India, the Durbar Room's ceiling is intelligible, but its secular showcases on the site of a former lawn detract all too quickly from its often excellent portraits. Osborne is neither an Indian palace, after all, nor a British one; its Italian garden is not in Italy and its Swiss Cottage not in Switzerland. As a home, it is vastly uncomfortable; as an art gallery, it presents too many mediocre, occasionally awful, paintings to the practised 20th-century eye.

Osborne House. Garden, from the Nursery Suite

Among its enthusiastic visitors, the loudest in their praise were the significantly aged, with hearing aids and crutches, in wheelchairs and clutching arms to stand upright. "Look, Mary!" squealed a dear old lady in her S-shaped nineties; "there's old Teddy!" She meant King Edward. Alan Leach and Linda Smith of English Heritage offered sterling information to those, and there were many, awestruck by the sheer quantity of things to see. David Roberts' excellent 'Street in Cairo' (1840) hung next to C.W. Cope's 'Cardinal Wolsey at Leicester Abbey' (1847), one of those group portraits which culminated in his 'The Council of the Royal Academy Selecting Pictures for the Exhibition' (1876) which was a picture selected for the 1876 exhibition by the Council of the Royal Academy. In a plethora of dull, loyal portraits the shimmering technique of Winterhalter proclaims its arrogant superiority: his 'Princess Alice' and 'Prince Ludwig of Hesse' in the dining-room and his 'Prince Philip of Württemburg' and 'Princess Charlotte of Belgium' in the royal nursery suite.

Barton Manor
Anthony Goddard, formerly a City accountant, tired of commuting to London and gave it all up, taking a one-year potted agricultural course at Cirencester in 1973-4. His wife Alix comes from a farming background in Devon, so the challenge would not have seemed quite as daunting to her. Together, they toured the area with a climatological atlas, and found a southtending situation here to be ideal. The Goddards manage, miraculously, to cope with 53,000 visitors a year (no coaches are allowed: they go to Osborne, next door) by employing two permanent gardeners, Judy the Girl Friday, two casual helpers five days a week, and a third in the holidays. Five acres of vineyard were planted in 1976, and the best harvest to date was in 1982, giving 20,000 bottles. Each season is unique, and in 1987 provided 17,000, while 1988 gave a miserly 7,500. Apple wine is a good sideline: they have had to give up Island apples, acquiring Merrydown's ready crushed from Sussex. Barton vineyard's enemies are starlings, so nets are now used, despite their expense; pheasants, and foxes. Luckily the local farmer Richard Orlik runs a pheasant shoot, and foxes, once seen on average twice a week, are now very scarce.

Barton Manor. Alix Goddard

The house, gutted and Victorianised by Prince Albert, has not been Elizabeth the Secondised by the Goddards and is not open to the public. Barton is mentioned in Domesday, but emerges from the shadows only in 1275, when an Augustinian oratory was founded; of this period we have a wall with blocked-up lancet windows near the modern front door. This oratory had the charge of St Catherine's on the Down from 1321.

In 1845 Queen Victoria bought Osborne estate, with Barton as an ancillary farm, and allowed Albert his head in designing Osborne as 'their' country retreat, while rebuilding Barton as a home for royal equerries and visiting royalty, among them King Leopold of the Belgians. Edward VII was one of those royal children who abominated Osborne, and avenged himself by giving it to the nation in 1902, while hanging on to Barton as his own, more modest, country retreat, and laying out terraces down to the lake. It was sold in 1922, and has been a private home ever since. A day could easily be spent in the gardens: the secret garden with a replica of Michelangelo's 'Bacchus', the water garden once Victoria's skating lake, the woodland walk through rhododendrons, in spring the yellow eiderdowns of daffodils, descendants of 225,000 planted in 1924.

I took lunch near Barton Manor at Crossways House, where waitresses in neat uniforms provided Dover sole. A high tea for £2.65 comprised cucumber sandwiches, home-baked scones, butter, jam and cream, a slice of fruit cake and a cup of tea. The only note that Edwardian time had not stood still sounded from the wall, where five prints of impossible drawings by M.C. Escher demurely posited insane simplicities to be studied at your peril, while a group of four breathless trippers arranged themselves in positions scarcely less complicated: "You'd better sit over there", "I'll sit next to you". "Will you be all right over there?" and "I'll sit over 'ere" repeated and subtly adapted till it all subsided again and the menu arrived.

Whippingham

Whippingham is the abandoned site by the Medina of Wippa's hamlet, where his Jutish folk would have fished, sailed, and even farmed. The earliest church has gone, and so has John Nash's, ridiculed by Percy Stone. Instead we have a curious design by the Prince Consort which always strikes me as royal more than religious, echoing to Osborne-like domesticity as one strives to be serious beneath the rising lantern, among creams and browns. Memorials abound like a churchyard turned inside out: there is plenty of food for thought about mortality, from Prince Henry of Battenberg's sarcophagus to memorial tablets for William Arnold, Rev. Matthew Arnold, and ninety Hesse soldiers who died of typhus in 1794. The dedication is to the Anglo-Saxon saint Mildred, great-granddaughter of St Ethelbert, King of Kent, converted by St Augustine in 597. She was born in 660 and educated for a life of discreet service at the Benedictine Abbey of Chelles. Returning from France at the age of 20, she could not become a nun until reaching 25, when she joined a convent on the Isle of Thanet, and was consecrated Abbess there by St Theodore in 690. She died in 725, and shortly thereafter became sanctified.

Whippingham has a churchwarden called R. Cav:s, evidently in harmony with the plentiful rooks all around. The chancel dates from the mid-1850s and the rest of the church from the early 1860s, with Prince Albert in charge of this Osborne estate church throughout, looking over the shoulder of Albert Humbert, who was also responsible for Sandringham. Humbert's too is the memorial to Albert (1864) and the whole place suffers from Persil automatic melancholia of the royal persuasion. It is difficult to ask Her Majesty to snap out of it, and Whippingham doesn't even try, unless one counts the exuberant Art Nouveau metal grille (1897) by Alfred Gilbert.

"I like it", affirmed a stout lady with a fat handbag that might have been stuffed with banknotes or game, and swung with the lethal potential of a ball-and-chain. She sat heavily down, gazing absently at the square crossing tower, suffused with light as if it had just been given a transfusion from heaven.

"Did I tell you our Moira's Dennis was putting string in his garden pond?"

"A lot of it?"

Whippingham. The Medina, from the churchyard

"When I went round Choosday he was filling it up with balls of string, fishing lines, gardening twine, anything he could lay 'is 'ands on."

"Oo-er".

"Said 'e wanted to see 'ow much string 'e could get into it."

"Guinness Book of Records?"

"Just plain pixilated."

I feel guilty about entering Whippingham Church, when I should be on holiday, like a vicar caught reading the Bible at the ballet. What place has more calm and silence, Hymn two hundred and thirty four, Psalm one hundred one five, when I am supposed to be enjoying myself? Eliot's *Four Quartets* made meditation respectable among atheists; Larkin's *Church Going* invited any sceptic to sit among the hassocks embroidered by the Townswomen's Guild. I avert my eyes from the crude daubs of Sunday School children asked to show the Holy Family on the Flight into Egypt: a few vague yellows and black shapes on sheets of crinkled white notepaper drawing-pinned up to honour kids who were there, inside, instead of larking on the swings and seesaw. Mrs Ribbett's turn to do the flowers. Sharon and Gary are getting married, if nobody can think of any good reason why not. Besides, they've lived together for the last three years, so it's nacheral innit? I mean, getting wed, speshally in a church designed by Prince Albert, with a German lantern tower to match and rose windows that shamefacedly copy those in Nôtre Dame de Paris, as if there were no new ideas in stained glass since then. Perish the generation that starts plagiarising for pleasure!

Whippingham. From St Mildred's

Two church ladies guarded the Christian books and pamphlets from thieves and vandals, while chatting in hushed tones at the west end, visitors pouring in from lines of coaches for ritual disappointment. "It's quite nice", said one whitehaired lady in a Norfolk accent, "but it's never St Peter Mancroft." It's quite frigid, actually, but at least the estate cottages and farmhouses the Prince Consort designed have a lived-in feel, their red-brick warmer at least from the outside. Their Germanic symmetry, so agonisingly far from the Englishness of Calbourne's Winkle Street, or the cottages dotted round Wellow or Ningwood, should be viewed charitably in the context of the time, when patronage extended to flush lavatories, wash-basins and a huge playground for the estate school.

Newtown

Newtown Old Town Hall, acquired by the National Trust in 1933, was used as a youth hostel, restored in 1969, then opened to the public from April to September, three afternoons a week, and two more in July and August. From the Old Town Hall steps at the back the view is flat, with wet, heavy clay that was never suited to farming in the first place. Though the main building style is of 1699, a kind of halfhearted Georgian with dull red brick (except for the yellowbricked back) has been grafted on to a much tougher, earlier stone base. The four-columned white wooden porch sits uncomfortably stunted below the tall hipped roof. But, as Dr Johnson observed of women preaching, "it is not done well: but you are surprised to find it done at all" in this rural corner between Newtown River and Clamerkin Lake, where birds outnumber people, and the rustling woods proclaim their antiquity by the gnarling of their twisted oak branches and the depth of bracken. In Walter's Copse red squirrels flicker uneasily in and out of view; droppings betray the presence of dormice. Bluebells and wood anemones snatch at the eye. The Town Copse, also National Trust property, grows hazel, between widely-spaced oaks, which are cut every seven to ten years for hurdles and fences. Organic farmyard manure is laconically advertised at 50 pence a bag. I spoke to a bearded youth of twenty helping out at Clamerkin Farm Park about the quiet life. "Ah," he said "but then you come from the

mainland: a hotbed of vice and perversity. To name but two."
Nearby the Romany Riding Stables offer horsedrawn caravan holidays, probably one of the ideal ways to clip-clop around the Island's 481 miles of road, once you get past the 1 km of dual carriageway, between Newport's Coppins Bridge and St Mary's Hospital. The last time I fenced and feinted with the Coppins Bridge traffic (to the Island what Piccadilly Circus is to London), the Elim Pentecostal Church announced "God can give you a new heart", indicating yet another entrant to the transplant business.

Newtown's mid-thirteenth century streets followed a grid plan similar to that in Newport and the other coastal towns: Brading and Yarmouth. Using the Town Hall as a landmark, its Broad Street is crossed by High Street and Gold Street. Church Street, crossing High Street, continued to the marshland. Aymer, Bishop-elect of Winchester, created Newtown in 1256 but ceded it to Edward I in 1284, except for the advowson of St Mary Magdalene's chapel. Listen as you catch faint glimmers beneath the fields of voices and creaking ships, to the memories of those who called their gull-marked streets 'Gold' and 'Silver' in hope rather than fulfilment. Seventy-three strips of land were marked out in Newtown, and seventy had been taken up by 1297, providing the canny landlord with rents and tolls from the local Wednesday market.

Saltworks are recorded in the Solent area from Saxon times, and may even have existed in the Roman period, but they are known from the Norman age in Newtown Creek, where seven operated in the 17th century and three up to about 1880, the salt being exported from Newtown Quay. Ken the harbour-master can point out the various little embankments where pans were formed to assist in the evaporation of salt.

An annual three-day fair was held almost without interruption until 1781, when ships up to five hundred tons could tie up on Newtown Quay. Jogging everyone's historical imagination, Newtown Randy was held on 12 August 1989, and so you might try around that date in later years, for Punch-and-Judy, fortune-tellers, stalls in and out of period, and a barndance starting at the strange time of 2.30 p.m. 'Randy' has a special meaning on the Island: as well as the usual significance of 'lustful' or 'sexy' it means a country fair, and applies predominantly to Newtown. Now it's sandpipers and oyster-catchers you will hear raising their song in the magical fields of Newtown.

Shalfleet

The New Inn at Shalfleet is considered by some to be the best on the island for seafood, and Nigel Simpson, mine host, catches quite a deal of it in his leisure hours. Mentioned in Domesday, the New Inn still boasts original flagstone floors, and if you're there in winter, log fires bring back times long gone when smugglers were hard to distinguish from innocent boatmen.

"My Frank didn't approve of the Falklands War", announced a fluffy pink cardigan with a Mickey Mouse brooch. "My Gordon did", snapped a tight blue two-piece.

"Your Gordon would. I say, my Frank didn't hold with it."

"My Gordon said he's no time for them Argies."

"What Argies?"

"Them Argentines."

"I'm not *talking* about Argentines. I'm talking about the war against the Falklands."

Oysters and mussels (when in season), lobster and crab make the New Inn something of a find off the beaten track, and its location near the creek offers birdwatchers and hikers a chance to amble up the Western Haven spit to Newtown River itself. Before you start, though, give a second (and third) glance to the magic of Shalfleet, a Saxon name meaning 'shallow creek', as in London's Fleet Street. The manor belonged to a certain Edric in the reign of King Edward the Confessor, but the Church of St Michael the Archangel has nothing Saxon to be seen: the oldest part is the tower, before 1086, with walls more than five feet thick and no outside entrance, until 1889, so that parishioners seeking refuge from sea invaders would be safe. In fact, the tower was built on clay, and the false security of its appearance led thirteenth-century builders to open too wide an arch in it, creating cracks which fourteenth-century buttresses did nothing to halt. A restoration programme in 1889 proved worse than useless, because when the great arch was opened again and a doorway cut into the north-eastern corner of the tower, it took only twenty-five

199

years for that same northeastern corner to cave in and fall. The majestic progress of Shalfleet's Archangel Michael continued with the north doorway (1150), south aisle (1190), Purbeck arcade and widening of the south aisle (1270), chancel (1290), south porch (1450), pulpit (1630), north porch (1754), steeple (replacing a cupola, 1800), removal of steeple (1912), restoration (1931 and 1952), culminating in the luxury of oil-fired central heating (1965) for the less hardy congregation of our days. Incidentally, the original dedication of the church is lost, and its recent dedication dates from 1964. The visitors' book repeats such adjectives, no doubt heartfelt, as 'charming and quaint', 'beautiful', 'peaceful and homely'. Mr and Mrs R. Worsley of Bembridge had inscribed: 'Lovely church, God bless you all!' An elegant slate memorial by David Kindersley commemorates 'Archibald Kindersley 1869-1955' – how far we have come since the riot of baroque fripperies that Sacheverell Sitwell taught us to appreciate in *Southern Baroque Art*! Outside, dandelions covered the grave of Benjamin Mew, departed this life June 13, 1841 aged 18 years. The first Rector of Shalfleet (1271-1309) was John de Insula, one of that family later known as de l'Isle, the frenchified version of the Latin 'Insula', island. Recent vicars have included E. Jenkins (from 1946), A.E. Ward (from 1967) and F.W. Crooks (1974-80), to whom is credited the saying at the time that the Inn was run by A. Monk and the Church by Crooks.

The manor house is regrettably empty as we go to press, but these matters have a way of righting themselves overnight, and the reader is recommended to see what it looks like, as it forms a tiny cluster with inn and church. We've no idea about the original manor house at Shalfleet, though one assumes it was made of wood and burned down, in common with a number of successors. The present house dates from around 1680 – you can see that date on the front porch – though it was clearly erected in at least two phases. The front is charming, but the back has been hacked about to no good purpose, unless you count half a dozen garages a good purpose.

Shalfleet's mixed blessing is that it lies plumb on the main road from Ryde, Cowes and Newport to Yarmouth. Bus no. 7 runs about 10 times a day through the village, and about six times on Sundays, so even without a car no villager need feel cut off. But why live in Shalfleet if you do not want to feel cut off? An idyllic seven-mile walk, with your car parked by the church, will take you south on the west bank of Caul Bourne, over the old railway line to Freshwater, to Eades Farm, Dodpits Lane, crossing the B 3401, recrossing the rail track, into Warlands Lane.

Wellow

West of Newbridge you will come to the little village of Wellow. Sixpenny Cottage used to be a bakery. The little Post Office is a general store. A pipe-smoker coughed hello inside. "A dozen eggs, a packet of firelighters, and an ounce of Bruno", he spluttered. Under the awning, bananas at 45p a lb and plums at 62p a lb yawned and went to sleep again. On the road, splashed with sunlight, a legless man with a knotted handkerchief covering his pate, was shoving himself along on a wooden wheeled tray, grunting spasmodically snatches from Gilbert and Sullivan's *A wandering minstrel, I,* closely followed by another man, also legless, on a similar tray, this

Wellow. Sixpenny Cottage

time painted garden-party white. Could there be a Paraplegic Road Race here, like the Isle of Man's T.T.? Residents of Wellow seemed as perplexed as I was. I never saw the contestants again.

Cranmore

If you relied on road signs, you would never reach Cranmore, or so the crafty locals hope, but the street boasts its own post office at West House, north of the Shalfleet to Yarmouth road, and the village its own vineyard, run by Annette and Norman Valentine, with guided tours over the vineyard, and group tasting in the medium-dry wine from the Mueller-Thurgau grape blended with Wurzer, Gutenborner, and Madeleine Angevine. The unadopted road is not for cars with delicate suspension, but my old Volkswagen Golf battled through to Bouldnor cliff edge, and then I plunged down bramble paths speckled with sunlight into broad Solent views, picking blackberries in early autumn's grace.

Back past Sunningdale Boarding Kennels (Tom and Hazel Laight), as I turned back into the Ningwood Road that evening, a streetlamp cast a downpour of light on the pentagonal side of a house: a whoosh of owlshine.

Swainston Manor and Calbourne

Swainton's Georgian splendour (a hotel open all the year round) stands on the base of the summer palace of the Bishops of Winchester, who owned Swainston from the eighth century to the time of Edward I, the bishop's guest. Edward subsequently became so unpleasant that, to rid himself of the importunity, Bishop John of Pontiserra surrendered it into the greedy royal hands. The ancient stone chapel is dignified and separate. Subsequently, Swainston passed to Mary, sister of Edward II and William Montacute, Earl of Salisbury, who accidentally killed a son of his with a lance while jousting.

But Swainston is not the only mediaeval building at Calbourne, for All Saints' Church has miraculously retained many of its features from that time, though a Norman church is recorded in Domesday and local families have seen fit and proper to alter the place from time to time, particularly the Simeons of Swainston, who rebuilt the north transept and

Swainston Manor. Mediaeval chapel .

burial vault below it in the 19th century, and the Holmeses of
Yarmouth who built the other local mansion, nearby Westover, in the late 18th and 19th centuries. The owners of the
Westover estate over the years have included the de Esturs,
the Lisles, the Erlismans, and the Urrys. The Montacute brass
of 1379 has been fixed to a wall but the tomb vanished, probably when the south transept was enlarged in the 18th century.

The tower has a 13th-century base, the rest – after a fire –
dating from 1752. One might try guessing which features of
All Saints are original and which historicizing imitations. The
simple heavy font is 14th century, but the 'Norman' dog-
tooth arch inside the north porch is conscientious Victorian.
The Barrington Chapel, apparently 13th century, is really the
work of Augustus Livesay in 1842.

I was accosted in the nave by a busy little man, who swivel-
led as he yapped, approving this and disapproving that, and
speaking to me much as he did to his non-committal wife, a
hard-suffering lady in a salmon-pink cardy with a thicker

green pullover over her arm 'just in case'. His tobacco finger waved in a feeble ellipse, sullying my private air like a silent piston.

A pity that a commonplace high white marble war memorial militates against the calm, restful weathered stone of Calbourne houses, as in the renowned Barrington Row, commonly known as Winkle Street. Two ladies with a little girl squeezed between a brand-new Vauxhall Nova (will antiques be called Veterrimae?) and a two-year-old Mitsubishi Colt, beside a little cascade. The eight-year-old girl, Sheryl, scooped up giggles in her cupped hands, but still some managed to escape. Her mother grimaced at the roofs, "pity about the TV aerials", as if it were impossible by a stroke of one's imaginary Tippex brush to erase them right away.

Some of the thatched cottages offer for sale postcards of themselves. At Brookside Cottage John Caudwell, whose wife Celia runs the Afton Gallery in Totland, showed me his prints and painted pebbles, and a grandfather clock by Edward Caudwell of Harwell. Overners, self-conscious like all the British, find it necessary to hold polite conversation with John in his shop, but do so in a predictable manner, revolving in his tidy room the same old questions. "Do you think they get the water from the stream?", "I suppose they have to hoover even in a place like this", "I wonder if they have toilets?", "What do they do in the winter?"

If you want to avoid the commonest questions in Winkle Street, these are they. "Do you get sick of people looking in at your windows?" "Does the stream ever flood?", "Do you have electricity?", "Do the cottages ever come up for sale?" and "Does it ever snow?" The least popular overners are those who park in Winkle Street.

Calbourne Water Mill, open seven days a week from Easter to the end of October, should not be missed even by the hasty. Mr Alan Weeks' family has been connected with the Island since 1878, when George Weeks – an accountant from Brixton – left London to start a new life at Calbourne. His father had been a miller, and the Weeks generations continued the tradition, adding a Museum of Rural Life and ideal picnic spots. The dissatisfied screeching of peacocks razors through the soft cooing of doves in sempiternal competition.

Calbourne. Barrington Row, called 'Winkle Street'

Calbourne has possessed a water mill or two since Saxon times, the first written record dating to Domesday, 1086. Caul spring feeding Mylplace Mill rises in Westover Park, crosses Winkle Street parallel with the cottages, and makes its way to Mylplace. Formerly, the Caul fed four other mills: a cloth factory, a paper factory, and two other cornmills. In the late 19th century, when stone-grinding was generally superseded by roller-mills, many of the traditional country mills went out of business, but Calbourne Upper Place Mill, as this mill was then called, replaced the old wooden wheel with an iron wheel in 1881, and installed a new roller plant in 1894, thus remaining competitive. Stoneground flour must be used quickly to avoid deterioration, so the mill added a bakehouse to its other activities up to 1894. The Museum and Teahouse, once an 1890 storage house, were removed from a farm in Brook, and installed at Calbourne in 1973-4. Domestic bygones, early typewriters, Home Guard memorabilia, a laundrette and a semi-undershot 9-foot diameter water wheel are among the other attractions at Calbourne Mill.

In the tea room, a woman in brown and green slumped aggrieved, farther down in her chair, squat, like a toad in a hole. "He made me play table tennis all weekend," she complained to an angular lady with a pointed nose. "I was like a wet rag. He only stopped for snacks and to go, you know, to be honest, to go to bed sort of thing, individually, in separate rooms." "Tut", responded the beak in a chasm full of boredom, "tut, tut."

Parkhurst

Parkhurst Forest, noted in Domesday Book, which once covered 1,250 hectares, now covers only 492 hectares, roughly its extent when enclosed by Act of Parliament in 1815. You can date some of the great oaks to that period, because earlier tree seedlings would have been destroyed by grazing animals. Nowadays, even more care is taken of oaks: foresters enclose the trunks in an open-topped plastic tube to protect the tree from the abundant rabbits and to accelerate growth.

To enter Parkhurst Forest, look for the Forestry Commission sign about a mile west of Newport on the main highway to Shalfleet and Yarmouth. Red squirrels have not left the Island yet (grey squirrels have not yet moved in) and reds feed on Scots Pine cones. Like most of the island woodlands, Parkhurst was ravaged by the October 1987 hurricane, and many fallen trees have not yet been replaced, but you will be able to find spruce, Japanese larch and Lawson cypress, with a fine stand of Corsican Pine planted in 1928. On Parkhurst's clay soil, conifers are generally being replaced with oaks.

If your blood curdles at the apparition of Abel Magwitch from the prison hulk in *Great Expectations*, think on this. The formidable bulk of Parkhust Prison opposite St Mary's

Hospital across the Newport-Cowes road is the distant offspring of two prison hulks, *Dido* and *Buffalo*, first moored in the Medina to confine between six and seven hundred men, who lived in appalling, inhuman conditions.

The old Albany Barracks hospital was converted for use from 1838 as a training prison for lads who would otherwise have been brutalised in the hulks before transportation. In that way, more than one thousand five hundred boys left for Western Australia and New Zealand with a smattering of school subjects, and practical skills such as farming, joinery, and bricklaying. This flow to the colonies ended in 1852, the last women left in 1869 and since then Parkhurst has remained a jail for men only.

Newport

The Romans inhabited Newport, as we can see from an excavated villa and site museum in Cypress Road, reached from South Street by following Church Litten south and continuing into Medina Avenue. Cypress Road is the third on your right. It is closed on Saturdays but every other day from Easter to September you can visualise life in 3rd-century Wight. This villa is of roughly the same period as Brading's Roman Villa.

The first building on the site is associated with a late first-century ditch; it combined wood and clay with straw, with a roof possibly thatched, as no tiles have been found. We think this home was destroyed by fire in the mid-2nd century, since fragments of burnt daub have been excavated in the ditch. Late in the same century the old ditch was filled in and a villa begun, conforming to the common winged corridor design common elsewhere in Britannia, Gallia and Germania. It is the west wing that contained the bath suite we see today, mostly of local materials, with Bembridge limestone for jambs, roof-slabs and cornerstones. Timber would have been used elsewhere, but all traces have long since perished. Late in the 3rd century, Roman-age Wightmen were attacked by Saxon raiders, and they hid coins, which are dated about 270 from hoards at Farringford and Ventnor. Part of the villa had become a blacksmith's shop by this period, and Newport villa never achieved the security and wealth of its counterpart of Brading, which was adorned by fine mosaics in the 4th century.

The villa was found on Mr. S. Cooper's property in 1926 and, refused by the Ministry of Public Building and Works in 1960, was saved only by the intervention of the Isle of Wight County Council, who still administer the Roman villa today.

These Roman baths correspond to thousands of similar houses and even palaces (like those of Diocletian near Rome's central railway station). From the cloakroom or apodyterium we proceed to the cold plunge-bath in the frigidarium, the cool tepidarium, the hot caldarium, and the sweat-room or sudatorium. An imaginatively-written tape reconstructs a Latin conversation between mistress and kitchen staff. A mid-3rd century corn-drier from Martin Boswell's Parsonage Farm at Newchurch discovered in 1982 is placed just outside the front door, completing the experience of Roman Newport.

The lady in charge, who comes from Niton, has only Saturdays off, working every other day in the season, and spends that day walking all over the island, and taking her camera to record changes, such as Newport before the Gateway development or Luccombe before the destruction of the 300-year-old trees in the furious hurricane damage of October 1987. Overners frequently enquire of her, "How did you get on during the War?", confusing the Island with the German-occupied Channel Islands. I felt regret that the County Council could not afford to buy the surrounding houses to expose the full extent of the Roman villa.

Mediaeval Newport grew up as a settlement serving Carisbrooke Castle, on which the inhabitants were dependent for security during raids by the Danes from 787 and by the French thereafter, up to Napoleonic times, in the last century. Richard de Redvers, Lord of the Isle of Wight, designed his 'new port' on the Medina as an adjunct to connect his capital town and stronghold of Carisbrooke with the Solent at Cowes, and in the 1120s and 1130s you can imagine a track linking Carisbrooke with a neatly laid-out town plan arranged in 'places' or building-plots leased by the Lord of the Isle at one shilling a year each. The regular street plan survives in John Speed's plan of Newport (1611) and thence until today, roughly speaking. The street frontages were built up by about 1600, filling in the meadows previously used for grazing and the pleasant gardens, as Sir John Oglander tells us in 1633. "Since my Memory it was a very poore Towne, the Houses most Thatched, the streets unpaved, and in the Highstrete where now be fayre Houses weare Garden Plottes."

Church Litten Park was the mediaeval archery butts, transformed into a plague cemetery during the outbreak of 1583-4, because up till that time all Newport people had been buried under the auspices of St. Mary's at Carisbrooke. The Tudor gateway still stands. I think of Newport's streets as arrows aimed from Carisbrooke towards the north-flowing Lugley Street, High Street, and Pyle Street (Pyle means 'ford') falling off into South Street. The bullseye would be St. James' Square, with Nash's 1819 five-bay Guildhall classically fronted by upper Doric pilasters. Originally a cattle market, St. James' Square has one of those frantic semi-planned frontages that make one long for the timeless beauty of Siena. Dewhurst's the Butchers is one thing, and the anorexic monument with cuddly lions another, but neither has anything aesthetically in common with the Guildhall (now a Magistrates Court), nor do the English seem to wonder why they should. It is all a mish-mash.

If you pass eastward along High Street by the Bugle Hotel, St. Thomas' Square has its own Victorian charms. The original St. Thomas' parish church of the 12th century was demolished in 1854 to make way for Dawkes's Decorated pile with an Early Victorian interior that looks just as it might have done when Prince Albert laid its foundation stone: a characteristic piece is the Turin sculptor Carlo Marochetti's contemporary memorial of Princess Elizabeth, daughter of Charles I, but the best elements are the much earlier pulpit and screen of 1636 by the Fleming Thomas Caper, and an alabaster monument of Sir Edward Horsey (1583).

The story of Princess Elizabeth, second daughter to King Charles I, is all the more poignant for being so brief. She was born in 1635, six years before her elder sister Mary married William of Orange in that fateful union. At the age of eight, little Elizabeth had given herself up to French and Italian, and could also read Latin and Hebrew. In the unequal struggle for power between the isolated Charles and the groundswell of popular anti-monarchical opinion fomented by the Parliamentarians, it was a foregone conclusion that the intransigent king, whose interests lay in the arts rather than in warfare and administration, would become the first English king to suffer judicial execution, in 1649.

Elizabeth had just turned fourteen and Sir Thomas Herbert noted how on 29 January 1649 she and her young brother, Henry, Duke of Gloucester (then nine, he would die of smallpox in 1660), "came to take their sad farewell of the King their father, and to ask his blessing. The princess, being the elder, was the most sensible of her Royal Father's condition, as appeared by her sorrowful look and excessive weeping... Most sorrowful was this parting, the young Princess shedding tears and crying lamentably, so as moved others to pity, that formerly were hard-hearted; and at opening the bedchamber door, the King returned hastily from the window and kissed 'em and blessed 'em; so parted."

Distracted by her father's death, young Elizabeth died of grief in the presence of her brother the following year at Carisbrooke, where the captain had been commanded "to see that no person should be permitted to kiss their hands and that they should not be otherwise treated than as the children of a gentleman". Carisbrooke was the last royalist stronghold to fall to the Parliament, capitulating in 1642, when the Countess of Portland reluctantly agreed to quit the chambers she and her five children were still occupying. Her garrison included Sir William Hopkins, who a month later accompanied her to Rouen. It was in his house that Charles I lodged while negotiating the Treaty of Newport of 1648.

Queen Victoria desired to create a monument to the tragic princess, and to fill the adjacent north wall windows with stained glass to soften the light falling on Elizabeth's tomb.

I am as scatty as the next Englishman, but the Revd. C.R. Farnsworth, Vicar from 1949 to 1957 must have been even scattier than the next one, for he spent every moment of his spare time constructing an exact scale model of the church, now displayed within. "As the church plans had disappeared", run the notes on the showcase, "Rev. Farnsworth had first to climb to the roof and drop plumb lines to ascertain the height of the walls and tower". (I love the "had to"). "18,808 lines are scratched on the roof to indicate tiles". The present incumbent is Canon J.F. Buckett, whose obsession with the bells recalls Quasimodo's in Victor Hugo's *Nôtre-Dame de Paris*. "They are part of an English tradition," urges the handout, quoting Psalm 127 in support of the English tradition, "sounding on occasions of national celebration or mourning, for Sunday services, for weddings, for funerals. We trust that bells will continue to ring out over Newport, and to that end an appeal has been launched to save the eight bells in St. Thomas' tower and augment the ring to twelve." As if twelve bells were in some way more ecclesiastical than eight. In fact, the original peal of 1674-5 consisted of only six bells, and increased to eight in 1808. So far, over £20,000 has been spent on new bells (they cost about £2,700 each), including £1,156 for fitting gudgeons to headstocks. The original purposes of church bells were to remind parishioners without timepieces that services were about to begin, and to warn them of impending invasion. Neither of these purposes seems to have any more relevance to the present day at St. Thomas' than the Revd. Farnsworth's scale-model.

St. James' Square is distinguished on its southern side by the beautiful God's Providence House, now a restaurant specialising in morning coffee and home-made cakes. Two ladies in competing shades of mauve were making their coffee last over scones and gossip.

"Mrs Golightly says her Bernard has been having more of that trouble."

"Viral meningitis?"

"One who thought he was an airline pilot."

"No!"

"Turns out he *was* an airline pilot. It was Sammy Linford who *thought* he was the airline pilot. Any road, Mrs Golightly's Bernard kept on trying to open the window."

"Bit of a draught".

"The one in the cockpit. They'd all have been dragged out in the upper atmosphere, twenty-seven thousand feet."

"So what happened?"

"They'd to put him in a desk job. Mrs Golightly says all the really crazy pilots are all on desk jobs."

You can immediately appreciate the connection between Carisbrooke Castle and Newport if you stand on the pave-

Newport. Castle Inn

ment at Castlehold, so called because the de Redvers family of the Castle 'held' 13½ of the town's building plots for themselves, without the control of Newport bailiffs. Castlehold consequently became for a time a sanctuary for outlaws. On the corner of Mill Street, the splendid Castle Inn of 1684 has typical blocked-up windows visible in the side wall and a low or 'catslide' roof dropping at the back. Mill Street was named for the Home Mill (now the Creameries): the mill cottages are preserved. Upstream, you can make out Westminster Mill, and downstream along Lukely Brook stands Towngate Mill, past which you can stroll over a bridge to Hunnyhill and the

Holy Cross or Saint Cross Mill, near the site of a Benedictine priory erected in 1120.

As I came round the corner into Chain Lane, two ladies with dogs swirling in yapping eddies around their legs were oblique in conversation, trying to get a word in smudgeways.

"No," interrupted the second, and the first kept her mouth open ready to continue at a tangent, "but I reckon that bloke in the choir'd do lovely for Marcia, he's clean, unmarried from what I hear, and speaks English. What more does she want?"

"He's," bleated the first, "an inSHORance salesman!"

"So what?", shrugged the first, wrinkling her nose to keep her specs up, "I know hundreds of nice inSHORance salesmen." And their helpless giggling in counterpoint reminded me of the uproar every Sunday before 1939 in the Chatsworth chapel. Even in Annigoni's bland portrait, Deborah Devonshire does not look like the kind of girl to keep a straight face in an emergency.

I don't suppose anyone who has visited busy Newport on a market day could ever forget, once heard, the *Recruiting Sergeant* ballad set graphically opposite (*auverright*) the wold Rose and Crown. It is a pity that the term 'gay' sergeant has been corrupted.

> I chanced to be i' Nippert town
> ('T wuz on a maarket day)
> An' auverright t' 'Rose and Crown'
> I met a zargeant gaay.
>
> Hes hair wuz iled, hes cap atop
> Wuz bunched wi' hribbons vine;
> Hes coat wuz laaced, hes trousies vaaced
> Each zaid wi' a hred line.
>
> Zhouts he, a ztridin' oop an' down,
> A gorgeous zight to zee,
> "Hroll oop, my lucky lads, hroll oop,
> An' jine our grand armee."

The farmer's lad proved too canny for the sergeant, however, preferring his stake or *zool* to which sheepfold hurdles were attached, to the sword or gun offered as a bait.

"Wi' zwords an' guns aw'm not acquent,
I'd liever use a zool.
Ten't in my waay, my zargeant gaay;
Goo: dry another vool.

None o' yer blood an' war vor me,
I'll baide at hwome I vow.
Cuckoo," zaays I, "Goo to, zaays I,
I'll ztick to meyaster's plough."

Newport F.C., alongside Church Litten, is the leading soccer club on the island. Where do soccer fans go when the season is over, and the F.A. Cup won and lost? The losers in 1989 were Everton, and at least one of their supporters, a middle-aged man of mournful countenance, was looking towards the empty pitch as though if he concentrated hard enough and rubbed his magic lamp, a genie would produce two teams, three officials and a ball. His blazer, starched into rigor mortis, displayed a sewn badge that cried out for attention. 'Nihil nisi optimum', it craved: 'nothing but the best'.

My favourite part of Newport is the Quay area, around Quay Street and Sea Street, with the Quay Arts Centre its focal point, overlooking the Medina. Exhibitions of local and international artists (quilters, photographers, Manet and Lowry) are supplemented by classes and courses in a wide range of activities from juggling and unicycling to writing and dance.

I took tea and buns in the café upstairs at the Quay Arts Centre (nothing substantial being on offer), where a furtive man and his mistress were discussing their next illicit meeting in tones that Agatha Christie fans would recognise as authentic St Mary Mead, and a girl of nineteen waved to a pair of chirping friends "Just goina ava blow-dry at Winkie's", a notable hairdressing salon in St James' St. A night-black cat peered round the doorway, its green eyes piercing as lasers, then as suddenly disappeared.

If the Island seems a sleepy backwater in arts terms, then Newport can offer traditional entertainment (plays, concerts and a piano-accompanied *Traviata* by Welsh National Opera at the elegant new Medina Theatre just outside Newport in the modern Mountbatten Centre, where parking – unlike elsewhere in Newport – poses no problem), but also the active support of the Quay for artists and writers. But the Quay Arts Centre suffers from the chronic underfunding usual in the provinces throughout Britain.

I met Paul Hancocks of the *Isle of Wight County Press* there, and enquired about live issues in the local community which recur in letters to the local paper. Unreliable ferries. Resentment among young people against the high prices overners are willing to pay for retirement homes, effectively pricing first-time buyers out of the market. Discrimination against islanders on the mainland. Headlines in recent weeks that I noted included '45 firemen fight blaze at Newport timber yard', 'Ombudsman drawn into Cowes town centre row', and 'Ryde heart swap mum tells of "will to live".'

I strolled along the Quay, and found a rabies notice on the column holding up the roadbridge above. It was in English, French, German, Dutch, Italian, Spanish and Russian, warning of the illegality of importing pets without lodging them first in quarantine. I had visions of two Russians cursing at

Newport. Quay Arts Centre

215

the ban on their pet poodle. Three young lads were slightly abseiling under the bridge with a length of car tow rope. 'The Harbour is Private', warned another notice. 'Parking Charge: £20 per day or part thereof'. Beside the Pirate Ship ("Don't leave the island till you've been to the wonderful world of pirates") I shook my head like any pious citizen at the glorification of Long John Silvers that dear RLS fostered. Shall we ever see paedophiles, mass rapists, or hijackers elevated to the romantic pinnacle occupied by Gilbert and Sullivan's Penzantine prancers, or Sir Walter Scott's Pirate, Captain Clement Cleveland? Good old savagery, that British standby since long

Newport. Pirate Ship

216

before Jack the Ripper and Dr Crippen, always seems to fire the imagination. I preferred the Riverside Multipurpose Centre, intended to promote wellbeing in work and leisure for the handicapped and disabled in Newport, with a stage, restaurant, workshop, and lounge.

I was sipping my rum and coke in the lounge at the Newport Quay Hotel, when my eye was caught by a whiff of Givenchy reminiscent of Pamela Stanton's perfumery on Scarrots Lane.

"What is it that you do?", purred a luxuriant fur coat with scarlet lipstick, suggesting that if I played my cards right she might not curl her lip in contempt.

I scratched first one hair on my head, then the other, in a vain attempt to appear blasé, like a flea-bitten mongrel at the threshold of Cruft's.

"Qu'est ce que c'est que vous faites?" she repeated, in the manner of Angela Rippon repeating that Yugoslavia had scored another 'nulle point' to add to their previous tally of zero.

"I suppose you could say that I amble fairly harmlessly round the globe looking around and chatting to people", I offered, a Muslim thief presenting his hand for amputation.

"Sacre bleu," she murmured in a mixture of apathy and admiration, "you must get very lonely."

"That's right," I said, offering my begging bowl for sympathy like a Buddhist in a sex parlour. "Only eight people died in the Great Fire of London. All the others escaped, but I never heard where they went. Their descendants might be scraping a meagre living somewhere near Totland to this day. One per acre. Lonely isn't the half of it: they must be dug in for a lifetime and hereafter in perpetuity of hesychasm."

"Hesy what?" sniffed the blonde.

"Chasm," I replied, cracking the bones in my knuckles to fill in the pause.

The following night I swam in black mud during eternal night eventually touching a wall: the cul-de-sac that is every travel-writer's terror. I turned over, and scribbled for six months in invisible ink that dried the moment it was written. No use: I switched on the bedside lamp and wrote salvation into tomorrow's script: Shangri-La over the horizon, the fabled city you have been seeking all these years. "No stranger has ever set foot across its four portcullises, and here are the four keys to the realm."

I digress because that is what travellers actually do, replacing accepted conventions with tropical colours and unexpected vibrancy, unfamiliar faces and names out of legend: Chimborazo, Tamanrasset, Khiva, Godshill and Yaverland. Instead of Natwest and Commercial Union you see Behari Lal's bazaar and masks by Giglioli di Venezia, sea-spume gathering and spattering, vivacious Masai and Koreans splintering your routine with their words and manners, like pierrots in a grocery.

I opened a *Cornish Times* that a recent arrival had left in the lounge. The classified advertisements column offered "Rabbit run, enclosed except for one end."

Lugley Street is one of those peculiar roads that gives English eccentricity a good name: Lazy Kate's Coffee Shop, with spinning lessons arranged at 23a, the Island Sugarcraft Shop with cake decorating demonstrations at 23, a restaurant called Top Cat at 48, where burgers and steaks can be found made of doubtless the traditional ingredients, and at 19 Not Just Gnomes, where other ornaments are indeed to be found, as well as macrame and chess sets. For bed and breakfast I recommend that atmospheric Seal House at 30 Sea Street if you want to be near Lukely Brook and the Medina. Within easy walking distance of Carisbrooke Castle is Martinique, 94 Carisbrooke Road, offering dinner on request, and a heated pool in season.

For shopping, Scarrots Lane abutting on the length of St. James' Street has its own special atmosphere, with the aroma of fresh bread from the Market Bakery and the gleam of fresh oils at the New Rembrandt Gallery. I did ask, but the new Rembrandt wasn't in. Outside the shop a little Chinese man scurried past masked in a gentle whimsical smile one remove from reality: very Deng Xiao Ping.

Newport is the best island starting-point for using a Southern Vectis Rover ticket, available on buses and Island BR trains in units of one day, one week or four weeks. It was at the bus station that two female overners were discussing the suitability of a suitor known to only one of them.

"I told 'er, I wooden 'ave nuthin to do with im, fiewozer."

"Why not?"

"Stans treason, dunni'? E's the kynoo car waiter grinniz vest an' lager to watch *Neighbours* withiz legs splayed out like a ruptured cart'orse." Beyond them I noted a kindred spirit. She was the kind of woman who pretends not to notice anything that happens in bus shelters, while avariciously hoarding every voice and gesture for a future novel of manners that would swivel between the suave acerbities of P.D. James and the gentle ironies of Barbara Pym, never making up her mind which until her deathbed scene, when, relaxing fully for the first time in her worried life she would at last realise that nothing matters, even realising that nothing matters.

They all got on to the number seven bus to Sandown.

Carisbrooke

Nothing on Wight is more magical than Carisbrooke, Wihtgarasburh, its late Roman fort underlying the present Norman stronghold, with two waterwells, one more or less in the centre of the complex, and the other deep in the keep. The Great Well of 1150 was sunk to a depth of 160 feet after Baldwin de Redvers' supply had failed. Water was brought to the surface by working a donkey pulling round a wheel 15' 6" in diameter. By such frail, vulnerable devices are islands won and lost.

At the well-house, Tracey introduced us to the latest generation of Carisbrooke donkeys: bone-idle Archie, Julia, Josephine, Jessica and her daughter Elizabeth, and the patient Jenny, three and a half years old. There is a five-second drop to the water level. The water is still drinkable, at a pinch, the table diminishing from forty feet in winter to twenty-two feet in summer, on average. The prisoners took $3\frac{1}{2}$ years to dig the well in 1587, and the oaken wheel, weighing $1\frac{1}{2}$ tons, is still in use more than four centuries later. Donkeys live up to the age of forty, but will be retired to Sidmouth's Donkey Sanctuary from Carisbrooke when they reach 27 or 28. 'In emergency', reads the notice, 'break the glass', behind which is a lone carrot.

The heart of Carisbrooke, however, is the Great Hall, and has been so for more than seven hundred years. Its life began

219

as a huge, austere stone hall, of one high storey, perpetually rank with smoke from a central hearth, for one slip of a hole in the roof would have made not a smatter of difference, despite all the good intentions. The 'modern' fireplace was provided about 1400, but it was not until George Carey's period in the 16th century that the upper floor was added and a porch introduced; in the 18th century the present staircase was provided. The Great Hall, the Governor's House until 1944, became the Castle Museum, incorporating the Isle of Wight Museum from Newport, together with the Island's premier museum.

Everyone will choose their favourite exhibits: mine are the 1549 cannon called 'The Carisbrooke Falcon' (on loan from the Tower of London) and an easily overlooked little early Norman ivory draughtspiece found in a nearby well, and bought in 1961 from the City of Norwich Museums. It shows a Norman soldier wearing chainmail at an open drawbridge, and must be from a sophisticated artistic centre of Norman art such as Rouen. On the stairs, enjoy C.W. Cope's oil painting depicting 'The Death of Elizabeth' (1855), a fine example of historical narrative. On the upper floor do not miss E. Hoffheimer's chamber organ of 1602, claimed to be the oldest operational instrument of its type; and a chair from Farringford, Tennyson's home.

At the lowest levels, the bastion walls date from the late 16th century, an Elizabethan precaution to protect the Norman middle level, the curtain wall, (1140-50), and the Norman keep on the highest level, which one has to imagine much higher in its heyday, reached at the farthest end opposite the western entry, through the massive gatehouse, its outer part of 1335-6. During the 14th century, the French attacked the castle several times, but it was never captured.

A teenage girl in a tight-fitting multi-coloured skirt, terrified of tripping over her highest of all heels, clung round the waist of her gum-chewing boy-friend and never looked up. Her hair was the colour of the sun's glory, but her voice was afflicted with the dead fall of a mousetrap clacking shut: sneering, ruthless, shrewd, egotistical, the Madonna of Pizzaburg.

Nobody will let alone the tragic ghost of Charles I, the

martyr-king of Stuart hero-worship. One November evening in 1647, he was helped to escape from close arrest at Hampton Court Palace and led away. Charles knew there were rumours of attempts by the Levellers to assassinate him, and sought refuge on the Island, where royalists were in a majority. The Governor of Carisbrooke then was the Parliamentarian Colonel Robert Hammond, nephew to the Royal chaplain Dr Henry Hammond and thus divided in loyalty. Cromwell was thought by Andrew Marvell to have been responsible for the king's 'escape' from Hampton Court:

'And Hampton shows what part
He had of wiser art;
Where, twining subtle fears with hope,
He wove a net of such a scope,
That Charles himself might chase
To Carisbrooke's narrow case.'

Cromwell wrote to his 'dear Robin', "Seek to know the mind of God in all that chain of providence whereby God brought thee thither, and that Person to thee." Charles found that he was under house arrest at Carisbrooke quite as effectively as at Hampton, when his riding privilege was withdrawn and his attendants dismissed with a contempt we recognise from Goneril and Regan in *King Lear*, after an attempt at rescue had failed and the attempter, Captain Burley, executed. We can visualise Charles walking the ramparts (*Hamlet* must be the operative play here), playing on the bowling-green laid out for him on the east bailey, and writing, meditating and reading to pass the time. We know he read the Bible, Herbert's *Divine Poems*, Tasso, Ariosto, and Spenser's *Faerie Queen*. Lines from Claudian struck a sympathetic note, and he copied them out:

'Fallitur egregio quisquis sub Principe credit
Servitium; numquam Libertas gratior extat.
Quam sub rege pio.'

(He is in error who believes submission to a good prince slavery; never does Liberty show more charmingly than under a pious king.)

History was passing by this most monarchical of monarchs, who – in the speech shortly before execution – impatiently denied the power of this temporal court to try him. Instead of answering the charge of High Treason 'and other High Crimes against this Realm of England,' he interrogated the Court's authority and jurisdiction. Charles answered, "When I was here last, it is very true I made that question. And truly if it were only my own particular case, I would have satisfied myself with the protestation I made the last time I was here, against the legality of this Court, and that a King cannot be tried by any superior jurisdiction on Earth. But it is not my case alone, it is the freedom and liberty of the people of England, and do you pretend what you will, I stand more for their liberties, for if power without Law may make laws, may alter the fundamental laws of the Kingdom, I do not know what subject he is in England that can be sure of his life or anything that he calls his own. Therefore when that I came here, I did expect particular reasons to know by what law, what authority, you did proceed against me here."

After another farcical attempt to escape, which failed simply because Charles was too large to get through the bars on his window, he remained at Carisbrooke till 6 September 1648, when he was removed to the Grammar School at Newport, as a prisoner on parole, attending meetings to negotiate a treaty with him which failed because he constantly reaffirmed the divine right of kings, and would not come to terms with Parliament, a firmness, or intransigence if you like, which led to his execution.

Even on a sunny August afternoon, shadows on the wall seem to mock at Parliament's justice, which killed a man because he would not conform, a judicial murder which would lead – some might think inevitably, though that would be a fallacy of hindsight – to the Restoration of the Stuarts and the long-term sympathy of the British with their monarchs whether Stuart, Hanoverian or merely capriciously selected from the commonalty.

A plump dumpling of a woman, with a wrestler's hairy armpits, was listening listlessly to a guide near the gatehouse. She slumped from foot to foot slowly, shifting her weight as if wearing wellingtons full of muddy water, her floral cotton frock challenging the island's gaudiest marquee.

A Roman villa was found in the Vicarage garden and part-excavated in 1859, justifying the supposition that remains of a masonry wall at the foot of pre-Domesday earthworks both east and west may be of Late Roman age.

It was at Carisbrooke Priory that the monks administered on behalf of the Norman Abbey of Lyre, near Évreux, William FitzOsbern's gift of the Island's wealthiest churches at that time: Arreton and Freshwater, Godshill and Newchurch, Niton and Whippingham.

They ran a farm using local labour, and a mill called Priory Mill, with a millpond still visible today from the gardens of the Eight Bells in the High Street.

In the pub itself, a woman Jezebelled in jade green, with a matching chiffon scarf, partially eclipsed by her barrelly husband, lunged words at her thin friend Greta as if they would only catch hold if delivered with a thrust: a naked rapier-point. Greta knew seven answers out of ten, but would always be vulnerable. Did you *really* want rotund Malcolm, set in his ways, desirable only because owned by her best friend?

Carisbrooke

A cloth-capped man stood outside on the pavement, in some dubiety, as if looking for the next train. But the last passenger train through Carisbrooke, Don Vincent tells me, was the 9.34 p.m. from Freshwater on Sunday 20 September 1953.

The Church of St Mary the Virgin soars up its more modest hill quite as proudly as the castle keep up the higher mound. Its associated ranges of buildings have gone, and the priory itself suffered nothing but problems from Isabella de Fortibus in the 13th century to Henry V, in 1414, who dissolved all alien priories, and gave Carisbrooke to the Jesus of Bethlehem Priory at Sheen (Surrey), who in turn leased the buildings to Sir John Leigh of Appuldurcombe, so that by marriage it passed to the Worsleys, then to Sir Francis Walsingham, subsequently Secretary of State to Elizabeth. Walsingham demolished the chancel on the strange grounds that the church would be quite large enough without it! In 1645 Charles I presented the living to Queens' College, Oxford, who are the present patrons.

The barnlike nave is light and spacious, with six pillars down the centre of 1190 replacing a plain wall. The irregular roof beams are five hundred years old. The magnificent ornate tomb of Lady Margaret Wadham depicts six of the cripples for whom she founded a charity hosptial. Aunt to Lady Jane Seymour, third wife of Henry VIII, Lady Margaret is an ancestor to the founder of Wadham College, Oxford. The 1658 pulpit is a rare example from the Commonwealth period, staid and solid as you like. The chart of the Vicars of Carisbrooke is a drumroll of names chanted out of the hazy past from Alvietus, 'Henry I being king' in 1114, to Michael Cooper from 1981, who wrote in his *Parish Press*: "Put your trust in Him, in God who is Father, Son and Holy Spirit. Ask Jesus Christ to come and live within you for to be born again is truly to enter into eternal life which nothing can remove or destroy. If you would like to know more of this wonderful God, please write to me at the Vicarage or phone 522095."

In the next column, on 522071, the *Press* advertises "Stevens Take Away for all the family, every evening but Sunday, visit us for lunch, even cold meats, noted for our gateaux, so why not give us a look in." Correspondents can become testy with the Victoria Sports Club. "I am one of these regular dog walkers and have always carried my doggy bag with me long before you placed the litter bins and I do agree with you that everyone should clear up after their dogs but I feel in all fairness to myself and the many doggy walkers who will agree with me that it would be so much more in aid of health if we could find the doggy litter in the grass that is becoming a jungle." Four irate signatories join pens: "Yes, we do agree that dog's excretia must be picked up and you'll find that the LADIES do so, but we do object to the verbal abuse that comes from various members of this Sports Club. There was no mention of the condoms that decorate the Recreation ground especially those that hang on the children's swings from time to time. Kiddies were actually seen playing with them." Parish magazines were never like this a hundred years ago.

Shide

Steak-and-kidney pie at the Barley Mow in Shide I found to be excellent for a sharpzet stomach, home-cooked in the authentic British style, with real ale served by Fred Clayton. In the *County Press* motoring ads I noted "Austin Allegro 1975, 1100cc, taxed May, MOT June, elderly driver must go". The elderly driver whose departure was thus peremptorily announced must have been first cousin to the decrepit pensioner at the next table, suffering from the hangdog air of an Englishman in a studio audience compelled to sit through yet another incomprehensible monologue by Billy Connolly.

A loud salesman in a bow-tie was trying to attract his attention. "Did you know," he nudged, "That in Britain we ate eight *billion* packets of crisps, nuts and nibbles last year alone?" The pensioner gazed into the mists of time, a TV junkie without a set. "I work it out," pursued the salesman, "correct me if I've made a bloomer, that's 140 bags of snacks for every man, woman and child in the land, straight up. What do you make of that, sir?" Little or no reaction, unless you call a slight sniff a reaction. "And what do you estimate to be Britain's favourite savoury snack?" Nothing. "Hula Hoops, my friend. Eighteen years old this year, dear sir. The best. One point three million packets eaten every day. Can't abide them myself, but what a slice of the market, eh? Now that's what I *call* selling."

I felt like shouting "Fire!" to rescue the stunned old man, whose only protection against verbal pollution seemed to be premature death, but as usual edged away into a universe temporarily deprived of shrill salesmen. As I emerged gratefully into the oxygen a woman in beige, with teeth to match, was suggesting to her hunched male companion that stages should be raised so ballerinas didn't have to dance on points to be seen properly. She ran her index finger thoughtfully over the bloody pool of tomato ketchup left on her plate, and sucked along its length with repressed abandon.

Another year I drove the single-lane road from Blackwater to Whitecroft Hospital for the insane opened in 1896, then after Whitecroft the road opened again to a double lane to Carisbrooke, signposted Newport, your first spectacular view across the fields to the castle being from St Dominic's Priory for Dominican nuns, a Dracula-period pile of 1865-6 in which you would not cheerfully incarcerate your worst enemy.

Arreton

I never visit the Island without halting at the place of Eadhere's folk, Eadhere's Tun, which by degrees was named Adrintone, Artone, Atherton, Adderton, and now Arreton, its last remaining Saxon burial mound on the Down a fitting reminder of the area's long history. The nebulous figure of St George, familiar to those who have lived in Lebanon as an early martyr, seems to possess few church dedications in England, despite being our patron saint. Alfred the Great named the manor in his will, read on his death in 901, and the manor has belonged to Edward the Confessor and many other monarchs, among them William I, William II, Henry VIII, Elizabeth, James I and Charles I.

The church has a Saxon doorway in the west wall forming the original entrance but within a few decades the land fell to the Normans, who continued the building. The great 13th-century tower was buttressed in the 15th, giving a peculiar stepped appearance. From 1131 to Henry VIII's reign four centuries later, Arreton was held as Quarr Abbey's jewel in their crown, rich agricultural land distant from embattled coasts

226

and politicking mainlanders.

St George's visitors' book has the usual right-hand column headed 'Remarks'. Eadie and Edna Connolly of Hartlepool had written "very nice", Mr and Mrs Broughton of Colchester had noted "peaceful", and R. and E. Croucher of Lowestoft had written "Suffolk".

Within the church, a tiny early Norman stained-glass window miraculously preserves a picture of the Crucifixion in that most fragile of all substances, above the Geary memorial plaque, delicate flesh tints gleaming amid startling crimson and heavenly blue. The other striking feature is the Sir Leonard Thomas Worsley Holmes memorial, celebrating the last in the line of Isle of Wight Worsley baronets. "He died on 10th January 1825 in the 38th year of his age and left to lament his loss a widow and three infant daughters of whom the youngest Isabella within a few days of his interment was consigned to her father's tomb." There is something both chilling and warming about such a monument, preserving for all time and for all visitors no matter how worldly or cynical the private grief of a matron and two inconsolable daughters. J. Haskell's carving (1829) represents the summit of local craftsmanship, each laconic arm almost weightless in sorrow, yet giving pulsating life to the compositional harmony. Haskell's drapery too is very fine, with its strong and subtle reminiscences of Greek sculpture.

Possibly the folk of Arreton are not excitably religious but the fact that their church is clearly also a material possession common to all signifies their tenacity through generations. God is with them, perhaps, but only on their terms: it is Arreton men who buttressed His church: without them it would have collapsed. Harvest festivals form a natural part of their seasons. Inertia is the pleasant obverse of fanaticism, contributing to permanence like an oak being left alone by loggers. At Arreton I felt the dull glow of reassuring stability defiantly beyond a world liable to conflagrations.

Five and a half centuries after the event I found a brass commemorating Harry Hawles, one of those who fought at Agincourt with Henry V and would have responded with more vigour than most to the exhortations of his royal namesake. Shakespeare asks his Oliviers to "Cry God for

Harry, England, and St George!" and this Harry, "long-tyme steward of the Yle of Wyght" as the verse describes him, survived the victory at Agincourt by a full fifteen years. The restless may employ their time at St George's rubbing brasses (enquiries to M.J. Flux at 14 Fort St., Sandown), but this parish church is a light, airy place to close your eyes and contemplate, emerging clarified.

Arreton Manor welcomes up to fifty thousand visitors in an eight-month season, and Wight magic works here as eloquently and ubiquitously as at Appuldurcombe or Carisbrooke, Borthwood Copse or Whale Chine. The surrounding downs teem with lolloping rabbits, Civil War battles rage around the Arreton Pageant (August's first Sunday) and a Museum of Childhood displays such rarities as Punch-and-Judy dolls and a Romanian jointed-limb doll of about 1900.

The manor house, lived in by Nicholas and Jeanne Schroeder with their young family, stands on the site of earlier inhabitants, very possibly Romans, certainly Saxon, but reached an apogee of fame and prosperity under the monks of Quarr in the 13th century. The house we see today, graceful yet solid, informal yet imposing, was begun in 1395 and completed in 1612, apart from the porch of 1639. The striking wolfhounds protecting the entrance are marble copies of Roman originals in the Uffizi dating to about the year 35. The eastern wing presents features of an earlier hall-house erected by Quarr monks, but there is no severity or austerity in the hollow chamfered mullion windows, the worn stone stairways, the oak-panelled screen said to date from 1396, or the magnificent dining-parlour, as intimate as Osborne is stately.

The monks' Great Hall once stood where the present Hall and Dining-Room preserve marvellous late Elizabethan oak panelling from the west bedroom. The wooden figures of Mercy and Justice represent the spirit of the law, and project from the mantlepiece where the coat of arms of Sir Thomas Bennet occupies the centre.

At the foot of the stairs is a sampler made by Ann Preston (1763) and on the stairs the owners have glassed over a section of 'wattle-and-daub'. A splendid Tudor four-poster bed can be seen in the west bedroom. An Echoes of Childhood Museum fills the attics, where woodworm ravaged floors and beams undeterred for centuries, but left the floor joists virtually intact.

Arreton Manor Library possesses what one might think of as a country squire's collection, with the complete works of Bulwer Lytton and Harrison Ainsworth. A lady in a smart cream cotton dress and pearls confided in her companion, softly as rumours, "My Roger was given the straight choice for promotion. He said it's either Hong Kong or Kidderminster. What shall it be, love, he said, to Linda, and she said..." They drifted out of earshot before I could catch the consummation.

I passed through a secret door, into the former gunroom, where smoothing-irons and early sewing machines will delight the serendipitously-minded. The 14th-century part of the house, on the site of the monks' main hall, displays wooden bygones and other treasures from the neighbourhood.

In a new Fabric and Fashion Accessories Museum I found examples of local lace, with examples from Malta and Honiton, and shoes made for Emily West, a full-term baby yet so small that she was cradled in a padded shoe box.

The National Wireless Museum of the Wireless Preservation Society brings back the curved horn loudspeakers from 1922 which feature on HMV labels, crystal sets with catswhiskers and headphones for – I recall – the apparent purpose of transmitting thunderstorms, and a wartime aircraft radio of the RAF type TR9 covered with barnacles after rescue from a single-seater sunk in the Solent. Arreton has one of the six surviving Logie Baird televisors which, after multiple developments, ended by changing our lives. Where better to take a cream tea than in the Jacobean tearoom? Especially if two gentlemen who can't resist an argument are dunking scones into their fresh cups of tea beside the great fireplace. They were speaking of the joys and sorrows of telly-watching, especially sport.

"Never watch cricket meself. I prefer team games like rugger or football."

"Cricket's a team game."

"Yerwo'?"

"Eleven a side."

"We got a right one 'ere. Ses cricket's a team game. 'Ave yer never watched it?"

"Aye".

"You *can't* 'ave. Does one bowler come on?"

"Aye".

"Does 'e aim at one batsman at a time?"

"Aye".

"It's one on one! If the batsman gets out, the bowler wins. If the batsman hits out, the batsman wins. One on one!"

"I never thought o' that. I suppose it's not allowed for the bowler to pass to someone on his side to get the batsman out."

"Sright. And if the batsman misses, there's nobody on his team to protect the wicket for 'im."

"The goalkeeper's like be'ind the stumps".

Haseley

Between Arreton and Newchurch, I stole a slight diversion, a couple of hours from eternity, for the manor at Haseley, owning the Island's longest stone barn, with one, two, three, four double-doors and – a bit of a let-down, perhaps – a corrugated iron roof instead of Island thatch. A pottery, craft-shop and

Downend, Arreton. The Hare and Hounds

tea-room invite the casual visitor, and indeed you may try potting yourself if you have never done so. A mini-railway carries you round the grounds, and within the house twenty rooms transport you back centuries, as if through the pages of English history.

Outside the restaurant, a white polo-necked beauty glanced with hatred at her white handbag. "O *Ba*singstoke! " she swore softly enough for all to hear, "I've left my Right Guard in the Ladies' at Farringford."

You enter from the west, though the ancient road from the north once provided the only connection that high green-sanded Haseley had with the surrounding world, cut off as it was on three sides by the marshy Eastern Yar. The origins of Haseley are lost in antiquity, but in 1136 it was granted by a Norman lord, de Bohun, to Quarr Abbey, who promptly extended the Saxon manor house with a new Wool Room, for the manufacture of woollen cloth, and added a fulling mill. After Henry VIII dissolved Quarr in 1536, it was bought by a Southampton merchant called John Mill, who acquired Haseley in 1538 and used some of the greenish-tinted stone from razed Quarr. After the Mills, the manor passed in the early 17th century to Sir Thomas Fleming, Lord Chief Justice, and the Flemings lived there or leased it to tenants until 1952, when it was sold, and by the mid-1970s stood empty. With the good fortune that Island manor houses seem to attract (except for Knighton Gorges, say, or poor burned out Black Pan, the smallest manor in Wight's Domesday), Haseley attracted Raymond and Krystyna Young, who moved into their restored Wool Room in 1977 and since then have conscientiously removed tons of rubble, revealing the old open fireplace, and repaired, renewed and restored in a delirium of dedicated hard work quite beyond praise. Haseley, like its close neighbour Arreton, should be held up as an object lesson to anyone questioning the value of private enterprise and the zeal of a couple seeking to allow history to speak in its own way.

Newchurch

After looking around the church in Newchurch, don't miss the historic Pointer Inn, dating back more than six centuries. Strong's country bitter may be your choice: I opted for a locally-caught trout while listening to a carful of sky-blue supporters from Coventry City ignoring the pub, the church, and the Island as a whole.

"We would've won the trivia quiz if Jack'd only remembered who Larry Lloyd was." Jack bridled with some heat, bolstered by another bitter. 'It was Steve Heighway I forgot." "Emlyn Hughes", interjected a third sky-blue scarf with a moustache. "Played right-back." "He never", admonished the first speaker. "We got everybody but the right back. Or was it right half." "Ar", agreed a fourth character in a greasy blazer with gilt buttons, "it was that one on the left wing, I can't never remember his name. Scored that goal on television. Jimmy Callaghan."

Havenstreet

Whenever I see a flapping bird black as creosote I always remember the wise words of my Uncle Giles who, with an inflatable red plastic parrot on his left shoulder, for the last fourteen years of his life felt certain he was a Long John Silver.

"Jim lad", he said to me when we were walking in the lanes

Havenstreet. Steam Railway

round Muskham, "if ever you see five crows together they be rooks, and if you see one rook together, be sartin it's a crow." Havenstreet by the station (1926), caw blimey, is one cacophonous Bisley of a rookery. For a bit of peace and quiet I clambered aboard the whooshing, pampered steam train pulled by the engine 'Calbourne' and we whistled our way through green fields by Great Briddlesford Farm and Woodhouse Farm. It doesn't take long to get to Wootton Station, which is actually quite a long way near Wootton Village, and is located south of Wootton Bridge and north of Wootton Common.

But Havenstreet is not only notable as the modern headquarters of Nostalgic Steam Trains Incorporated. It is also a starting-point for the exploration of Firestone Copse, north of the railway line. Take the turn at the end of the village and you will plunge into 66 hectares of pure and mixed stands of broadleaved and conifer trees, herons throughout the year, and waders in winter. Spring is the time to admire wild daffodils and primroses. Summer is for butterflies – not the reddish-orange Glanville Fritillary confined to southern downs, but Marbled Whites, Small Tortoiseshells, White and Red Admirals. Autumn provides guelder-rose berries for hungry woodland birds.

Away Again

Just as a connoisseur of paintings will change the display on his walls so regularly that every painting he owns becomes an unexpected revelation, with details that he had forgotten, like the little dog in Carpaccio's *St Jerome*, so I feel it is necessary to live on the mainland to enjoy the Isle of Wight, coming across fresh views and changing aspects which an islander will take for granted.

A lady stock auditor from Cowes joined me on the Sealink ferry *St Cecilia* from Fishbourne. Her husband is an islander and she, born in Portsmouth, crossed the Solent to marry him in 1963. Their children went to Cowes High School but, typically of the younger generation, had to (or chose to) find employment beyond Wight. Fifty per cent of her friends are overners, and she does not find the antagonism towards incomers that is encountered for instance in Wales, or the Lake District

National Park, where house prices are forcing local people out of the market-place. She is a member of the Ladies' Circle, equivalent to the men's Round Table, and of the Cowes Tangent Club, a ladies' version of the 41 Club. She takes holidays in Cornwall, and goes shopping in Southampton by hydrofoil. The atmosphere in Cowes fostered in her son a lifetime's passion for sailing. Her local beach is Gurnard. Everyone is friendlier on the Island than on the mainland; crime is petty and the occasional vandalism silly rather than vicious. But she does lock her front door when she goes out these days; earlier generations did not bother.

The *St Cecilia* (gross tonnage 2968; crew 13; maximum passengers 1,000) eased itself on to the quay at Portsmouth. A cormorant (*could* it have been a cormorant?) dived away, behind the stern, challenging me to follow it. It flew straight – whatever it was – across the Solent, the way we had come. I felt again that tug of desire to see Chale and the Needles, Brading and Newtown, all that Wight magic.

Epilogue

A little scene in St Mary the Virgin, Brighstone.

I have a benevolently clerical look about me, and was taken for a Catholic priest even while excitedly holding hands with my wife in a Maltese bus at the age of thirty. In my black polo-neck sweater a Mosta-bound farmer addressed me as 'Father'.

One late afternoon, while the sun tried to get in through the windows of St Mary's for one last glance, an eighteen-year-old lad with a cheerfully questing face but a heart ponderous with foreboding came up to me diffidently, a humble agnostic, as I sat in the front pew, writing quickly like a spy, struggling against time to encode a formula before it is forgotten forever. He asked with a rush of urgency:

"It is all a parable, isn't it, Father?"

To which I answered dreamily, for I always expect the sudden leap of consciousness of the Zen master, "Yes my son, it is all a parable."

I could not bear to humiliate him into realising that he was incapable of recognising an apparent cleric for a real one. "All of us," I encouraged him, "Every one."

At another time I was in the churchyard of St John the Baptist at Niton, waiting for twilight to signal I should go home. Thirty birds above and beyond me had chattered their usual homilies about death and transfiguration, their meeting-place as one and all, before gradually drowsing into soliloquy.

Two lovers, fingers entwined, walked in shadow (Sali and Vrenchen) and I heard their conversation, which I could never transcribe, for it was holier than Scripture and more private than fire at a lonely woman's hearth. They spoke of themselves, of each other, of commonplace wonders like devotion and marriage, patience and serenity. They held each other close. Time slowed to a stop. I felt my cheeks burning with cowardly tears again. I am not man enough to take up the burden of life's rigorous happiness without confessing the intense poignancy of such chance encounters, and the inadequacy to sum them up of our word 'bliss'.

THE EMPEROR'S GUEST

is Don Peacock's diary of 1276 days as a British prisoner of war of the Japanese in Indonesia during World War II, spent mainly as a white coolie on the tropical island of Haruku. The tale opens in Singapore as the young Yorkshireman is patriotically drinking gin, to prevent it from falling into enemy hands. Fleeing on a ship bound for Australia, he is ordered off in Batavia (now Jakarta) to defend Java, but the island surrenders and, after rejecting a guerrilla life behind Japanese lines, he is persuaded to join a slave-labour battalion.

After conversion to a rice diet, and toughening up to withstand Nip brutality, he joins a party transforming Haruku into an aircraft carrier. The island of disease, despair and death is run by a half-crazed Nip sergeant as his own little kingdom. Survivors run the gauntlet of American bombers and submarines to regain Java. The author is bound for Indo-China when the Allies blocked the seas and he ends his war in Singapore.

DONALD PEACOCK was born at Stapleton, N. Yorks., in 1919, and educated at Darlington Grammar School in County Durham. His career as a trainee journalist on the *Northern Despatch* was interrupted when he was called up for World War II a week before Chamberlain even blew the whistle.

After his years as a guest of the Emperor, he returned to journalism, retiring in 1984 as deputy night editor at the *Daily Mirror*'s Manchester office. Don Peacock married in 1948, and has a son and daughter. His first wife died in 1976. He now lives with his second wife in Cheshire.

ISBN 0 906672 55 4
40 illustrations
£14.95 (plus £2.00 P & P) Hardback

A DOCTOR IN SAUDI ARABIA

is the autobiographical account by Dr. G.E. Moloney of his years in Saudi Arabia, where he was Professor of Surgery to the University of Riyadh, 1977-82, following years as a relief Surgeon in Shetland, surgeon at Hackney Hospital during the blitz, Stoke Mandeville Hospital, and Radcliffe Infirmary in Oxford. Fourteen years on the Council of the British Medical Association and a busy life as consultant, writer, and surgeon in private and public practice led him at first to reject an offer to Head the Surgical Unit in Riyadh, but he eventually spent five happy years there, organising, teaching and operating. *A Doctor in Saudi Arabia* deals with his medical and surgical experiences, but takes an intelligent look at Saudi history and development, the rôle of the royal family, the cult of T.E. Lawrence, and many travels within the country, near and far.

ISBN 0 906672 81 3
365 pages. 150 illustrations
£14.95 (plus £2.00 P & P) Hardback

ALSO IN *ARABIA PAST AND PRESENT*

ARABIAN GULF INTELLIGENCE, being 'Selections from the Records of the Bombay Government', New Series, no. XXIV, 1856, concerning Arabian, Bahrain, Kuwait, Muscat and Oman, United Arab Emirates and Islands of the Gulf. 728 pp. 6 maps. ISBN 0 900891 54 8. £48.75. Hardback

ARABIAN PERSONALITIES OF THE EARLY TWENTIETH CENTURY, being the primary biographical sourcebook (formerly classified confidential) on leaders of the Arabian Peninsula, the Syrian Desert and Sinai, written by Lawrence, Bell, C.E. Wilson, Carruthers, Cox, Craufurd, Davenport & Storrs, among others. 384 pp. ISBN 0 906672 39 2. £29.75. Hardback

SOJOURN WITH THE GRAND SHARIF OF MAKKAH (1854) by Charles Didier, now first translated, with a new map and illustrations. A journey to Sinai, Suez, Tor, Yanbu', Jiddah, Ta'if and back to Jiddah. ISBN 0 906672 11 2. £22.50. Hardback